Expectations of Equality

The Western History Series
SERIES EDITORS

Carol L. Higham
University of North Carolina at Charlotte

William H. Katerberg
Calvin College

Expectations of Equality
A History of Black Westerners

Albert S. Broussard
Texas A&M University

A CO-PUBLICATION OF

Harlan Davidson, Inc.
773 Glenn Avenue
Wheeling, Illinois 60090
www.harlandavidson.com

The Buffalo Bill Historical Center
720 Sheridan Avenue
Cody, Wyoming 82414
www.bbhc.org

Copyright © 2012
Harlan Davidson, Inc.
All rights reserved.

Except as permitted under United States copyright law, no part of this publication may
be reproduced or distributed in any form or by any means, or stored in a database or any
retrieval system, without prior written permission of the publisher. Address inquiries to
Harlan Davidson, Inc., 773 Glenn Avenue, Wheeling, Illinois 60090.

Visit us on the World Wide Web at www.harlandavidson.com

Library of Congress Cataloging-in-Publication Data

Broussard, Albert S.
Expectations of equality : a history of Black westerners / Albert S. Broussard.
       p. cm. — (The western history series)
Includes bibliographical references and index.
ISBN 978-0-88295-284-0 (pbk. : alk. paper)
     1. African Americans—West (U.S.)—History. 2. African Americans—West
(U.S.)—Social conditions. 3. African Americans—West (U.S.)—Biography. 4. West
(U.S.)—History. 5. West (U.S.)—Social conditions. 6. West (U.S.)—Biography. I.
Title.
     E185.925.B76 2012
     305.896'073078—dc23
                                                                    2011039511

Front cover art: Charles Alston, "*The Negro in California History: Exploration and
Colonization*," panel 1, mural at the Golden State Mutual Life Insurance Co.,
9'3" x 16'5", 1949.
Cover design: Linda Gaio, Harlan Davidson, Inc.

Manufactured in the United States of America
14 13 12   1 2 3 MG

I dedicate this book to my children,
Valerie and Matthew Broussard,
and to the memory of my godchild,
Rebecca Ellison Wright.

Contents

Acknowledgments

All research projects are collaborative endeavors and this book is no exception. Carol L. Higham and William H. Katerberg, the editors of this series, invited me to contribute a short volume on African Americans in the West and deserve my biggest debt of gratitude. I wish to thank Donald Pisani, a friend and former colleague at Texas A&M, who encouraged me to press on in writing histories of African Americans in the West long before they became fashionable. Quintard Taylor, a colleague at the University of Washington, shared my enthusiasm for writing this book and encouraged this project from the start. I have interacted with many western historians on professional panels, in libraries, museums, archives, and through e-mail in the course of researching and writing this book, and I have profited from their suggestions. They include Darlene Clark Hine, Leon Litwack, Richard White, Douglas Flamming, Josh Sides, S. R. Martin, Matthew Whitaker, and Steven Danver. I wish also to thank William Tuttle, who invited me to serve as the Langston Hughes Professor of American Studies at the University of Kansas in 2005, where I conducted the initial research for this project. George C. Wright, president of Prairie View A&M University, invited me to his campus on two occasions to share my research with his students. Stephen Chandler, head archivist at the Black Women's Archives in Washington, D.C., granted me access to the papers of the National Council of Negro Women and made his staff available to field each of my requests. Bill Page, research librarian at Texas A&M, helped me to sort out the genealogy of several black westerners. Walter L. Buenger, my department head at Texas A&M, consistently encouraged this project and provided travel funds to conduct research at several western libraries. I will always owe a special debt of gratitude to the late David J. Weber, who embraced me as a friend more than three decades ago and encouraged me to join the faculty at Southern Methodist University, where I taught from 1981 to 1984. I will miss his friendship and wise counsel. Andrew J. Davidson at Harlan Davidson, Inc., assisted me as a copyeditor and Linda Gaio Davidson helped to find suitable images and artwork for this book. I have profited from each of their suggestions. Finally, I wish to thank my family for their encouragement over the years. Most of all, I thank my wife, Mary Broussard, who saw this book blossom and take on its own life over the past five years.

—Albert S. Broussard
College Station, Texas

Introduction

The history of people of African descent in the West predates the arrival of the first recorded African slaves in Jamestown, Virginia, in 1619 by approximately nine decades. Esteban de Dorantes, an African slave, sailed west with the earliest Spanish settlers through the Gulf of Mexico before local Indians captured him near Galveston Island. Numerous mixed-race African men and women followed in Esteban's footsteps over the course of the next century and settled in the vast Spanish empire in North America known as New Spain. Although these men and women lived under the purview of Spanish law, they intermarried with Europeans, Indians, and other mixed-race peoples, raised families, helped to establish schools, churches and communities, and served as scouts and soldiers. Spanish officials either widely disregarded or enforced haphazardly Spanish laws that discouraged miscegenation, or race-mixing, for Africans, Indians, and Spaniards intermarried and mingled openly for centuries.

"The American West is a product of conquest and of the mixing of diverse groups of people," the historian Richard White observed in his important book, *"It's Your Misfortune and None of My Own": A New History of the American West.* My book argues, in this vein, that African Americans also have comprised part of the region's rich diversity, despite their small numbers relative to other racial and ethnic groups in the West. More specifically, black westerners were only one of many racial minorities who suffered discrimination, an abridgement of their citizenship rights, and intermittent racial violence. American Indians fared perhaps the worst of all racial minorities, but Hispanics, Japanese, and Chinese immigrants also faced widespread discrimination and inequality. Such an argument implies many questions, both large and small.

How did African Americans and people of African descent fare in the American West? Did they perceive the region as a place free of the pernicious racial restrictions that African Americans faced in the southern, midwestern, and eastern states? Did the presence of Indians, Asians, Hispanics, or white immigrants hinder or assist the progress of black westerners? Were gender restrictions as severe for African American women in the West as in other parts of the nation? What cultural contributions did black men and women bring to the western states and territories? Did black westerners emulate their counterparts in other regions of the nation and vigorously fight segregation and racial inequality? Finally, did race relations in the region differ markedly from those of the South, which did so much to shape how Americans think about race? In pondering these questions, it is important to note that the West has been distinct in the United States, historically, because of the comparatively larger and defining presence of Hispanic, Native American, and Asian communities, along with those of African Americans and whites.

Expectations of Equality: A History of Black Westerners will attempt to answer these pivotal questions. To do so, it examines how African Americans over the course of nearly five centuries attempted to find their place in the states and territories west of the ninety-eighth meridian. Although black westerners, like white immigrants or native-born whites, defy easy characterization because they came to the West for a variety of reasons, blacks have shared certain commonalities with these groups. The majority of African Americans who settled in the West saw the region as a place where they could fashion a better life for themselves or their families. Some naively viewed the West as an oasis, a place free of racial or class restrictions. While many white immigrants, native-born whites, Hispanics, and Asians also saw the West as a place of opportunity, the experiences of

African Americans differed profoundly from those of whites, people who never faced such a pervasive pattern of discrimination based solely on their race. Indeed, no western state or territory ever passed laws that barred whites from voting, employment opportunities, buying or renting houses or apartments in certain neighborhoods, or frequenting public accommodations. These racial restrictions were, however, very much a part of the world in which black westerners lived and their children or grandchildren inherited. Numerous western laws and racial bigotry consistently reminded African Americans that their skin color, rather than their ability or the content of their character, designated them as second-class citizens.

Like their counterparts in other parts of the nation, black westerners challenged hostile white attitudes and racial discrimination and exclusion by insisting that they, too, deserved to enjoy all of the rights and privileges of citizens under the United States Constitution. Thus, the persistent struggle that black westerners waged for racial equality emerges as one of the major themes of this book. Whether they settled in small rural communities like Helena, Montana, or Greeley, Colorado, or in large cities such as Los Angeles, San Francisco, Denver, or Seattle, black westerners fought vigorously for full equality. Black men and women organized protests and campaigns for racial justice in churches, political leagues, women's clubs, and national organizations such as the National Urban League (NUL), the National Association for the Advancement of Colored People (NAACP), and the Congress of Racial Equality (CORE). African American women felt especially aggrieved and insulted by segregation laws and second-class citizenship, and they organized to abolish segregation throughout the West. I have attempted to interweave their stories and campaigns throughout the narrative, for black women, to their credit, challenged the narrow and racially exclusive view of citizenship that relegated them to a separate and unequal status. Black westerners also believed firmly in the principles of the U.S. Constitution and trusted that it was a color-blind document. Thus the fight for basic civil rights—such as the right to

xiv ಄   **Expectations of Equality**

vote, attend the school of their choice, and live in an integrated community—were important priorities for black westerners. Indeed, the consistent level of civil rights activity in the West, despite the small black population, is one of the major conclusions of this book.

The relatively small number of African Americans who migrated West sets them apart from whites or Hispanics. With the exception of Texas, no western state or territory contained a sizable black population until World War II. The successive waves of white migrants and immigrants who populated the Great Plains, the mountain states, or the West Coast between 1848 and 1900 did not produce a corresponding wave of black migrants. African Americans trickled into these regions after 1848, some as gold miners, and others as homesteaders, cowboys, cattlemen, scouts, and mountain men. The vast majority of black westerners, however, settled in urban areas, large and small, that stretched from San Antonio, in Texas, to Seattle, in Washington. Adventurous black men and women also were among the homesteaders in states and territories such as Kansas, Nebraska, and the Dakotas.

World War II changed the West dramatically, perhaps more so than any single event of the twentieth century, as war production shifted to the West Coast and the Sunbelt states stretching from Florida to southern California. After facing more than a decade of economic hardship during the Great Depression, migrants of all races and nationalities traveled great distances and flocked to the West to work in shipyards, airplane factories, and a broad array of defense industries. These new economic opportunities also brought large numbers of African Americans, the majority of them from the southern states, to western cities like San Francisco, Oakland, Portland, and Seattle for the first time. Emboldened by a new commitment from the federal government to abolish racial discrimination in defense industries during the war, African Americans worked alongside white workers throughout the West. These black workers not only settled in western cities, but also competed with white war workers for scarce housing, recreation facilities, and public space.

The postwar years brought even higher expectations for black westerners, as they pushed with even greater vigor to end racial discrimination in employment and housing, and to open doors to new opportunities. African American leaders also slowly began to link their local struggles for equality with the broader struggle for civil rights that was sweeping the nation. Thus it was two western cities, Oklahoma City and Wichita, Kansas, that saw the first student sit-ins in the nation to protest segregation in public establishments. It was also in a western city, Topeka, Kansas, where seven-year-old Linda Brown attempted to integrate an all-white school in defiance of the 1896 *Plessy* v. *Ferguson* decision, which mandated separate-but-equal facilities for blacks and whites. When the United States Supreme Court overturned *Plessy* in *Brown* v. *Board of Education* (1954), it unleashed a torrent of expectations of equality among African Americans in the West and throughout the nation. Many black westerners believed that racial discrimination would soon be a thing of the past.

Reflecting the importance of this issue and the era, the final two chapters of this book reveal how black westerners responded to the challenges of the national civil rights movement and describe the multiple roles they played in it. Indeed, many significant and pivotal events of the civil rights era traced their origins to the West, including the 1965 Watts race riot, the founding of the Black Panther Party, and demonstrations led by the CORE. In 1966 Maulana Ron Karenga, a black nationalist leader in Los Angeles, invented the tradition of Kwanzaa (the Swahili word for "first fruits"), which today African Americans throughout the nation observe as a celebration of the harvest in Africa's traditional agricultural societies.

Historians will probably always disagree over the precise definition of "the West." Herein, I define the West as the nineteen states and territories west of the ninety-eighth meridian. For most historians, Texas and Oklahoma represent the most problematic states that fall under this definition. The majority of the Oklahoma Territory, which opened for American settlement in 1889, exists east of the ninety-eighth meridian. Texas's vast territory divides almost equally between the East and West. Yet both Texas and Oklahoma, I argue, contain many attributes that conform to the majority of western states, such as a westward-moving frontier, cattle drives, aridity, and sites where the U.S. government stationed soldiers, both black and white, to fight hostile Indians and protect American settlers. Texas possessed each of these features as well as racial slavery. Thus Texas represents a hybrid of both the South and West.

Finally, readers should not lose sight of the stories of individual people told in these pages. So, the many questions and issues notwithstanding, *Expectations of Equality* tells the stories of black westerners. I designed this book to introduce students to scores of African American men and women who lived in the West from the early 1500s until the turn of the twenty-first century. Many of these people led ordinary lives that are difficult to reconstruct in detail–working, raising families, attending church, and educating their children. Yet some of them forged colorful careers as scouts and mountain men, Buffalo Soldiers, businesswomen, athletes, activists, and politicians that we can study in a good amount of detail. An even smaller number led important campaigns for racial justice and emerged as respected leaders in their communities. I hope that all who read this book will gain an appreciation for the long struggle for full equality that all black westerners—those who earned some measure of fame as well as those who lived quieter, largely unsung lives—waged to try to help make the West a place free of racial boundaries and restrictions. I would also encourage students and scholars alike to continue their research into the saga of African Americans in the West, for their collective struggle represents a vital piece of the canvas we know as United States history.

Suggested Readings

Barr, Alwyn, and Robert A. Calvert, eds. *Black Leaders: Texans for Their Times.* Austin: University of Texas Press, 1981.

De Graaf, Lawrence B. "Recognition, Racism, and Reflections on Western Black History," *Pacific Historical Review* 24 (February 1975): 22–51.

De León, Arnoldo. *Racial Frontiers: Africans, Chinese, and Mexicans in Western America, 1848–1890.* Albuquerque: University of New Mexico Press, 2002.

Flamming, Douglas. *African Americans in the West.* Santa Barbara: ABC-Clio, 2009.

Porter, Kenneth W. *The Negro on the American Frontier.* New York: Ayer Company Publishers, 1971.

Savage, W. Sherman. *Blacks in the West.* Westport: Greenwood Press, 1976.

Taylor, Quintard and Shirley Ann Wilson Moore, eds. *African American Women Confront the West, 1600–2000.* Norman: University of Oklahoma Press, 2003.

Taylor, Quintard. "From Esteban to Rodney King: Five Centuries of African American History in the West," *Montana: The Magazine of Western History* (Winter 1996), 2–23.

———. *In Search of the Racial Frontier: African Americans in the West, 1528–1990.* New York: W. W. Norton, 1998.

Taylor, Quintard, Lawrence B. De Graaf, and Kevin Mulroy, eds, *Seeking El Dorado: African Americans in California, 1769–1997.* Seattle: University of Washington Press, 2001.

CHAPTER ONE

Black Settlers

African Americans have had a long, rich, and complex history in the American West. Among its earliest non-native settlers, people of African descent arrived in the West in the sixteenth century with Spanish explorers who conquered New World societies. Accompanying Spanish soldiers and sailors, African peoples exhibited the same assertiveness, arrogance, and basic motivation as the Spanish. They, too, wished to conquer and exploit the resources of a new society and its people as thoroughly as possible. The earliest record of the black presence in the American West was a slave by the name of Esteban de Dorantes who, though ill-advised, made first contact with the native peoples of the Southwest. After surviving the failed expedition of conquest led by Pánfilo de Narváez to Florida in 1528, Esteban, his master, Captain Andrés de Dorantes, and a small group of explorers sailed west through the Gulf of Mexico. The Karankawa Indians quickly captured these interlopers near Galveston Island, but Esteban and four members of the party, most famously Alvar Nuñez Cabeza de Vaca, all of whom had learned to survive through their wits, escaped in 1534. By 1536, the group reached Mexico City. In 1539, Don Antonio de Mendoza, the viceroy of New Spain, organized an expedition to New Spain's northern frontier in search, some say, of the fabled Cities of Cíbola. The group was led by a Franciscan friar who purchased Esteban to serve as his guide. Esteban, who had also acquired a reputation as a healer, interpreter of Indian languages, and liaison, led a small party in advance of the main expedition. When he and his party reached a Zuni pueblo, native elders advised Esteban not to set foot in the village. Disregarding the warning, he pushed on and the locals killed him in May 1539. Although Esteban's adventurous life did not end happily, it illustrates the significance of African peoples to western and borderlands history and their role in the exploration and settlement of New Spain's northern frontier. That Spanish officials permitted Esteban to lead the small expedition reveals how much confidence they had in his ability to serve their interest and interact favorably with local Indians. While relatively few in number, other black men on this frontier played multiple roles, serving as liaisons, scouts, interpreters, soldiers, and healers.

Black women also made their way to the Spanish frontier, but their story was quite different. Unlike their male counterparts, these women, both free and slave, tended to lead less violent lives, helping to settle communities and establish churches, and intermarrying as they moved northward. Isabel de Olvera, a free *mulatta* (a person of mixed African and Spanish or Indian ancestry) of Querétaro, Mexico, joined the relief expedition (dispatched to help colonize present-day New Mexico) of Juan Guerra de Resa to New Spain in 1600. As one of the hundreds of Spanish-speaking black settlers listed by Spanish officials in their census records of the frontier, Isabel de Olvera's experience as a servant to a Spanish woman and as a *casta* (a person of mixed blood) bore a remarkable similarity to that of many other women who lived and settled in the far northern provinces of New Spain. Neither her race nor her skin color posed an obstacle in her quest to advance. Isabel displayed the confidence of many free women of color when she filed a deposition with the *alcalde* (mayor) of Querétaro, demanding official protection of her status as a free person on her journey up to New Mexico in the event that others might mistake her for a slave. The daughter of a black father and an Indian mother, Olvera represented a rather substantial mulatto and mixed-race black population in New Spain's Far Northern provinces. The important affidavit that she so carefully requested to have signed and certified reveals how Olvera, and perhaps many other mixed-race people in the West at this juncture, construed race. They viewed themselves as neither black nor white, but rather a combination of Spanish, African, and Indian. Their status as free people gave them confidence they would be protected by the laws of the Spanish government, which they considered their government.

Mixed-race African women such as Olvera dotted the landscape of Spain's North American colonial settlement, from Albuquerque to San Antonio to Los Angeles. These women proved to be much more, however, than petitioners for protection and justice. They settled communities, raised families, served their neighbors as *curanderas* (practitioners of folk medicine) and worked as domestic servants. Black women also intermarried with Native Americans and members of the various Spanish castas who settled the New World, including *mestizos* (half-Indian, half-Spanish) and Spaniards. Attempts by the Spanish authorities to control these mixed-race unions proved unsuccessful, rendering obsolete a 1527 Spanish law mandating that blacks could only marry other blacks. Spanish authorities tolerated mixed-race marriages in part due to the shortage of European women in the New World colonies. They realized that they needed the contributions of women of all races and nationalities to ensure the success of their colonial settlements.

New Spain

African Americans, whether having come from Spain itself or within the Spanish colonies, went to the region we consider the West in a quest for a better life. Although they predated the arrival of African slaves on the East Coast of what is now the United States, black westerners were relatively small in number and performed a multitude of roles. Like Esteban and Olvera, persons of African descent more likely moved north from Mexico and its provinces than west from the Atlantic Coast. Individuals like these scattered across the vast territory known as New Spain. Some of them entered New Spain's northern province of *Tejas* (Texas) in the late seventeenth century, such as the black bugler who accompanied the missionary expedition of Domingo Terán de los Rios to the villages of the Indians of East Texas. Others, such as a free black interpreter whose name has been lost to history, assisted Friar Juan de Padilla in 1541 during the expedition of Francisco Vásquez de Coronado, which, like several others, searched for the Seven Cities of Cíbola. Similarly, high-ranking Spanish military officials such as Domingo Ramón included blacks in their expeditions. Ramón served as commander of a military unit whose purpose was to re-establish a Spanish presence in East Texas, notes historian Donald E. Chipman, in order to check French influence in the area from Louisiana. The Ramón expedition, which totaled seventy-five persons, included Juan Concepción, a black man of undetermined status. Among other things, the expedition is credited with helping to establish the mission of Nuestro Padre San Francisco de los Tejas, east of the Neches River. To be sure, some blacks arrived in colonial Texas as slaves or servants, but others who found their way there served in the military, worked as scouts, traders, and trappers, or farmed the land.

Similarly, the earliest Spanish settlements in Alta California (present-day California) included persons of African ancestry who helped create the rich racial diversity of the province. The black presence in California dates to 1579, when four black men landed in the San Francisco Bay with the English explorer Sir Francis Drake. The number of blacks in California grew slowly as compared to other regions of New Spain, as Spanish authorities in California focused on building and maintaining missions to Indians, not on settlement, in the 1770s. The famed Franciscan missionary Junípero Serra, who established a mission at Monterey in 1771 and worked to convert local Indians to Christianity, noted the presence of mulatto sailors in the area. When the Spanish began to promote the development of *ranchos* (ranches) in the 1780s, many Spanish settlements in California became racially mixed communities that comprised mulattos, mestizos, blacks, and individuals of various Indian groups.

Historians know little about the lives and roles of these early black Californians. It is likely that they worked in occupations similar to those of their Spanish or mixed-race counterparts. At least two things, however, are certain. As many as one in five of the Spanish-speaking settlers or soldiers in California by 1790, according to historian Jack Forbes, were of African descent. Some of these early black settlers in California probably classified themselves as either mulatto or mestizo, others as Indian or Spanish, depending on their skin color and social status. The same was the case in New Spain generally and in its other North American colonies (what is now New Mexico, Texas, and Arizona) between 1528 and 1848, with mixed bloods, blacks, and Hispanicized Indians composing the vast majority of the population. Disregarding Spanish laws or edicts that discouraged miscegenation, Africans, Spaniards, Indians, and mixed race peoples intermingled, intermarried, and procreated freely for centuries. And even though "whiteness" remained the norm, and generally defined the political and social status of an individual, racial intermixture was widespread.

Black and mixed-race westerners composed a significant percentage of the original settlers of some western towns and cities, places where race mattered but racial identities remained fluid and changeable. Western cities such as San Francisco, Monterey, Los Angeles, and San Jose contained sizable black and mulatto populations during the Spanish period. The founding of Los Angeles in 1781 serves as an excellent example, for twenty-six of the original forty-six settlers of the *pueblo* (village) had either African or part African ancestry. Apparently, skin color initially posed no barrier to their success, for Francisco Reyes, a mulatto from central Mexico, became the alcalde of Los Angeles in 1781. Even more impressive was the fact that the Spanish government appointed two mixed-race brothers, Andres Pico and Pio Pico, military commander of the Mexican California militia and governor of California, respectively. The grandsons of a mestizo and his mulatto wife, Andres and Pio provide evidence that the frontier population, as historian David Weber writes, became whiter over time as "Indians and mulattos declared themselves mestizos, and mestizos declared themselves as espanoles." In other words, individuals like the Pico brothers possessed the ability to define their own race and ethnicity in early western history, and, apparently, mixed-race ancestry was more desirable than declaring oneself an African or having visible signs of African ancestry.

Northern California also attracted a small number of people of African descent, most of whom, like their counterparts in southern California, possessed mixed-race ancestry. In the period after Mexico gained its independence from Spain in 1821, West Indian-born William A. Leidesdorff, of Danish-African ancestry, is one of the most notable examples. A successful merchant and ship captain, Leidesdorff arrived in Yerba Buena (as the Spanish originally called San Francisco) in 1841. Sailing his schooner *Julia Ann* on voyages between California, Mexico, and Hawaii, he became a large landowner, a successful merchant, and one of the city's early political leaders. President James K. Polk, a rabid white supremacist who was unaware of Leidesdorff's mixed race ancestry, appointed Leidesdorff, a Mexican citizen, to the post of American vice-consul in 1845. In 1847, the public elected Leidesdorff to San Francisco's city council, where he served as city treasurer. Leidesdorff also helped to establish the city's first school system and served on its first school board. A street in San Francisco in the Embarcadero district bears his name today, representing the magnitude of his service.

Not every African American who went to California had the good fortune to captain a ship and accrue land and notoriety, but many blacks served as crew members on ships that came to California. Upon their arrival, these individuals occasionally deserted their ships and became Mexican citizens. Allen Light followed this path in 1835 and became one of the most prominent otter hunters along the southern California coast. Because of his considerable skill in hunting otters, Light obtained a prominent political post. California governor Juan Bautista Alvarado in 1839 appointed him *comisario-general* and assigned him the responsibility of halting the widespread practice of illegal otter hunting (i.e., done without a license from the government) in the Mexican state. Light's significance to California's early history is twofold: he was among the earliest group of English-speaking blacks to arrive in California; and he became the first known U.S.-born African American to serve as a Mexican official. Thus, throughout the Spanish and Mexican periods, African Americans served in governmental capacities as well as acted as settlers, servants, and slaves.

Hawaii

African Americans occasionally migrated west even beyond California to seek opportunities and improve their lives. Some ventured as far as Hawaii, coming to the islands as seamen, fugitive slaves, and missionaries. Anthony Allen, a fugitive slave from Schenectady, New York, fled to Hawaii in 1810 in an attempt to escape the oppressive conditions that both slaves and free blacks faced in northern states such as New York and Pennsylvania. In Hawaii, Allen became a respected merchant, married a Hawaiian woman, and served as one of the trusted advisers of Kamehameha the Great, the king of the Hawaiian Islands. African American women, though less likely to migrate quite this distance, also came to Hawaii in rare circumstances. Betsey Stockton, the first African American female reported in Hawaii, arrived there in 1823 to work with Christian missionaries. Born a slave in Princeton, New Jersey, in 1798, Stockton worked in the household of Ashbel Green, who served as president of the College of New Jersey (later renamed Princeton University). Green proved more benevolent than most slave owners, and he encouraged Stockton to learn to read and educate herself in a broad number of subjects. She also attended evening classes at Princeton Theological Seminary. Green granted Stockton her freedom when she became a missionary, joining the American Board of Commissions for Foreign

Missions (ABCFM). Stockton remained in Hawaii for two years, teaching native Hawaiians and their children the rudiments of reading and writing and the Christian gospel. Stockton also established a school for Hawaiian children at Lahaina, Maui, perhaps her most enduring achievement on the islands. She returned to the mainland in 1826 at the request of Charles Stewart, her sponsor, and devoted the remainder of her life to teaching and missionary work in Philadelphia, Pennsylvania, Grape Island, Canada, and Princeton, New Jersey. Generally, opportunities existed in Hawaii for African American immigrants but only within limited parameters; the same would be the case in Gold Rush California.

California

Gold Rush
Soon after the United States gained control of California in 1848, the California Gold Rush brought approximately one thousand African Americans to the territory amid the larger international frenzy to strike it rich. This movement to California, which became an American state in 1850, composed the largest voluntary migration of African Americans prior to the Civil War. By 1860, five thousand black persons lived in California, where less than a thousand had been recorded in 1852. Black migrants continued to settle in some of the state's major cities, such as San Francisco and Sacramento, where they interacted with people from all nations, including China, Chile, and Europe, and worked in integrated settings. Unlike earlier settlers of African descent and their progeny who originated from either New Spain or Mexico, the majority of these black migrants spoke English and had migrated to California from the United States. Like their white or foreign counterparts, black miners occasionally worked collectively by race or nationality. Locals commonly referred to some mining sites as Negro Hill or Negro Bar because of the prevalence of black miners in that area near the American River. The Gold Rush offered the same opportunities for success or failure

to African Americans as it did to whites. Ultimately, obtaining quick wealth proved as elusive for most African American miners as it did for their white and foreign counterparts, the majority of all miners abandoning the gold fields after several years of back-breaking work. Most black prospectors chose to stay in California after quitting the mine, particularly in the major cities.

Slavery

Some white miners brought their black slaves to the gold fields of California, confident that their human chattel would be protected by federal law and the presence of enslaved persons in the western states and territories. California, which entered the Union as a free state in 1850, serves as a case in point. By 1860 as many as five hundred black slaves resided in California by some estimates (compared to the five thousand free black residents), despite a state prohibition against slavery enacted in the California State Constitution of 1850. This figure may be inaccurate, however, because the prohibition against slavery in the state constitution also prevented slaves from being counted in the census. Nonetheless, slaveowners brought slaves to California during the early stages of the gold rush and continued to bring them after the Golden State entered the union. George McKinley Murrell, born into a comfortable slaveholding family in Bowling Green, Kentucky, completed the arduous overland journey from western Kentucky to California in 1849 and set up operations on the north fork of the American River. A male slave named Rheubin accompanied Murrell on the journey and assisted him in this mining enterprise. Yet Murrell also permitted Rheubin to be hired out and work independently, a common practice among slaves in the southern states. Their relationship underscores the acceptance of slavery in the mines and the similarity of California slavery to the institution as it existed in the South.

Although a few western states such as Texas freely permitted and even encouraged the growth of slavery, some Californians found the practice of owning human beings abhorrent. Thus, a small but committed group of white abolitionists and free blacks used every opportunity to assist fugitive slaves, an activism driven by the state's relatively large and politically astute free black community. The black leader Peter Lester, a native Philadelphian, invited slaves into his San Francisco home to lecture them on their rights. "When they left," he boasted, "we had them strong in the spirit of freedom. They were leaving [slavery] every day." On a number of occasions San Francisco's small African American community raised money to hire attorneys to mount legal challenges on behalf of individual slaves. For example, in 1851 San Francisco's black leaders hired Samuel W. Holladay to defend a fugitive slave named Frank, incarcerated prior to his pending return to Missouri, a slaveholding state. The prevalence of slavery in California suggests that slaveowners confidently believed that Californians would not tamper with their human property. And, for the most part, this assumption proved correct. As Rudolph Lapp writes in his history of blacks in gold rush California, "the lack of law enforcement made it possible for slavery to exist in many parts of the state." But several sensational fugitive slave cases in California, centered in San Francisco, gave southern slaveholders pause. The Archy Lee case, which involved an eighteen-year-old African American slave who had been brought to California from Mississippi in 1857 by Charles Stovall, the son of Lee's owner, proved to be the most significant.

Archy Lee probably never envisioned himself at the center of a dramatic fugitive slave case. When Lee arrived in California in 1857 with Charles Stovall, master and slave settled quietly in Sacramento, where Stovall taught school and permitted Lee to hire out his own time in order to earn a wage. As time passed, however, Stovall grew increasingly concerned about Lee's loyalty and the detrimental effect that residing in California might be having on his bondman. When Stovall attempted to locate Lee and transport him back to Mississippi, he discovered that Lee had disappeared. Lee initially hid in the Hotel Hackett, a business owned by free blacks in Sacramento, which had, next to San Francisco, the most politically active black community in the state. In time, California authorities arrested Lee under the federal Fugitive Slave Act of 1850 and brought him to trial. Much to Stovall's surprise, several white anti-slavery supporters defended Lee and attempted to prevent his return to Mississippi. After a series of highly publicized trials, the state brought Lee before a United States commissioner, who had been authorized under the federal Fugitive Slave Act to decide the merits of the case. The federal commissioner ruled that Archy Lee was a free man, not a fugitive slave, because he had not fled across state lines to obtain his freedom, but rather sought out his freedom within the state of California after his arrival there in 1857. This case revealed the groundswell of biracial antislavery support in San Francisco and Sacramento. It also illustrated that slaves brought by their owners to California, a free state, were not content with their bondage and occasionally sought out white and black allies who, they believed, could help them obtain their freedom. Most important, the fact that the commissioner sided with Lee in his quest for freedom seriously undermined the rights of slave owners who brought their slaves to California and reinforced the state's own constitution. Cases like that of Archy Lee laid the groundwork for battles over civil rights in the coming century.

Texas

The war between Mexico and Spain (1810–1821) that resulted in Mexico's independence initially promised to have a positive effect on the status of blacks who lived in the province of Tejas. Following Mexico's independence from Spain in 1821, the new national government, based in Mexico City, abolished slavery throughout the nation. Mexico also offered free blacks full citizenship rights, land ownership, and other privileges denied to them in the United States. A small number of African Americans lived in the Mexican province of Tejas, including free blacks, fugitive slaves, and mixed-race African Americans who had intermarried with Mexican citizens. Mexico tolerated mixed marriages more than did any state in the southern

United States because Mexico did not practice slavery or depend on slave labor for its economic livelihood. Nor did Mexico pass segregation laws based on race and skin color or develop a firm adherence to the principle of white supremacy.

Following Spanish colonization policies, in the 1820s Mexico began to allow Americans to set up colonies in Tejas in order to increase the population of the isolated province, promote economic development, better protect existing settlements from raids by hostile Indian peoples, and prevent annexation by a rapidly expanding United States. American settlers had to agree to follow Mexican law and eventually become Roman Catholic. Most of the American settlers who came to Tejas under the immigration program were white. Despite Mexican law, many of these white settlers intended to establish plantations with slave labor, generally disdained Mexicans as racially inferior, and had no intention of ever becoming Roman Catholic. Nonetheless, a few African Americans also received land grants directly from the Mexican government. In one interesting case, the noted white abolitionist Benjamin Lundy sought approval for the establishment of a black colony from the United States, and the Mexican government supported the idea. The project met with widespread opposition from whites in Tejas, who had illegally been establishing slavery in the province.

Whites in Tejas discouraged the growth of a sizable free black population in part because they had hoped to reinstate slavery, and they felt encouraged when Mexican officials permitted them to import blacks as contract laborers. Whites also viewed free blacks as a negative influence on slavery, as a group who might potentially incite slaves to run away or rebel. In addition, white settlers in Tejas were uncomfortable with the idea that free blacks enjoyed the same Mexican citizenship rights as whites. Many white Americans had come to Tejas, in their words, to establish an empire for slavery. Having migrated from the southern United States, where slavery flourished, they also believed in white supremacy and innate black inferiority (as well as disdained most Mexicans, many of whom were mixed-race). Thus the racial views of whites in Tejas resembled those of white southerners, and Tejas, because of the presence of slavery, would be drawn increasingly into the sectional crisis that brewed in the United States during the 1850s. The Mexican government's decision in 1821 to grant a colony to one Moses Austin of Missouri would set the stage for a massive migration of whites into Tejas. The land grant to Austin encouraged white settlement as well as a rise in the number of slaves there. The obligation to establish an American colony, however, fell on Stephen Fuller Austin, Moses' son, following Moses' death in 1821 after having contracted pneumonia.

Several African Americans, such as Greenbury Logan and Lewis B. Jones, obtained land as part of the prominent colony set up in Texas by Austin. Other African Americans, such as William Goyens, a North Carolina blacksmith and land speculator, also optimistically settled the region. Goyens amassed a considerable fortune by the time of his death in 1856. He also possessed an aptitude for speaking Indian languages. Between 1835 and 1838 he served as an interpreter with the East Texas Indians for Sam Houston, the first president of the Republic of Texas, which would fight a war and win its independence from Mexico in 1835–36. Similarly, the four Ashwood brothers, William, Aaron, Abner, and Moses, although born in South Carolina, migrated to Texas between 1831 and 1835, and they earned considerable wealth in land and cattle, a testament to the fact that race did not necessarily prohibit success in the lives of African Americans in Mexican Tejas.

Despite Mexico's ban on slavery, both white Texans and many Mexican officials believed that slavery would be vital for the growth, development, and maturation of this region. The Mexican government reported about 5,000 slaves in Tejas in 1836, and Tejas slavery resembled the *peculiar institution*, a nineteenth-century term for slavery as it existed in the U.S. South, where it had been established for centuries. The majority of enslaved people in Tejas worked the fields and picked cotton, already the major staple crop in the region. Slaves also worked as skilled tradesmen and artisans in the small towns and urban centers, as well as labored as cooks, domestics, and laundresses. Some planters hired out their bondmen, a profitable business and a practice especially popular with women, children, or elderly persons who owned slaves but could not supervise them properly. The majority of slaves resided on Anglo plantations on the fertile lands near the Colorado, Trinity, and Brazos rivers in Central and East Tejas. Pockets of slaves also worked plantations near Nacogdoches and in small white communities near the Red River. White planters, as well as small farmers, attempted to control their human chattel by the lash, threatening to sell family members, withdrawing visiting privileges, and cutting their weekly rations of food. Slaves attempted to improve their condition by running away, and a small group succeeded in joining Indian tribes or Mexican settlements.

By 1835, the American population in Tejas, both black and white, had reached around 30,000 residents, of whom about 5,000 were slaves. By this time, tensions between Tejas and Mexico had reached the breaking point, both with Anglo-Texans, most of whom always had disdained Mexicans on racial and religious grounds, and among many *Tejanos* (Hispanic-Texans), who had long felt frustration with first Spanish and then Mexican governance based in distant Mexico City. The following year, Texas declared its independence from Mexico, and the Texas Revolution set in motion the formal break from Mexico and the expansion of slavery in this far-flung, breakaway region.

Like whites and Tejanos, African Americans fought for Texas independence, although the latter faced considerable uncertainty about what an independent Texas would mean for their future. Ironically, some free blacks shared the prevailing beliefs of whites about the Mexican government and its people. Like white Texans, African American Texans were disgruntled with a distant national government that did not seem to serve their interest. Some had developed a stronger attachment and identity to Texas than to Mexico, although scholars cannot be certain if black Texans felt their status would improve should Texas gain its independence. Nevertheless, the majority of black Texans pledged their loyalty to the Republic of Texas. Samuel McCullock, Jr., a free black who had migrated to Texas from Montgomery, Alabama, along with his three sisters and white father, Samuel McCulloch, Sr., became the first casualty of the Texas Revolution. A musket ball severely wounded him in the shoulder when Texans stormed the Mexican officer's quarters at Goliad. Free blacks as well as slaves also fought in the famous battles of San Antonio and San Jacinto, and the Texans granted freedom to a slave named Peter when he volunteered to use his own wagon to transport military supplies. Black Texans who were unable to fight due to advanced age or circumstances beyond their control contributed money and supplies to the war effort. Despite their loyalty to the Texas government, free blacks saw their status move backwards after the successful revolution.

With strong ties to the U.S. South, the new Republic of Texas systematically pushed to restrict many of the freedoms and privileges that free blacks had enjoyed under the Mexican government. For example, in the Constitution of the Republic of Texas, white Texans stripped citizenship rights from free blacks and restricted black property rights. In an effort to solidify white supremacy, the new Republic prohibited interracial marriages. The constitution also banned the permanent residence of free blacks within the Republic of Texas without the approval of Congress. The authors of the Texas constitution designed this provision to curtail the growth of a sizable free black population, for white Texans viewed free blacks as a potentially troublesome presence, although Texans seldom enforced the provision. The same could be said for the anti-miscegenation statute, as Samuel McCulloch, Jr., the first casualty in the revolution, married Mary Lorena Vess, a white woman, and the couple had four children, thereby increasing the free-black population. In 1840, the Texas Congress passed its strictest law against the presence of free blacks, giving them two years to leave Texas or risk being sold into slavery. Sam Houston, the president of Texas, postponed implementation of the punitive law and it never went into effect. Nevertheless, the other restrictive laws had a chilling effect on the growth of Texas' free-black population, which reported only 397 persons in 1850 and a mere 355 a decade later. White Texans had placed free blacks on notice that the Republic did not welcome them and would go to considerable lengths to prevent the growth of a sizable free-black community.

Texas's independence did not, as many had hoped, bring about immediate recognition from the United States. Following the Missouri Compromise of 1820–21, when Congress agreed to restrict any future slave state to the geographical region south of the 36° 30′ north latitude, lawmakers carefully balanced the number of free and slave states admitted to the Union. In the politically charged atmosphere of the 1840s, in which any new state entering the Union proved a contentious issue and opened a wedge between the North and South, nearly a decade passed before the United States formally annexed Texas. On December 29, 1845, Texas entered the Union as the twenty-eighth state. It entered as a slave state.

The outbreak of the War with Mexico in 1846, following a border dispute between the United States and Mexico, also had a profound impact on settlement in the West. The Treaty of Guadalupe Hidalgo, signed in 1848 following the defeat of Mexico by the United States, significantly expanded the territory of the United States and further strengthened the position of white slave holders in Texas. In fact, the land acquired by the United States in the 1848 treaty with Mexico was the third largest territorial acquisition in the nation's history, exceeded only by the Louisiana Purchase (1803) and the purchase of Alaska (1867). Few whites disputed the legality or the necessity of slavery in Texas. In fact, the number of African American slaves in Texas grew at a faster rate than did any other segment of the population, from 58,161 in 1850 to 182,566 in 1860. This spectacular growth in the slave population in a single decade confirmed the views of many that Texas had become a major cotton-producing state and that slave labor represented a critical factor in that success. On the eve of the Civil War, which began in1861, enslaved people made up roughly one-third of all Texans. In sharp contrast, only 355 free black resided in Texas in 1860, a sign that many African Americans no longer viewed Texas as a place where they could hope to live freely, raise and educate their children, and prosper.

In less than fifty years, between 1820 and the 1860s, blacks in Texas witnessed rapid and violent changes. Originally granted citizenship and land by the nascent Mexican government, black Texans soon lost those rights with the rise of the Republic of Texas. By the time the United States annexed Texas, enslaved blacks vastly outnumbered free ones, who retained few of the rights that had drawn them to Texas.

Employment: Opportunity and Restrictions

Although African Americans encountered and decried racial restrictions in many areas of employment in the West, they also acknowledged that western states and territories sometimes provided them the opportunity for a fresh start. As noted earlier, the California Gold Rush presented some African Americans with the chance, however slim, to make their fortune as miners. San Francisco also offered economic opportunities. The city so impressed one black migrant that he called it the "New York of the Pacific." Many of San Francisco's early black settlers found work plentiful during the city's formative years. Mifflin W. Gibbs, a free-born African American from Philadelphia, although lured to California by gold, ran a successful business in San Francisco for a number of years. Gibbs was, however, only one of three African Americans listed among 3,100 merchants in San Francisco in the 1852 census. The vast majority of black residents worked unskilled jobs, as white artisans and white labor organizations prohibited blacks from working in the skilled trades. The city's small African American community also competed for jobs with Chinese workers, who outnumbered blacks significantly in California. Here was a significant difference between the West and other regions of the nation. The western states and territories, especially the West Coast, contained large communities of Chinese and Mexican workers in addition to relatively small African American communities, all of whom competed for unskilled jobs.

Just as the gold rush attracted African Americans to California, the mountain fur trade attracted adventurous African Americans to other parts of the West. Under any circumstances, fur trapping and trading was a difficult occupation, but some rugged black men flourished in this rough and tumble undertaking. These mountain men, as others called the fur traders, faced isolation, danger from wild animals and the natural environment, hostile Indians, and unpredictable incomes. Peter Raney, who worked with the famous mountain man Jedediah Smith, came to California in 1826 and established a reputation as a successful fur hunter before Indians killed him in an undetermined conflict. James Beckwourth, who worked for the Rocky Mountain Fur Company in the 1820s and visited California on a number of occasions prior to statehood, surpassed Raney's exploits. An adventurous and daring man by nature, Beckwourth led several groups of migrants on the westward overland migration. During one exploration of the Pit River valley, he discovered the mountain pass (or trail) that allowed overland covered-wagon trains to reach the upper Sacramento Valley. The pass still bears his name. Beckwourth himself sought new challenges and moved to Colorado, where he conducted a number of businesses in Denver and acted as a government agent in negotiations between Indian nations and the United States during the Civil War. Beckwourth lived his final years working as a scout for the U.S. Army in Colorado and died at the age of sixty-six.

Not every black westerner looked to the West as a beacon of opportunity. Some fared so poorly there prior to the Civil War that they returned to their states of origin. Others criticized the restrictions that western state and territorial governments imposed on their civil rights. California, for example, denied African Americans the right to vote, attend integrated schools, testify in court in cases involving whites, and use either public accommodations or public transportation on an equal basis. San Francisco's black leaders were especially troubled by an anti-immigration bill that passed the California State Assembly overwhelmingly and seemed destined to pass in the state senate. This bill would have severely restricted the ability of African Americans to leave the state, even to conduct business or to join family members, for it imposed a heavy monetary tax to reenter California. To the relief of African American leaders in California, a technicality defeated the passage of the bill in the state senate. Other western states and territories passed laws that prohibited free blacks from even entering their communities. The Oregon territorial legislature, for example, passed a Negro Exclusion law as well as numerous restrictive laws that discriminated against free blacks already in Oregon. Likewise, territorial legislatures in Kansas, Utah, and Nebraska passed racially restrictive legislation.

During the turbulent decade of the 1850s, the narrowing of economic and political opportunities and California's anti-Negro immigration bill prompted some black westerners to reassess their relationship with the West. In the most dramatic example, in 1858 several hundred black westerners, the majority of whom lived in San Francisco, emigrated to Victoria, British Columbia, in effect swapping one western community, where they had become dissatisfied, for another. One of these immigrants was Archy Lee, the former slave who had gained his freedom in 1858. Lee apparently found Victoria to his liking, for he became a successful drayman (transporting goods in a flat, horse-drawn wagon) and property owner in the city. The former black merchant from San Francisco, Mifflin Gibbs, also prospered in Victoria, writing that Canada (then known as British North America) drew blacks like himself "by the two-fold inducement of gold discovery and the assurance of enjoying impartially the benefits of constitutional liberty." Many of these African American settlers prospered, built homes, and enjoyed the respect of their contemporaries. African Americans also enjoyed political rights in British Columbia denied them in California and most other western states and territories. Neither British Columbia nor any other locale, however, attracted more than a small number of disaffected African American western migrants prior to the Civil War. The majority of black westerners remained in the U.S. West, guardedly optimistic that their condition would improve over time.

Civil War

Black westerners viewed the Civil War as a time of great promise for the young nation and an opportunity to rid it of slavery. They also hoped the war would give them a chance to prove their loyalty to the nation. Thus, black westerners took a keen interest in the outcome of the war and in President Abraham Lincoln's remarks regarding the connection between slavery and the conflict. Black westerners followed the course of the war through black newspapers such as *Douglass' Monthly*, published by Frederick Douglass. Although blacks in the far western states and territories did not commit troops to fight for the Union army, they supported the Union by raising funds and collecting food and clothing to assist fugitive slaves who came West during the war, and for such organizations as the U.S. Sanitary Commission (created by President Abraham Lincoln to coordinate women volunteers who wanted to contribute to the war effort).

Because a large number of African Americans had come west as slaves prior to the outbreak of fighting in 1861, the outcome of the war, particularly in Texas, had a critical bearing on their future. Texas had the largest number of slaves of any state or territory in the West. That number, 182,556 in 1860, actually increased during the course of the Civil War, as white planters from neighboring states brought their bondmen to Texas for safe keeping. Because so many of the early Civil War battles occurred in the East or later in border states such as Kentucky and Tennessee, Texas appeared far removed from the destruction of life or the devastation that plantation society faced between 1861 and 1865. As the number of free blacks in Texas was never large, black Texans played only a marginal role in supporting the Union army, contributing a mere 47 men to the fight.

The African American population in Kansas, although not nearly as large as that in Texas or California, played an important role in the Civil War. Only 627 African Americans were reported in the territory of Kansas in 1860, but that number increased significantly as the war progressed. Black Kansans contributed many soldiers to the Union army and established stations on the Underground Railroad to support fugitive slaves. The voters of the Kansas Territory had rejected the institution of slavery in their constitution on three occasions prior to the Civil War, and the towns of Lawrence and Leavenworth were highly sympathetic to fugitive slaves. As many as 5,000 fugitive slaves were reported in Kansas in 1862, with many of these runaways coming from neighboring Missouri and Arkansas. One such fugitive who "stole himself" was Henry C. Bruce, whose brother, Blanche K. Bruce, would become a United States senator from Mississippi during Reconstruction, one of two African Americans who served in the Senate during this time. Henry arrived on a ferryboat in Leavenworth, a town whose black population had increased significantly during the Civil War. When he arrived at Fort Leavenworth, after crossing the Missouri River, Bruce proclaimed for the first time, "I then felt myself a free man." The town of Lawrence also welcomed fugitive slaves. The "sack" or destruction of Lawrence in 1856 by eight hundred armed pro-slavery intruders still resonated strongly with many residents of the town, which had opposed slavery repeatedly prior to Kansas' admission into the Union as a free state in 1861. These black newcomers organized the Freedmen's Church in 1862 and labored zealously to gain the basic rudiments of literacy. African American women in Lawrence contributed as readily to the war effort as their male counterparts and organized the Ladies Refugee Aid Society, which collected food and supplies to help former slaves. The society was a precursor both to the Freedmen's Bureau, which distributed aid nationally to all freedmen and refugees, irrespective of race, and numerous statewide black women's organizations that provided assistance to needy African Americans throughout the second half of the nineteenth century.

Kansas' most significant contribution to the war effort, however, was the formation of a colored regiment of six hundred troops, the First Kansas Colored Infantry, in August 1862. Kansas senator James Henry Lane played a pivotal role in the organization of black troops, encouraging African Americans to fight for their own freedom as well as the collective Union effort to unite the nation, his exhortations predating President Abraham Lincoln's commitment that the Civil War was fought to abolish slavery as well as save the union. The Union promised each black recruit, of which there was no shortage, $10 a month in regular army pay, provisions, and certificates of freedom for the enlistee and his family. Although black recruits received $3 less per month than did white enlistees, a policy that remained in force throughout the entire U.S. military until 1863, black troops in the West took tremendous pride in serving their country. As historian W. E. B. Du Bois would write later about the heroism of all black Civil War soldiers, black soldiers could only gain recognition of their manhood through combat. As part of the Army of the Frontier, the First Kansas Colored Infantry also included Indians loyal to the Union and white regiments from the West. Free blacks from northern states also joined this unit, and the men in the First Kansas Colored Infantry became the first black soldiers to fight and die in service to their country during the Civil War. A portion of the regiment fought a rebel force at Butler, Missouri, in the fall of 1862, and the local press noted their bravery and heroism. The *Lawrence Republican* wrote that the black soldiers "behaved nobly," and "have demonstrated that they can and will fight." The regiment engaged a rebel force in October 1862 at Island Mound in Bates County, Missouri, and although ten black soldiers were killed in the fighting, their courageous stand forced the Confederates to retreat. The unit was formally mustered into federal service on January 13, 1863, under the command of Colonel James M. Williams. The First Kansas Colored Infantry represented the fourth African American unit to be mustered into the federal army, and their inclusion predated that of the famed

54th Massachusetts regiment by several weeks. The Fifty-fourth, led by Colonel Robert Gould Shaw, the son of a Massachusetts legislator, fought valiantly in numerous Civil War campaigns and led a famous assault on Fort Wagner, which guarded the entrance to Charleston's strategic harbor. The heroism of these troops and their commanding officer was captured in the academy-award-winning film *Glory* (1989).

Acquitting themselves bravely in combat, the First Kansas Colored Infantry fought in numerous battles in Indian Territory in the American West. In July 1863, the black regiment fought alongside whites for the first time, at Cabin Creek in present-day Oklahoma, where they turned back Confederate troops. As historian Dudley Cornish writes, "this engagement seems to have been the first in the Civil War in which white and colored Union soldiers fought side by side, and it is recorded that the white officers and men allowed no prejudice on account of color to interfere in the discharge of their duty in the face of an enemy alike to both races."

The First Kansas Colored's most significant engagement against Confederates troops, however, remains the successful engagement at the Battle of Honey Springs in July 1863. Considered the largest Civil War battle fought in Indian Territory, the Battle of Honey Springs was a brazen attempt by the Confederate army to drive all Union troops from Indian Territory. The First Kansas Colored, under the command of Major General James G. Blunt and fighting alongside allies from the Cherokee Nation and white Union troops, routed Confederate forces. The black regiment held the Union center during the fierce fighting and moved within fifty steps of the Confederate line before they exchanged volley fire for twenty minutes, forcing the rebels to break ranks and run. The First Kansas Colored even captured the colors of a Texas regiment. By all surviving accounts, these five hundred black troops fought bravely and courageously, but Major General Blunt paid his men the highest compliment of all. In a letter published in the *Cincinnati Daily Commercial* in 1863, he wrote that "I never saw such fighting as was done by the negro [sic] regiment." The black soldiers, he continued, "fought like veterans, with a coolness and valor that is unsurpassed."

The First Kansas Colored's valor would be tested again in April 1864 at the battle of Poison Springs, Arkansas. This time the regiment did not fare so well, suffering heavy casualties: 117 men dead and 65 wounded. Confederate soldiers executed all wounded or captured black troops on the battlefield, spiking the casualty numbers. Following the battle, black soldiers in the West adopted the battle cry, "Remember Poison Springs." The battle of Poison Springs put to rest any lingering doubt about the willingness of African American troops to die for their country. By the conclusion of the Civil War, Kansas had enlisted more than 20,000 soldiers in nineteen regiments and four batteries. One of these batteries and two of the regiments were "Colored." A total of 2,080 African Americans represented the Jayhawk State (Kansas) during the Civil War.

The Civil War thus marked a major turning point in the history of the U.S. West. African Americans had shown their bravery and valor on the battlefield, and they were poised to take their place as full-fledged citizens in their respective communities. As they returned home to support their families, educate their children, and participate in local and statewide politics, black westerners generally felt optimistic, believing that their futures would be brighter. At the same time, they were aware that the end of the Civil War also left them with an array of new challenges, including testing the limits of the newfound freedom and securing political rights that many black westerners previously had been denied. Despite their contribution to the war effort, black westerners knew also that white racial attitudes would not change overnight. For those in Texas, the conclusion of the Civil War also meant casting off the shackles of slavery and finding a meaningful place in society as free persons.

Suggested Readings

Baker, T. Lindsey and Julie P. Baker, eds. *Till Freedom Cried Out: Memories of Texas Slave Life.* College Station: Texas A&M University Press, 1997.

Barr, Alwyn. *Black Texans: A History of Negroes in Texas, 1528–1971.* 2d. ed. Norman, OK: University of Oklahoma Press, 1996.

Berwanger, Eugene. *The Frontier Against Slavery: Western Anti-Negro Prejudice and the Slavery Extension Controversy.* Urbana: University of Illinois Press, 1967.

Bonner, Thomas D., ed. *Life and Adventures of James Beckwourth.* Lincoln: University of Nebraska Press, 1972.

Bragg, Susan. "Knowledge is Power: Sacramento Blacks and the Public Schools, 1854–1860." *California History* 75 (1996): 214–21.

Broussard, Albert S. *Black San Francisco: The Struggle for Racial Equality in the West, 1900–1954.* Lawrence: The University Press of Kansas, 1993.

Bruce, Henry Clay. *The New Man: Twenty-nine Years a Slave, Twenty-Nine years a Free Man.* Lincoln: University of Nebraska Press, 1996.

Campbell, Randolph. *An Empire for Slavery: The Peculiar Institution in Texas.* Baton Rouge: Louisiana State University Press, 1989.

Castel, Albert. "Civil War Kansas and the Negro." *Journal of Negro History* 52 (April 1966): 125–138.

Chandler, Robert J. "Friends in Time of Need, Republicans and Black Civil Rights in California during the Civil War Era." *Arizona and the West* 24 (Winter 1982): 319–40.

Fisher, James. "The Struggle for Negro Testimony in California, 1851–1863." *Southern California Quarterly* 51 (December 1969): 313–34.

Forbes, Jack. "Black Pioneers: The Spanish-Speaking Afroamericans of the Southwest." *Phylon* 27 (Fall 1966): 233–246.

Jackson, Miles M., ed. They Followed the Trade Winds: African Americans in Hawaii (entire issue) *Social Process in Hawaii* 43 (2004).

Lapp, Rudolph. *Blacks in Gold Rush California.* New Haven: Yale University Press, 1977.

Rawley, James. *Race and Politics: "Bleeding Kansas" and the Coming of the Civil War.* Philadelphia: J. B. Lippincott, 1969.

Rampp, Lary C. and Donald L. Rampp. *The Civil War in the Indian Territory.* Austin: Presidial Press, 1975.

Telfer, John H. "Philip Alexander Bell and the San Francisco Elevator." *San Francisco Historical and Cultural Society Monograph* (August 1966): 1–11.

Weber, David J. "A Black American in Mexican San Diego: Two Recently Discovered Documents." *Journal of San Diego History* 20 (1974): 29–32.

Wollenberg, Charles. *All Deliberate Speed: Segregation and Exclusion in California Schools, 1855–1975.* Berkeley: University of California Press, 1976.

CHAPTER TWO

The Era of Reconstruction

As the Civil War drew to a close, free and enslaved African Americans lived in communities throughout the West, principally in California and Texas, where blacks would pursue new political and economic freedoms immediately after the war. Soon, black migrants from the South joined existing communities of black westerners or created new communities on the Great Plains. Wherever they settled, the migrants worked hard to establish themselves and better their new communities, believing in the promise of new rights and freedoms.

The Civil War years and the postwar era of Reconstruction that followed transformed the whole nation profoundly, but it changed the American West in specific ways. The Thirteenth Amendment to the U.S. Constitution, passed by Congress in 1865, abolished slavery throughout the nation, including Texas, where the overwhelming majority of western slaves had been held in bondage. The Fourteenth Amendment, ratified by the states in 1868, clarified for the first time who, irrespective of race or nationality, was a United States citizen, and the Fifteenth Amendment, ratified in 1870, granted black men the right to vote. The passage of three constitutional amendments in the space of five years constituted a political revolution, and black westerners acknowledged the importance of their newfound political and civil rights with passionate celebrations.

Perhaps nowhere did the end of slavery in the West resonate

more powerfully than in Texas. When, on June 19, 1865, Union general Gordon Granger sailed into Galveston Bay and issued General Order No. 3, known as the Texas Emancipation Proclamation, the Lone Star State's 183,000 slaves suddenly became aware of their freedom. Throughout the remainder of the nineteenth century and into the twentieth, "Juneteenth," as this day has become commonly known, was the most popular celebration held in the United States to mark the end of slavery. During the nineteenth century, public celebrations of Juneteenth varied widely from community to community throughout the state, but they generally commenced with a ceremonial reading of the Emancipation Proclamation issued by President Abraham Lincoln on January 1, 1863, followed by a featured speaker, then a locally organized public festival or celebration such as a picnic or a parade. Amid the revelry of good food and good music, African American ministers typically held church services to mark the significance of the occasion. Such public celebrations of Juneteenth represented a form of activism on the part of Texas freedpeople, for, as historian Elizabeth Hayes Turner writes, "In venerating Lincoln and in rejecting Jefferson Davis, freedpeople presented an emergent dissenting view. Lincoln's Emancipation Proclamation epitomized the freedpeople's dissenting view." In short, the annual statewide Juneteenth celebrations dramatically illustrated that freed people valued liberty over bondage and saw their emancipation as the dawning of a new era, one full of exciting possibilities.

Although General Granger's order made it clear that slavery in any form had been abolished in Texas, the same mandate also encouraged black Texans to sign labor contracts, plant crops, and remain settled on their present plantations. Neither General Granger nor white Texans welcomed the prospects of tens of thousands of black people wandering the countryside looking for jobs or displaced family members. In its massive postwar policy known collectively as Reconstruction, the federal government failed to provide freedpeople with land or any form of meaningful compensation for their years as forced laborers, which, understandably, deeply disappointed many

black Texans. Still, African Americans felt encouraged that they now possessed control over many aspects of their lives, such as legalizing marriages and signing contracts to work for wages. Very soon after war's end, black men and women began to assert their new freedom in areas such as education and politics.

Education

Hope that freedom would evolve and grow for African Americans blossomed with the establishment throughout Texas of the first schools for blacks, many of which were one-room schoolhouses founded by the Freedmen's Bureau.

Established by Congress in March 1865, the Bureau of Refugees, Freedmen, and Abandoned Lands, commonly known as the Freedmen's Bureau, was designed as a temporary agency, a branch of the U.S. Army. Its primary function was to assist anyone, black or white, who had been displaced or left homeless by the Civil War. But the agency also supervised the affairs of freed slaves in the southern states, administered all land abandoned by Confederates or confiscated by the Union army during the war, and established a system of public schools for the former slaves in the South. In January 1866, the bureau supervised sixteen schools for black students, some of whom were adults, who showed a desire to learn. Within six months, the Freedmen's Bureau in Texas reported that they had set up ninety schools, which instructed 4,590 students and employed forty-three teachers. By 1870, there were eighty-eight freedmen schools in Texas, employing eighty-five teachers, which included forty-five African Americans, who instructed 4,468 students.

Freedmen schools were staffed by both black and white teachers, the majority of whom were supplied by the American Missionary Association (AMA) and most of them, at least initially, came from northern states. Since most black Texans were newly freed slaves and resided in rural areas, freedmen schools amounted to little more than one-room schoolhouses. Yet freedmen schools also operated in towns, where they were afforded military protection, and some operated out of African American churches. Freedmen schools faced enormous challenges, however, wherever they were located, including difficulty in recruiting teachers, a shortage of school supplies, and attempting to educate African American students in a racially charged atmosphere, particularly in the wake of the defeat of the Confederacy.

The Freedmen's Bureau also operated in Kansas, but there, the challenges the bureau agents and its educators faced were significantly different than those facing their counterparts in Texas. Unlike Texas, which had fought for the Confederacy and possessed the dual status as both a southern and a western state, Kansas entered the Union as a free state in 1861 and the Jayhawk State contained an active and committed abolitionist movement. In August 1865, Charles Henry Langston, a prominent African American, was appointed as a Freedmen's Bureau agent for the states of Kansas and Missouri. A prominent educator, politician, and civil rights leader, Charles Henry Langston, the grandfather of Langston Hughes, arguably one of the leading American poets of the twentieth century, was a remarkable man. Charles and his brother John attended Oberlin College in Oberlin, Ohio, an institution which from its inception permitted women the same educational opportunities as men. Yet Oberlin also allowed African American students to enroll on an equal basis with whites and to attend classes on an integrated basis. Viewed by some as a hotbed of radicalism on many issues, the college as well as the surrounding community had numerous black residents and stations on the Underground Railroad to assist fugitive slaves on their journey to freedom. Langston's responsibility as a Freedmen's Bureau agent included general supervision over the schools of freedmen as well as their moral and religious condition. The vast majority of the freedmen under his supervision were refugees who had fled from Missouri to Kansas during the Civil War.

Remarkably, not long after the bureau set up and began to operate the first schools for African Americans in Texas, black leaders there pressed successfully for the creation of several public and private colleges. The most notable became Paul Quinn in Austin (1872), Prairie View A&M (1876), and Tillotson College, also in Austin (1877). Since public and private colleges in Texas remained segregated by race until the second half of the twentieth century, these institutions trained the majority of college-educated African Americans in the Lone Star State, including many of Texas's future political leaders and the vast majority of black teachers in the state, a critical component of the black professional class. Through a succession of small victories, black teachers, who had far fewer resources at their disposal than their white counterparts, achieved remarkable success in educating hundreds of thousands of black children in the wake of slavery, despite the disadvantages those students faced. The achievements of the black teachers were all the more remarkable because they operated in a system that expected them to fail. In addition to instructing African American children, black teachers served as role models, community spokespersons, and mediators between the African American and white community. They also represented models of decorum and respectability, teaching black children how to persevere during difficult times, earn a respectable living, fight for full equality, and maintain one's dignity.

Politics

As with education, African Americans in Texas and elsewhere in the West took a keen interest in politics after 1865. Blacks viewed participation in the political process as a means to gain power, respect, and dignity, not only as individuals but as a race, preparing black men and women to function as responsible citizens and to fight aggressively for their civil rights. African Americans believed, too, that engaging in the political process would elevate their status socially, economically, and educationally. That said, African Americans had little prior experience in political affairs before 1865, and they stood at a severe disadvantage compared to their white counterparts. Not a single black westerner, for example, had held a major political office before the era of Reconstruction.

The elections of 1866, 1868, and 1870 swept the Republican Party into power nationally, and African Americans, who cast votes for the first time in most western states and territories, elected an impressive number of black men to state legislatures. Texas led all western states in the number of black officeholders, electing Matthew Gaines and George T. Ruby to the state senate in 1870 and twelve other Africans Americans to the state house of representatives, the majority of them coming from counties with a high percentage of black population along the Gulf Coast, the Brazos and Colorado rivers, and in Northeast Texas.

Several black legislatures played important roles. Gaines and Ruby, for example, served on several senate committees and wielded considerable influence within the state Republican Party. Both men supported bills to strengthen economic development and public education, and Gaines expressed strong opposition to separate facilities for African Americans. Gaines gave his spirited support to Senate Bill No. 276 in the Texas legislature (1871), which created Texas A&M University, one of the premier public universities in Texas. Ironically, nearly nine decades would pass before Texas A&M permitted its first African American student to enroll.

While no other western state rivaled Texas in electing black officeholders, several of them did pass laws that strengthened black political and civil rights. Nevada became the first state in the Union to ratify the Fifteenth Amendment, in large measure because Republican senator William Stewart was a principal congressional sponsor of this important, though controversial, legislation. Born in rural New York, Stewart briefly attended Yale before moving to California in 1850 during the gold rush. Like most miners, Stewart achieved only moderate success, so he shifted course by studying law, then entering politics. The attorney general of California, who had been Stewart's law partner, chose Stewart to serve as the acting attorney general when the former was forced to take a leave of absence from office. Lured by the momentous discovery of silver known as the Comstock Lode, in 1860 Stewart moved to Nevada, where he worked in mining litigation. Although favoring more moderate policies toward the readmission of the Confederate states to the Union, Stewart detested President Andrew Johnson, and his disdain for the President led him to support voting rights for African Americans. Nebraska, which contained a small black population, also permitted black suffrage as early as 1867, as a condition of its admission as a state to the Union, and Kansas, which had been fervently anti-slavery prior to the Civil War, also strongly endorsed the amendment. Neither California nor Oregon ratified the Fifteenth Amendment, however, as Democrats controlled the legislatures in both states and vehemently opposed African American suffrage. By initially denying African Americans the right to vote, these states also prevented African Americans from gaining political office prior to the ratification of the Fifteenth Amendment in 1870.

Other western states also elected African Americans to elective office, two of the most capable of whom were Edward McCabe and John Lewis Waller. Edward McCabe, a native of New York who had migrated to Kansas during the "Exodus," won election as state auditor of Kansas in 1881, the highest elective office achieved by an African American in nineteenth-century Kansas. John Lewis Waller, a former slave from Missouri who moved to Kansas in 1878, received an appointment as ambassador to Madagascar in 1891, thereby becoming one of the first African Americans in the West to gain an appointment to national office. Waller, a Republican, served three years with the consular service, and, in 1882, established the state's first black newspaper, *The Western Recorder*, in Lawrence. During this era, even states without large African American populations, such as Kansas, Nebraska, Colorado, and Wyoming, elected or appointed black men to office.

African Americans also began to play prominent roles in Republican Party politics at the state level. Again, Texas led the way. When Texans called a new constitutional convention and elected delegates to it in February 1868, they seated nine African Americans. These men and their Republican supporters succeeded in including provisions in the new state constitution that rejected legal discrimination and ensured free public schools for all Texas students, irrespective of race. The Twelfth Legislature (1870) passed bills creating the State Police and a state militia to control the rampant lawlessness and crime in Texas, some of which was racially motivated. To the displeasure of white Democrats, African Americans composed a majority of the new state militia and 40 percent of the state police, an indicator that racial violence had taken its toll on black Texans, more and more of whom would no longer stand idly by when whites threatened their lives and communities. Thus, within five years of the end of the Civil War, African Americans in Texas acted on their new freedom by actively pursuing political power.

Black political leaders in Texas also played significant roles in the affairs of their party, none more so than G. T. Ruby and Norris Wright Cuney. Ruby, a northern-born journalist and educator, migrated to Texas from Louisiana in 1866. He joined the Freedmen's Bureau in Galveston and became the administrator of the schools. He also taught school at the Methodist Episcopal Church in Galveston and later became a traveling agent for the bureau throughout numerous Texas counties. He served in this capacity until October 1867. Ruby also helped establish the Loyal Union League, an organization designed to seek political rights for black Texans and foster

African American support for the Republican Party. By the time of the convocation of the Twelfth Legislature in 1870, in which Ruby served in the state senate, many people already regarded him as one of the most prominent black politicians in Texas.

While in Galveston, Ruby also published the *Galveston Standard*, a short-lived African American newspaper. Yet it was Ruby's work in the Texas state senate that earned him the greatest degree of respect. As historian Merline Pitre writes, "As a senator, he became one of the most influential men of the Twelfth and Thirteenth legislatures." Ruby's colleagues appointed him to many important committees, including judiciary, militia, education, and state affairs. A strong advocate of organized labor, Ruby organized the first Labor Union of Colored Men at Galveston. Although little is known about Ruby's personal life, he married a mulatta (a fair-skinned woman of African descent) who many persons mistook for white.

During this same time, Norris Wright Cuney emerged as the most influential African American politician in Texas. The son of Philip Cuney, a prominent white Texas planter, Norris had been raised and educated to lead from a young age. Unlike Ruby, Cuney never held a major elective office within the state, but through his leadership within the Republican Party, Cuney secured the prestigious position as collector of customs for Galveston, Texas, where he distributed federal patronage to both white and black Texans. Cuney also served on the Galveston City Council and dedicated himself to improving the condition of African American workers in Texas. When state representatives selected Cuney as national committeeman for Texas at the state convention in 1886, he became arguably the most powerful Republican politician of any race in the state.

One can see the enthusiasm with which African Americans embraced politics in Texas after the Civil War on a smaller scale in several other western states, particularly California. Prior to the Civil War, between 1855 and 1865, black leaders in California organized four statewide conventions with political rights, civil liberties, employment, and education topping their agendas. When those leaders in San Francisco organized a statewide political convention

in 1865, suffrage was the foremost issue. The assembled black delegates based their argument for the right of black men to vote on
their important contributions to American society, most recently the
invaluable service that black soldiers had rendered for the Union
army. The delegates formally petitioned the state legislature, request-
ing an immediate repeal of California's racially discriminatory
suffrage law. These political protests by black Californians stand as
the first steps in the civil rights movement by black westerners.

California, which entered the Union as a free state, quickly
emerged as the center of western civil rights activism, with San
Francisco and Sacramento serving as strongholds. San Francisco,
a boomtown following the discovery of gold at Sutter's Fort near
Sacramento in 1848, had attracted African Americans from across
the nation, as well as blacks from Mexico, Jamaica, and Latin
America. It continued to do so after the Civil War. Black migrants
to California from the East Coast, particularly those from New
England, had long exposure to radical abolitionist newspapers such
as William Lloyd Garrison's *Liberator*, the *Colored American*, and
Frederick Douglass's *North Star*. Some of these new arrivals, such
as Philip Alexander Bell, had edited black newspapers before their
arrival in San Francisco, while others had worked tirelessly to end
the legal exclusions against free blacks. As a result, organized black
protest in San Francisco had predated the Civil War, beginning
as early as 1851, when African American leaders printed a resolu-
tion in a local newspaper protesting the denial of suffrage and the
inability of blacks to testify in court cases involving whites. In 1871
black San Franciscans protested segregated schools for black children and their inability to use public accommodations on an equal
basis. The campaign that the city's black leaders waged throughout
the 1860s to give blacks the right to ride on public transportation on an equal basis with whites interested African Americans of
all social classes, but particularly black women, who depended on
local transportation to get to their jobs and to stores to purchase
food for their households. Small wonder, then, that black women
frequently lay at the center of these disputes. The San Francisco

Pacific Appeal, a local black newspaper, reported in 1863 that "two of our most respectable females were denied seats in one of the city railway cars."

As it turned out, neither of the women to whom the paper was referring, Mary Ellen Pleasant and Charlotte L. Brown, took the matter lightly, for each of them brought a suit against the local railway companies and collected damages after having been ejected from city streetcars solely because of their race. Although many details regarding the life of Mary Ellen Pleasant remain shrouded in mystery, such as where she was born and if she had ever been enslaved, she insisted that she had been born free in 1814 in Philadelphia, the locale of a large free black community as well as a station on the Underground Railroad. A striking woman physically, surviving accounts describe Pleasant as a tall, fair-skinned woman and a formidable presence. Like the majority of black women who were gainfully employed in the West, Pleasant worked as a domestic when she first arrived in San Francisco. But unlike most black domestics, Pleasant worked in the homes of wealthy white families, including that of Selim and Lisette Woodworth, where she managed to learn the intricacies of San Francisco's business community, accumulated a small savings, and invested her money wisely. (A former commander in the U.S. Navy, Selim Woodworth was reputably one of San Francisco's wealthiest merchants.) In time, Pleasant was engaging in mining stock and precious metals speculation, running a boarding house, and the owner of three laundries. Even though she was clearly a woman of means, San Francisco's black community embraced Pleasant as one of their own, for she contributed to charitable causes in the community and supported the local black press. Much less is known about Charlotte M. Brown's background; nevertheless, her ability to bring a successful legal challenge against a streetcar company suggests that she belonged to San Francisco's small black middle class. Black women also predominated in San Francisco's early civil rights and social organizations, such as the Ladies Union Beneficial Society and the Daughters and Sons of the Zion Benevolent Association.

Although barred from participating in the black state conventions because of their gender, African American women contributed to the early civil rights struggle in the West in important ways. Not content to passively accept second-class citizenship, these women challenged racially discriminatory laws directly in the courts and, in so doing, challenged the meaning of citizenship in the West. By demanding their rights as American citizens, they exposed the hypocrisy of California's professed racial liberalism and tolerance. Denied seats at political conventions and unable to vote, African American women typically worked for racial equality and reform within female organizations such as women's clubs and literary societies.

Black women contributed significantly to the support and maintenance of African American institutions in other areas of public life, notably churches. In small and large western communities alike, African American women organized bake sales, bazaars, and fund-raisers to sustain their churches. For example, in 1860 the small African American community in Marysville, California, supported the day-to-day activities of the Mount Olivet Baptist Church through the collaborative support of its parishioners and a committee of church women who conducted regular fund-raisers. In similar ways, black women raised money to provide crucial economic support to *The Mirror of the Times* of San Francisco, the first African American newspaper published in California.

Finally, it was women who led the campaign to gain educational equality for black children in California's public schools. By allowing themselves to be named as plaintiffs in case after case, the dogged persistence of African American women eventually forced the California Supreme Court to strike down the state's segregated school law in 1880. The campaign to end legal segregation in California's public schools reveals that black women's activism operated outside the boundaries of politics, conventions, and other male-dominated organizations. Rather, western black women challenged racial exclusion in the courts and willingly worked with middle-class white women, concerned parents, friends, and female organizations in their quest to receive racial justice. They demanded that African American women, like all respectable women, be treated civilly and granted access to schools and public accommodations on an equal basis. Before and after the Civil War, men and women in the black communities in the West sought political influence over their lives and the lives of their children. They believed that they could make the West, unlike the South, a place with fewer restrictions on their rights. Other African Americans sought influence over the lives of others through the military.

The End of Reconstruction

The era of Reconstruction came to an end in the late 1870s and, as historian Adam Fairclough concluded, signaled the triumph of white supremacy. Whites throughout the South, including Texas, had resisted and sought to contain black freedom as soon as the Civil War ended, but after the end of Reconstruction every southern state legislature passed a series of repressive and discriminatory laws known as Black Codes, which were followed by a more lasting system of racially discriminatory laws and customs known collectively as the "Jim Crow" laws. These laws physically separated Africans Americans from whites in states like Texas literally from the cradle to the grave. Blacks and whites were born in separate hospitals, raised in separate communities, attended separate schools, generally worked in separate jobs, and seldom if ever attended the same social functions. Segregation even followed blacks and whites into the afterlife, as they were buried in separate cemeteries. The era of Reconstruction also unleashed a flood tide of violence, retribution, and discrimination against African Americans in the former Confederate states. Even as 4 million slaves turned freedmen attempted to form stable families, acquire property, educate themselves and their children, and find meaningful employment, white southerners viewed any assertion of even the most basic civil rights by blacks as a threat to white supremacy and their way of life. Lawlessness abounded in every southern state, as white Confederate soldiers came home bitter and unrepentant over the defeat of the Confederacy, often directing their rage, contempt, and fury at African Americans through a variety of grisly methods.

The federal government's inability to protect the lives of African Americans in Texas and throughout the South after the end of the war in 1865 represents one of the greatest failures of Reconstruction. As early as 1866, race riots erupted in Memphis and New Orleans, where dozens of African Americans died at the hands of lawless white mobs and vigilantes. Nor did the Freedmen's Bureau protect the lives of African Americans in remote rural areas of the South. The agency's official records reveal that whites brutally attacked black men, women, and children, and that these victims and their family members had little recourse to justice. Any time, for example, that white southerners suspected black voters threatened white authority, they resorted to intimidation, violence, and orchestrated campaigns of terror. Some of this violence operated through secret organizations like the Ku Klux Klan (KKK), a white supremacist organization established in Pulaski, Tennessee, in 1866. The KKK and dozens of similar organizations, threatened, beat, and killed hundreds of black southerners, some of whom were lynched, a new and brutal (both physically and psychologically) form of racial violence that emerged after the Civil War. Thus, exercising their newfound rights as citizens in this highly charged atmosphere proved to be very difficult.

Black men in Texas and the South found it increasingly difficult to vote, a right that had been guaranteed them with the passage of the Fifteenth Amendment. White southerners used a variety of devices such as literacy tests, Grandfather clauses, residency requirements, and poll taxes to keep African Americans away from the polls. Typically these tactics proved to be effective, but when they did not, whites resorted to violence and intimidation. Collectively, these tactics, both legal and extralegal, assured second-class citizenship for African Americans, stripped them of political power, and served as a stern warning to other blacks not to challenge white authority. Moreover, white supremacist groups, including terrorist organizations such as the KKK, emerged as influential institutions in the twentieth-century West in such cities as Houston, Denver, Los Angeles, and Portland, where their membership harassed not only African Americans but Jews, Catholics, and European immigrants. The white supremacists could not take away black freedom, but they could and often did limit and circumvent it to a great extent for almost a century after the end of the Civil War. Therefore, the final push of the civil rights movement in the 1950s and 1960s—in the West as in the South and the rest of the nation—would serve as a second era of Reconstruction (see below, in Chapters Four and Five).

Buffalo Soldiers

In the decades after the Civil War, the U.S. military represented an important outlet and source of employment for African Americans. It afforded them an opportunity to assert their manhood, gain status, earn a steady wage, and, for many, their first chance to attain literacy. Serving in the military also permitted some soldiers to command and lead men and advance through the ranks of their units. Therefore, many black men voluntarily joined the army. In Texas and other western states and territories during Reconstruction and throughout the rest of the nineteenth century, the number of blacks who served in the military varied from year to year, but their numbers usually exceeded 1,000. The U.S. Army garrisoned the Ninth Cavalry, composed largely of black troops who had served in the Civil War, in the border forts along the Rio Grande. In the summer of 1866, Congress decreed that the army's regular forces should include six black regiments composed of four infantry regiments and two of cavalry. The army further consolidated these units in 1869, combining them into two regiments of cavalry, the Ninth and the Tenth, and two regiments of infantry, the Twenty-fourth and Twenty-fifth.

Despite the fictitious stories spread by white soldiers that African Americans soldiers lacked discipline and performed poorly in the heat of battle—stories allegedly about incidents in the Civil War—black soldiers as a group performed ably. Most of these soldiers proved brave and dependable, and black regiments maintained the lowest desertion rate and the highest rate of re-enlistment in the Army. Despite the poor treatment, insults, blatant acts of racial discrimination, unequal military justice, and indiscriminate violence that followed black soldiers in virtually every community or post in which they settled, nothing dampened their spirit or killed their enthusiasm to serve their country. Black troops of the Ninth and Tenth cavalries became known as "Buffalo Soldiers," a term of respect bestowed upon them by American Indians who likened the kinky hair of the black cavalrymen to that of the buffalo, an animal that the Plains Indians revered and considered sacred. Buffalo Soldiers took considerable pride in this honorific title.

The Buffalo Soldiers performed numerous military functions in the American West. They protected American settlers from hostile Indians as well as outlaws. They fought in numerous frontier wars against the Cheyenne, Kiowa, Apache, and other Indian nations. And they patrolled the Texas-Mexico border and the Texas Panhandle. White officers such as Colonel Benjamin Grierson, who commanded the Tenth Cavalry, and Colonel Edward Hatch, a Maine native who organized the Ninth Cavalry, had great respect for their men and confidence in their ability to fight.

The Buffalo Soldiers demonstrated their courage and fighting ability in numerous battles and skirmishes in the western states and territories. For example, the Tenth Cavalry played a key role in General Philip H. Sheridan's winter campaign of 1868–1869. After Sheridan's soldiers drove Southern Plains tribes onto reservations in Indian Territory (currently Oklahoma), the general assigned black soldiers the job of making sure the Kiowas, Kiowa-Apaches, and Comanches stayed on their reservations. Similarly, the Red River War in 1874 gave the Tenth Cavalry an opportunity to prove its mettle in combat. During a five-month military campaign, the black regiment, working in tandem with men from the Ninth Cavalry, destroyed more Indian lodges and property and captured more hostile Indians than any other regiment in the U.S. Army. In 1875, military authorities transferred the Tenth Cavalry to the Texas frontier and stationed the regiment at Fort Concho, Texas. For the next decade, these Buffalo Soldiers served as the major military presence in far West Texas.

By 1873, several companies of Buffalo Soldiers were garrisoned at forts on the northwest Texas frontier. In just four months of duty they managed to recover 1,200 stolen horses and head of cattle from ruthless rustlers, Mexican, Indian, or white. Buffalo Soldiers were also used to settle disputes in frontier communities as well as in urban areas where traditional modes of law enforcement proved to be ineffective. In 1877, the government used the Ninth Cavalry to stop an episode known as the Salt War in El Paso, Texas. This civil dispute arose between Anglo and Mexican American settlers when a group of whites who hoped to profit from the large deposits of salt, located one hundred miles east of El Paso, proposed to levy a tax on them, even though the salt deposits had been accessed freely for decades by residents on both sides of the Rio Grande. Colonel Edward Hatch was ordered to assume command of all troops in El Paso, as this local conflict had rapidly escalated and eleven persons had been killed. Only with the assistance of the Ninth Cavalry was this violent conflict resolved. In its wake, no less than seventeen Buffalo Soldiers received the Medal of Honor for heroism, an official acknowledgement of the bravery of these men.

In addition to the more famous Buffalo Soldiers, black infantrymen also fought admirably in the West. The Twenty-fourth Infantry served for many years in Indian Territory. Black infantrymen, like their white counterparts, built roads, constructed forts, escorted wagon trains, guarded army posts, and strung telegraph wire. By protecting stage routes, cattle drives, and mail riders, all tempting targets for Indians and outlaws, they acted as peacekeepers on the frontier, guaranteeing the safety of settlers and migrants moving west.

Despite their courage and outstanding service, black soldiers met with racial prejudice and violence no matter where in the West they were stationed. And despite the numerous roles black soldiers performed, they found themselves unwelcome in many western communities. They received little protection from local lawmen, and black military patrols even came under fire from or were ambushed by hostile whites and Mexicans. In 1875, a black sergeant named Edward Troutman and his detachment came under fire while searching for cattle rustlers in Texas. As the black soldiers fought their way through the ambush, two of them were shot to death. When the commanding colonel, Edward Hatch, learned of the attack, he dispatched to the scene sixty troops along with a deputy sheriff, where they found the mutilated bodies of the two Buffalo Soldiers. Hatch and his men then attempted to retrieve the uniforms and other equipment of the slain soldiers. Hatch arrested nine Mexican suspects, including two men who had bullet wounds, only to see a local grand jury release eight of the men and the other win a speedy acquittal, a sad commentary on frontier justice. Adding insult to injury, local authorities charged Hatch with false imprisonment of the men he had arrested, and a grand jury indicted him along with his patrol for burglary because he had illegally entered a private residence to recover property belonging to the two dead troops. Colonel Hatch correctly charged the residents of Starr County, Texas, with creating "a system of terror—to control the county in their interest."

The Buffalo Soldiers faced numerous obstacles in West Texas, perhaps the most formidable of which was fighting Apaches. On August 6, 1880, African American soldiers of the Tenth Cavalry combined with a detachment of soldiers from the Twenty-fourth Infantry to fight the notorious Apache leader Victorio. The United States Army did not take Victorio lightly, regarding him as one of the ablest of Apache chieftains, a smart tactician, and an effective leader of men. That the U.S. Army ordered the Buffalo Soldiers to pursue Victorio and his small band of warriors surprised no one. The military engagement that became known as the Battle of Rattlesnake Springs began after numerous Apache raids into settlements and towns in New Mexico, West Texas, and Mexico. American military officials grew especially alarmed in late July 1880 when Victorio and a band of his followers brazenly crossed the Rio Grande with the intent to find refuge in the Guadalupe Mountains on the Texas–New

Mexico border. Victorio had advanced in part to halt the advance of the Buffalo Soldiers across the western section of the Pecos. Colonel Benjamin H. Grierson, commander of the Tenth Cavalry and the District of the Pecos, decided initially not to pursue Victorio, but instead stationed black troops at strategic water holes and crossings that they had scouted carefully. Not long thereafter, however, Grierson permitted his men to engage Victorio in battle in the mountain passes, valleys, and plains of West Texas. At Rattlesnake Springs, located north of present-day Van Horn, Texas, the Buffalo Soldiers defeated Victorio decisively in a three-hour skirmish in which they fought bravely and once again demonstrated their combat effectiveness and ability to adapt to constantly changing conditions. Defeated and demoralized, and short of supplies and water, Victorio and his men withdrew into Mexico. As Grierson's soldiers pursued him, they left guards at the water holes and mountain passes to make certain that Victorio could not resupply or reenter the United States. Rattlesnake Springs marked the last appearance of Victorio on American soil. Shortly thereafter, Mexican forces killed the Apache raider in the Tres Castillos Mountains, a site Victorio had frequently used as a refuge, ending any remaining threat to West Texas or the Southwest. By the end of 1880, peace had finally come to the Texas frontier, and the Buffalo Soldiers, no longer needed at Fort Concho, were moved farther south in Texas to Fort Davis.

At the turn of the twentieth century, the Buffalo Soldiers would take on new roles. For one, black soldiers protected the American West's national parks prior to the creation of the National Park Service in 1916. Colonel Charles Young, a West Point graduate and the highest ranking black officer in the U.S. military until World War II, led troops in 1903 to Wawona, California, at the southern boundary of Yosemite National Park. In addition to building roads, Young and his fellow Buffalo Soldiers protected and guarded the park from outsiders who wished to despoil the area's natural beauty or harm its wildlife. The federal government subsequently appointed Young acting superintendent of Sequoia and General Grant national parks in

California, making him the first black superintendent of a national park. His responsibilities included directing the activities of all the park rangers as well as the construction of roads to California's Giant Forest, a stand of some of the oldest and tallest trees in the world.

African American soldiers thus lay at the center of the story of the "winning of the West." If this meant, ironically, that they played a role in the suppression of dissent and the imposition of social order that also denied them their own rights, it is also true that black soldiers contributed to the building of American society in the region. As historian William H. Leckie's excellent history of the Buffalo Soldiers, notes in summary: "The Ninth and Tenth Cavalry were first-rate regiments and major forces in promoting peace and advancing civilization along America's last continental frontier. The thriving cities and towns, the fertile fields, and the natural beauty of that once wild land are monuments enough for any buffalo soldier."

Despite their valor, racial prejudice also conspired to destroy the military careers of a number of black soldiers stationed in the West, with the career of Henry O. Flipper serving as a case in point. For the reasons enumerated above, African American soldiers took great pride in their military service, and during Reconstruction, a small number of black men attended the nation's military service academies. Between 1870 and 1877, twenty-seven African Americans received appointments to West Point Military Academy. Only twelve of the candidates passed the rigorous entrance examinations, and none of them had graduated when Henry Ossian Flipper entered the Academy in 1873. Although Flipper endured numerous hardships and considerable racism as a cadet, he graduated from West Point in 1877, giving him the distinction of becoming the first African American to do so.

Following his graduation, Lieutenant Flipper served in the Tenth Cavalry for five years and worked as the commissary officer at Fort Concho, Texas. An inept bookkeeper, Flipper faced charges of embezzlement, although the accusations were dismissed at his court-martial. Instead, the U.S. Army found Flipper guilty of making false statements and recommended his dismissal from the military. Flipper maintained his innocence, claiming that his friendship with the sister-in-law of a white officer—consorting with a white woman, one of America's most revered racial taboos—had produced these charges. Nonetheless, his promising military career came to an abrupt end. Flipper worked as a mining engineer in New Mexico and Mexico for the remainder of his life. Although he labored in vain to clear his name, he never succeeded in his lifetime. Ninety-five years after his dismissal, however, the army reversed its decision and granted Flipper an honorable discharge. In 1999, Flipper received a full presidential pardon. Though an unusual case in that Flipper had graduated from West Point, his treatment exemplified the challenges faced by all black soldiers of his day and, unfortunately, for many years thereafter.

Cowboys

Just like whites and Mexicans, African Americans became cowboys, bronco riders, wranglers, and cooks in the cattle industry in the nineteenth-century West. Every western state and territory contained some black cowboys and ranch hands, but Texas emerged as the center. Performing a wide array of tasks, these men, and occasionally women, proved to be highly competent workers and made a significant place for themselves in the cattle industry. African Americans, for instance, made up as much as 20 to 25 percent of the men who participated in the cattle drives from Texas to the Kansas railheads. Although the work was physically difficult and dangerous, black cowboys earned the respect of their fellow white and Mexican counterparts by performing their job as well as the next person. Working as a cowboy or ranch hand afforded a black man a higher degree of freedom and autonomy than enjoyed by the typical tenant farmer or a sharecropper. Black cowboys probably also faced less racial prejudice than their African American counterparts in other occupations, even if only a few of them managed to acquire land or sufficient herds to become ranchers or foremen.

Many black cowboys were remarkably accomplished horsemen. Ike Word, a former slave, had the reputation as the best roper on the Charles Word ranch near Goliad, Texas. Bose Ikard worked for the legendary cattle baron Charles Goodnight in West Texas, where Ikard herded cattle, fought off Indians, and guarded money. Ikard also accompanied Goodnight on his first long cattle drive, which opened the famed Goodnight-Loving Trail. Black cowboys excelled in the arts of taming mustangs, breaking horses, and bulldogging steers. An African American cowboy won the steer roping contest at Mobeetie, Texas, in 1884, and Bill Pickett, a native Texan and the son of former slaves, became widely known by the turn of the twentieth century for perfecting the technique of bulldogging, known today as steer wrestling. A man of black and Indian descent, Pickett's technique involved riding alongside a longhorn steer, dropping suddenly from his mount to grab the steer's head, then twisting it slowly while biting the powerful animal's upper lip. This method permitted Pickett to easily control the steer and soon was widely adopted by other steer wrestlers. Pickett performed for many years with the 101 Ranch Wild West Show in Oklahoma, and he worked at that prestigious ranch for much of his adult life. Because Pickett was featured in motion pictures, many film scholars regard him as the first African American western star. Pickett's acclaim among cowboys of all races resulted in his selection as the 1972 honoree of the National Rodeo Hall of Fame in Oklahoma City, the first African American to receive that honor. Finally, in 1994, the United States Post Office issued a postage stamp in his honor, although the stamp incorrectly displayed the image of Ben Pickett, one of Bill's brothers.

Not surprisingly, black men composed the overwhelming majority of African American cattle herders in this decidedly male culture, yet several black women, such as Johanna July, a Black Seminole woman, and Henrietta Williams Foster, also earned respect among their male counterparts of all races for breaking horses. As part of the migration of Black Seminoles from Mexico to Texas between 1870 and 1871, July and a community of Black Seminoles settled at Fort Duncan near Eagle Pass, and Fort Clark at Brackettville, both in Texas. Although Johanna performed the domestic duties expected of all young women, she also eagerly learned how to herd stock and manage cattle. Over time, she became an accomplished horsewoman: breaking wild horses was her specialty. Shunning the time-tested techniques cowboys had used in Mexico and Texas for generations to break broncos, Johanna would lead horses into the Rio Grande, making them swim about until they were too tired to buck during training. There is no record that black women accompanied male cowboys on the long trail drives, for the roles of black female hands were, on the basis of their gender, confined largely to working ranches and herding small stock of horses, goats, and cattle. The West provided African American men and women with opportunities they might not have had in the East or South. Both the military and the cattle industry allowed blacks to develop new skills and participate in ways barred to them in other parts of the United States.

Farmers

Throughout much of the post–Civil War era, the majority of black westerners lived in cities, but significant numbers of them resided in rural areas and worked in agriculture in places like Texas. Indeed, in 1900 nearly two-thirds of all black Texans labored in agriculture, the majority of whom (69 percent) as sharecroppers or tenant farmers. These men and women, often illiterate or poorly educated and less than a generation removed from slavery, scratched out a meager living. Black tenant farmers earned little profit for their labor, due to the small plots that they farmed but also the result of the exorbitant rates that the landowner and storekeeper (sometimes the same person) charged tenant families for things they needed every year— things such as seeds and equipment they needed to work the land, as well as food and sundry goods they needed to live. They gambled, in effect, that they would produce a large enough crop and that prices for that crop would be high enough come the harvest to repay the loans they had taken out from the storekeeper during planting season. Often they were unsuccessful and ended up in a vicious cycle of debt from which they could not escape. These cycles of debt trapped entire families, for not even a wagon or a farm animal could legally cross state lines unless the debt owed on it had been settled in full. Interest rates could run higher than 25 percent, and few black farmers possessed the wherewithal to challenge the balance sheets that white landowners presented to them at the end of each growing season.

Sharecroppers typically fared just as poorly as did tenant farmers, and some sharecropper families remained tied to the land they worked because of a recurring debt they never could satisfy, an oppressive social pattern known as debt peonage. Southern planters viewed sharecropping as the replacement system for slavery, for it guaranteed low wages and kept the majority of black southerners bound (practically in "bondage") to the land. For their part, many African Americans were hesitant to leave sharecropping because they risked being arrested for vagrancy, a Jim Crow law that if "violated" could land blacks in jail and then, perhaps, hired out as prison farm workers by the county or state. In addition, locating a better-paying job might be perceived as a sign of assertiveness on the part of black farmers, who thereby risked violence or economic retaliation.

Some categories of black farm workers fared slightly better than did tenants or sharecroppers but remained in poverty nonetheless. Black farm workers in Texas, for example, worked for operators of large farms for a wage, earning an average of $10 to $20 a month in the late nineteenth century. These were low wages, to be sure, but they provided the wage workers better economic status than sharecroppers. By earning wages, the former also escaped the crippling debt faced by sharecroppers, who, as mentioned, continuously had to take out loans for farm supplies. That said, the hours black farm hands put in were long and the work was tedious and difficult. Some planters in Texas also continued to employ white overseers who whipped workers for a variety of alleged offenses. African American farm workers could potentially improve their position by moving to another farm or into an urban area, just as whites and other migrant workers could. But unlike whites and others, the majority of black farm workers, men and women, possessed few marketable skills, making relocation difficult. Additionally, the pull of family and their lack of resources (compared to white migrants) further complicated relocation.

In response to the conditions they faced, black farmers made several attempts to improve their wages and the prices they received for their crops, in Texas pulling together to form the Colored Farmers Alliance and a Colored State Grange, similar to the farmers' organizations formed by white farmers of the day. Both organizations sought to provide their members support and a pooling of resources for the sale of crops or the purchase of land. These organizations also provided members a way to engage in what today we would call social networking, as black farmers from outlying regions came together in local chapters to socialize and discuss common grievances. The Colored Farmers Alliance, a national organization, was established in Houston County, Texas, in 1886 by R. M. Humphreys, a white Baptist minister. Its African American members soon took control over the alliance, which spread to twelve states and reached a membership of more than 1 million at its peak in 1890, following its merger with the National Colored Alliance, a rival group. J. J. Shuffer, a black Texan, served as president of the alliance, and H. S. Spencer as its secretary. These men and the other officers encouraged alliance members to learn new farm techniques, acquire ownership of their homes, improve their level of education, and operate cooperative stores. The Colored Alliance also published newspapers and raised money to provide longer school terms for black children, which showed that even farmers recognized the importance of the education of their children for the advancement of their race. In concert with the message that the majority of black organizations delivered to their members during this time, known generally by scholars as the age of agrarian discontent or Populism, the alliance instructed members to uplift themselves through diligence, thrift, good character, and sacrifice. Alliance members also learned that by owning their own homes and minimizing debt they could avoid economic forms of discrimination. The alliance also achieved some important interracial gains in the short run, such as the cooperative purchasing and marketing of goods and farm supplies between black and white farmers. Despite these achievements, the Colored Farmers Alliance failed in 1891 due to a lack of funds, the inexperience of managers who ran some of the local exchanges, and the failure of a cotton pickers' strike that the alliance had called in September 1891. It should be noted, however, that farmer's movements in general failed during the era.

Black farmers shared hard work and frustration with the pricing schemes of purchasing agents and railroads with white farmers of the period. But black farmers also suffered disproportionately under the sharecropper system, inherent racism of landowners, and a greater lack of skills, making things harder for them. Finally, white southern planters and their supporters felt threatened by the alliances of black and white farmers during the populism of the 1890s. This biracial grass-roots movement to improve the economic plight of all farmers, irrespective of race, swept through the southern, midwestern, and western states. The Populists (or People's Party, as they were also known) endorsed candidates for political office who supported the objectives of the farmers' alliance. Ultimately, southern white planters and politicians felt threatened by the cooperation of black and white farmers they witnessed, so they resorted to a call for white solidarity and backed it up with violence, a common tactic used to undermine any demonstrable unity between blacks and whites. For this reason, some African Americans farmers in Texas sought new opportunities in other parts of the West.

African American Communities

After the Civil War, the prospect of living outside what had been the slave South pushed a small percentage of black migrants who preferred the solitude of rural life west, expanding the black population of the region and creating new African American communities in the Great Plains. In his occasional visits to western cities, Booker T. Washington, the renowned black leader and president of Alabama's famed Tuskegee Institute, urged African Americans to promote the formation of black communities through economic self-sufficiency and free enterprise. Washington's message, which he preached widely between 1881 and 1915, spurred the growth and development of all-black towns in western states such as California, Colorado, Oklahoma, and Kansas. These communities, of which at least sixty were established between 1865 and 1915, attracted African Americans with the lure of free or inexpensive land, the opportunity to vote, superior schools for their children, and the absence of segregation and racial violence, sweet relief from the pernicious racism in other parts of the United States. Most of those who migrated to these western black towns came from the South, where they had worked as sharecroppers or tenant farmers. Not unlike other migrants and immigrants, they headed west in order to improve their economic condition.

The first sizable migration of African Americans out of the South to the West pointed to the state of Kansas, to which blacks began migrating almost immediately after the Civil War. By 1870, more than 17,000 African Americans had migrated to the Jay Hawk State. The black population would reach more than 43,000 a decade later. By 1879, this migration became known as the Kansas Exodus, and in that year alone about 6,000 African Americans migrated to Kansas in the space of several months. Grassroots leaders such as Benjamin "Pap" Singleton, a former slave from Tennessee, and Henry Adams, a former slave from Georgia, encouraged their fellow African Americans to leave the South and head west. Although Adams never settled in Kansas, Singleton incorporated a colony there in 1877, and other black migrants established five more black colonies that same year. The largest such colony, or town, was Nicodemus, founded by African Americans from Lexington, Kentucky, who arrived in five groups in 1878 and 1879. Within two years, Nicodemus reported a population of 700 residents.

Taking up a homestead on the Kansas prairie proved a difficult process for many black settlers, who faced unfamiliar surroundings, isolation from friends and family members, and some hostility from already established white ranchers. While black settlers shared these challenges with migrants of all races, black settlers often suffered from a unique problem: a lack of capital with which to purchase land. Nonetheless, a small number of black migrants accumulated enough money to rent or purchase small plots on which they farmed. Others remained in towns such as Topeka, Wichita, or Lawrence, working for the railroads or in other types of unskilled labor. Largely free from the vicious pattern of racial violence and segregation that the majority of African Americans experienced in the South, most of the "Exodusters" remained in Kansas, where they raised families, voted, and sent their children to better schools, reveling in the relative freedom of the Plains. Like migrants of other groups, the Kansas Exodusters stood as proof that even lowly sharecroppers possessed the capacity to improve their lives by moving West.

California, Nebraska, Colorado, and Oklahoma also attracted small numbers of black rural settlers. Lieutenant Colonel Allen Allensworth, recently retired from the U.S. Army, actively promoted farming for black Californians as a means to gain economic self-sufficiency. Unlike in the South, in California African Americans had made few inroads into agriculture by 1870, this despite the industry's importance in the state economy, the prodding of black newspapers that more blacks should take up farming, and the prevalence of other minority groups working in the industry. By 1890, however, about one-fourth of all employed black males in California worked in agriculture, fishing, or mining. For example, modest numbers of black farmers and ranchers worked the land in the rural communities of the Central and San Joaquin valleys. In 1907, Colonel Allensworth joined with a small group of investors and purchased farmland in the San Joaquin Valley, where they established the all-black town of Allensworth. Like the Exodusters who settled in Kansas, migrants drawn to Allensworth envisioned an all-black community in which the residents could live free of racial discrimination and have the chance to prosper economically. Despite its promise, Allensworth had attracted only 200 settlers at its height between 1908 and 1920. Periodic droughts, the lack of water for irrigation, and competition from other black towns all contributed to Allensworth's gradual demise.

The black community of Boley, Oklahoma, founded in the former Creek nation in 1904, followed a different path from that of Allensworth. Located at an advantageous crossroads on the Fort Smith and Western Railroad, and possessing ample water and timber, Boley experienced few of the privations of Allensworth. Although Boley's black residents faced occasional violence by Creek Indians and hostile whites, the community generally thrived. Boasting churches, a school, restaurants, women's clubs, and fraternal organizations, Boley reached a population of 1,000 in 1907 and attracted the endorsement of Booker T. Washington. Yet even the ringing support of the Wizard of Tuskegee could not halt the tide of African Americans throughout the nation who steadily left rural areas, including Boley, and began moving to cities. By 1910, the population of Boley had stabilized, but its African American residents probably did not anticipate the effect that statehood would have on Oklahoma's race relations, in rural areas as well as cities. After Oklahoma entered the Union as a state in 1907, the Democratic-controlled legislature adopted numerous Jim Crow restrictions, stripping African Americans of their right to vote and segregating schools and public accommodations. But even if Boley never was the utopia that many black settlers had envisioned, it provided a significant number of African Americans a fresh start, autonomy, and the opportunity to make a decent living.

Women

African American women adapted remarkably well to rural life in the West. They found the separation from family members and friends difficult; and like their white counterparts, they complained about their isolation from the culture of the black middle class. But they also established networks and support groups such as churches, women's clubs, and literary societies to make life tolerable. These institutions and organizations also eased the transition to their new communities. Willianna Hickman, a thirty-one-year-old Exoduster from Kentucky, traveled to Kansas with her husband, a minister, and their six children. The Hickmans and 140 other homesteaders settled in the all-black town of Nicodemus. After a difficult beginning and the shedding of tears when she first laid eyes on the community, Willianna and her family carved out a new life in Nicodemus. The black settlers lived in dugouts (houses built below the ground), which Willianna found strange, but after some time she adapted to these conditions. "Days, weeks, months, and years passed and I became reconciled to my home," she wrote later. Willianna's observation was in fact an understatement. The Hickman family eventually made improvements on their farm, which they occupied for nearly twenty years. Women like Willianna coped with the isolation of rural life by making visits to town to attend church and social events. Eventually Hickman's three daughters became respected teachers in the community.

Ava Speese Day and her family, homesteaders in the Sand Hills region of northeastern Nebraska, received 640 acres in 1907. At first the family braved the harsh climate of the Plains in a sod house, which consisted of one large room. In time, however, the Days built on to the house, doing so when their finances improved. Ava's family, like other black pioneering families in the region, grew corn, beans, vegetables, and raised cattle. They also raised horses and mules. The Day children attended an all-black school staffed by African American teachers. This tight-knit community engaged in numerous social activities such as dances, picnics, and rodeos. Both Willianna's and Ava's experiences mirrored those of other women in the West, be they white, black, or immigrant.

Attending church for black women in rural areas was especially important, for much of their lives and social activities revolved around religion. In their churches, predominately Baptist and Methodist, African American women organized fund-raisers, bake sales, musicals, and established women's clubs. They also sang in choirs, performed concerts, and organized public programs. Black church women hosted speakers from outlying communities and provided much needed day care for young children. By teaching Sunday school and leading choir rehearsals, African American women imparted the culture, traditions, and religious values of their churches to the larger community and the next generation. In some instances, as they did in Great Falls, Montana, black women took the initiative to obtain church property, even if only the names of male trustees appear on the deed of the Great Falls African American Methodist Episcopal Church. Like other western women, black women helped to create and run their communities and the institutions that sustained them.

Despite the promise of freedom, race and gender combined to restrict severely the range of occupations for black women in the West, the majority of those who worked for wages outside of the home did so as domestic servants. Before the Civil War, African American women had worked in domestic service, both as slaves and free women; in the decades after the war the majority remained in these menial jobs, doing so long after many white women, including white immigrant women, had left these positions to work in factories and even white-collar jobs. Whereas in cities such as San Francisco and Minneapolis domestic service acted as a launching pad for immigrant women into the wider work world, domestic service represented the entire work world for many black women. Thus, in every western community, African American women served as cooks, maids, housekeepers, seamstresses, and laundresses, positions that paid the most menial wages and offered virtually no potential for advancement. Western cities also offered all residents less opportunity for industrial employment than either the Midwest or the Northeast. Therefore, African American women in the West made almost no advancement in factory jobs before U.S. entry into World War II. Outside of teaching in segregated schools, western black women also made few inroads into professional employment in the nineteenth century.

The low wages and difficulty black women faced in finding employment contributed to the disproportionate number of them imprisoned in the western states and territories. Black women in all regions of the West felt the brunt of western justice more sternly than did their white counterparts. When measured by their rate of incarceration in western prisons, African American women, historian Anne M. Butler notes, "faced a frontier more hostile than expansive, more oppressive than egalitarian." Local authorities more vigorously prosecuted black women than they did women of other backgrounds for crimes ranging from petty thief and grand larceny to prostitution. Throughout the nineteenth century, authorities thus were more likely to send black women convicted of crimes to state penitentiaries to serve longer sentences than white convicts. They were also far less likely to grant African Americans pardons. That most of the incarcerated women were young, uneducated, and possessed scant economic resources supports the conclusion that many western black females had turned to criminal activity out of economic necessity. Once apprehended, they faced a penal system every bit as brutal as any that existed in the Jim Crow South. Finally, when serving a prison sentence black women reinforced the dominant society's prevailing stereotypes about ethnic women in general, that they were lazy and prone to theft and acts of violence. These stereotypes were even more pernicious when applied to African American women.

Conclusion

The era of Reconstruction marked a new beginning for black westerners, but it hardly erased racial prejudice or inequality. Indeed, the violence and intimidation used by whites, most famously in vigilante organizations such as the KKK, revealed their continued power to dictate the racial, social, and economic order of society despite the end of slavery and the rights guaranteed to black Americans in the Fourteenth and Fifteenth amendments to the U.S. Constitution, a phenomenon solidified by the imposition of "Jim Crow" racial segregation in the South as well as places such as Texas and Oklahoma in the West. The legacy of violence and inequality would continue to shape the experiences of African Americans in the West into the second half of the twentieth century. Nonetheless, black westerners proceeded to strengthen their communities, construct schools and churches, and broaden the range of jobs they worked. They also encouraged their brethren to vote, run for political office, and realize the importance of politics in obtaining power and access to resources. They also organized all-black towns as refuges from racial violence and discrimination and slowly began to secure employment in white-collar positions and the professions. Despite racial restrictions, African American women saw new possibilities in the West, where they organized the social structure of their communities, taught their children, and passed on the values and traditions of African American culture from one generation to the next. To be sure, the three decades following the end of the Civil War were fraught with difficulties, but they also offered great promise.

Suggested Readings

Athearn, Robert. *In Search of Canaan: Black Migration to Kansas, 1879–1880*. Lawrence: The University Press of Kansas, 1978.

Barr, Alwyn. *Reconstruction to Reform: Texas Politics, 1876–1906*. Austin: University of Texas Press, 1971.

Brophy, Alfred L. *Reconstructing the Dreamland: The Tulsa Riot of 1921: Race, Reparations and Reconciliation*. New York: Oxford University Press, 2003.

Butler, Anne. "Still in Chains: Black Women in Western Prisons, 1865–1915." *Western Historical Quarterly* 20 (February 1989): 18–35.

Cantrell, Gregg. *Feeding the Wolf: John B. Rayner and the Politics of Race, 1850–1918*. Wheeling, IL: Harlan Davidson, 2001.

Dobak, William A. and Thomas D. Phillips. *The Black Regulars, 1866–1898*. Norman: University of Oklahoma Press, 2001.

Franklin, Jimmie Lewis. *Journey Toward Hope: A History of Blacks in Oklahoma*. Norman: University of Oklahoma Press, 1982.

Hamilton, Kenneth. *Black Towns and Profit: Promotion and Development in the Trans-Appalachian West, 1877–1915*. Urbana: University of Illinois Press, 1991.

Heintze, Michael R. *Private Black Colleges in Texas, 1865–1954*. College Station: Texas A&M University Press, 1985.

Hornsby, Alton. "The Freedman's Bureau Schools in Texas, 1865–1870." *Southwestern Historical Quarterly* 76 (April 1973): 397–417.

Hudson, Lynn M. *The Making of "Mammy Pleasant": A Black Entrepreneur in Nineteenth-Century San Francisco.* Urbana: University of Illinois Press, 1968.

Leiker, James. *Racial Borders: Black Soldiers Along the Rio Grande.* College Station: Texas A&M Press, 2002.

Lemke-Santangelo, Gretchen. *Abiding Courage: African American Migrant Women and the East Bay Community.* Chapel Hill: University of North Carolina Press, 1996.

Massey, Sara, ed. *Black Cowboys of Texas.* College Station: Texas A&M University Press, 2005.

McLagan, Elizabeth. *A Peculiar Paradise: A History of Blacks in Oregon, 1788–1940.* Portland: Georgian Press, 1980.

Pitre, Merline. *Through Many Dangers, Toils, and Snares: The Black Leadership of Texas, 1868–1900.* Austin: Eakin Press, 1985.

Reid, Debra. *Reaping a Greater Harvest: African Americans, the Extension Service, and Rural Reform in Jim Crow Texas.* College Station: Texas A&M University Press, 2007.

Robinson III, Charles M. *The Fall of a Black Officer: Racism and the Myth of Henry O. Flipper.* Norman: University of Oklahoma Press, 2008.

Turner, Elizabeth Hayes. "Juneteenth: Emancipation and Memory." eds. Gregg Cantrell and Elizabeth Hayes Turner, *Lone Star Past: Memory and History in Texas.* College Station: Texas A&M University Press, 2007.

Wayne, George H. "Negro Migration and Colonization in Colorado." *Journal of the West* 15 (January 1976): 112–17.

Winegarten, Ruthe. *Black Texas Women: 150 Years of Trial and Triumph.* Austin: University of Texas Press, 1995.

"A Cutting Horse at Work." *Black Cowboys Photo File, American Heritage Center, University of Wyoming*

"Andy" an African American placer miner, at a sluice. *Courtesy of the Huntington Library, San Marino, California.*

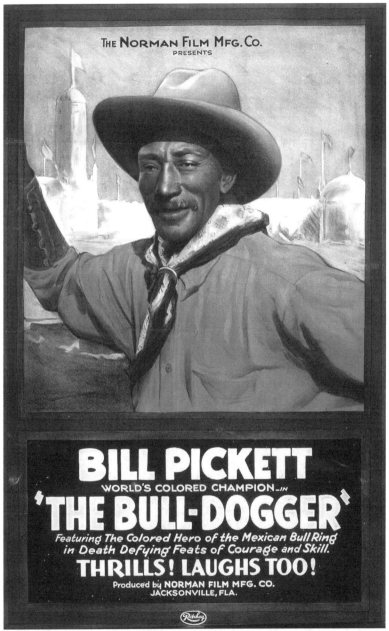

Bill Pickett, champion bulldogger, 1921 movie poster. *Buffalo Bill Historical Center, Cody, Wyoming. U.S.A. Museum Purchase, 1.69.2030*

Buffalo soldiers of the 25th Infantry, some wearing buffalo robes, Fort Keogh, Montana. Chr. Barthelmess, photographer. *Gladstone Collection of African American Photographs, Library of Congress, LC-USZC4-6161*

Esteban, also known as Estevanico, was a Muslim slave from northern Africa and an early explorer of the Southwestern United States. *David and Carol Weber Collection*

Nat Love, James Bama painting. Love, cowhand and reknowned roper, identified himself with dime novel hero Deadwood Dick, often using that name. *Buffalo Bill Historical Center, Cody, Wyoming; William E. Weiss Memorial Fund Purchase, 5.04*

James Beckwourth, early Western trapper and fur trader.
Beckwourth fought in the Seminole War (1837), helped put
down an insurrection (Taos, 1847), died in 1866 and was buried
by the Crow as a warrior. *Print after a daguerrotype housed in the
Smithsonian Institution, Washington, D.C.*

A young Carlotta Stewart Lai at about 19 years of age. *Courtesy: Moorland-Spingarn Research Center, Howard University*

Nicodemus, Kansas, 1885. A settlement founded by Exodusters in 1877 showing a number of townspeople and the Williams Mercantile store. The building on the far left is believed to be the First Baptist Church. *KansasMemory.org, Kansas Sate Historical Society, #526*

The first meeting of the Montana Federation of Colored Women's Clubs, Butte, Montana, 1942. *Montana Historical Society, PAC 2002-36.1-14*

Carlotta Stewart Lai, Principal, with students of Hanamaulu School, Kauai, HI *Courtesy: Moorland-Spingarn Research Center, Howard University*

Golden State Mutual Life Insurance Company Headquarters, 1949–2010. In 1948 a new home office on Adams Boulevard was designed by architect Paul R. Williams, the first certified African American architect west of the Mississippi River, and first African American member of the American Institute of Architects. Williams also served on the first Los Angeles Planning Commission in 1920. The building houses two significant murals, depicting the African American experience in California (see page iv). *Courtesy, Golden State Mutual Life Insurance*

The men and women of the Moses Speese family on their homestead in Custer County, Nebraska, in 1888. *Photo by Solomon Butcher. Nebraska Historical Society, [Digital ID, nbhips 10963]*

Actress Hattie McDaniel, 1941. *Courtesy, Myra Wysinger, McDaniel Family Photo Collection*

Lillian Smith, Mary McLeod Bethune, and Eleanor Roosevelt, Washington, D.C., 1945. *Courtesy DC Public Library, Star Collection, © Washington Post*

Destruction following the Tulsa riot. Thousands of armed whites attacked African Americans on the streets and burned virtually every home and business in the thirty-five-block section centering on Greenwood Street. *McFarlin Library, Department of Special Collections and University Archives, University of Tulsa*

"Captured Negroes" being taken into detention by vigilante whites, June 1, 1921, during the Tulsa race riot. *McFarlin Library, Department of Special Collections and University Archives, University of Tulsa*

Mary Ellen Pleasant, age 87, ca. 1901. *San Franciso History Center, San Franciso Public Library*

Buck Colbert Franklin (right) and fellow attorney I. H. Spears (left) with secretary Effie Thompson, in the tent that functioned as their office following the Tulsa riot. Lawyers like Franklin and Spears fought to keep the property of burned-out black residents from takeover by real-estate developers and other opportunists operating with the aid of new city ordinances aimed at preventing the riot's victims from rebuilding their homes. *Courtesy John Whittingham Franklin*

"A Negro Regiment in Action." An Illustration from pages 168–169 of the March 14, 1863 issue of *"Harper's Weekly." KansasMemory.org, Kansas Sate Historical Society, #433*

Black Masons, Stromsburg, Iowa, late 1920s. George Albert Flippin is in the fourth row, second from the left. *Courtesy: Moorland-Spingarn Research Center, Howard University*

CHAPTER THREE

Urban Communities, 1910–1940

Immediately after the Civil War, free blacks in the West sought to protect their civil rights, even as newly freed persons from the South went west to seek new economic opportunities. The new arrivals joined existing African American communities or, homesteading, created new ones, all of them holding out hope for a new or better life free of restraint. But even as the promise of the Emancipation Proclamation faded, and Jim Crow laws spread across the West, as they did in the South, black westerners increasingly turned inward to develop new leadership and institutions within their respective communities. These organizations, which included churches, community centers, women's clubs, and protest organizations such as the National Association for the Advancement of Colored People (NAACP) and the National Urban League (NUL) served collectively as bulwarks against racial discrimination. They also trained a new generation of black leaders, united black westerners with other African American communities throughout the nation, and assured black westerners that they were not alone in their quest to achieve full equality.

At the turn of the twentieth century, the overwhelming majority of black westerners lived in cities and earned their living working in urban occupations. A small percentage of African Americans continued to farm during the early decades of the twentieth century, and the fishing and mining industries employed an even smaller number. Only in Texas and Oklahoma did blacks farm in large numbers. Cities proved to be a powerful magnet for African Americans, for in urban settings blacks found opportunities to work in a variety of occupations, earn higher wages, send their children to schools that instructed them on a year-round basis, and participate in numerous social, religious, and fraternal activities. Black westerners changed jobs with far greater frequency in urban areas, exercising a freedom commonly denied to them in the South. City life also offered one the chance to meet new people, renew old acquaintances, and cluster in ethnic or racial enclaves—neighborhoods where they felt safe and accepted and could nurture their own traditions even as they tried to gain acceptance in the mainstream society. Large western cities like San Francisco, Los Angeles, Denver, Seattle, Tulsa, and Houston had a rich tradition of black commercial and cultural institutions that dated from the nineteenth century. Although few of these businesses rivaled the scale of black banks or insurances companies in southern cities such as Durham, North Carolina, or Atlanta, Georgia, they were impressive given the relatively small black populations in western cities.

With the exception of Houston, Dallas, and Los Angeles, western cities contained relatively small black populations prior to World War II. San Francisco and Oakland, for example, reported two of the largest black communities in the state of California but contained only 1,642 and 3,055 African Americans respectively in 1910. By 1940, Oakland's black population had increased to 8,462, while San Francisco reported 4,806 African Americans. Los Angeles, in contrast, contained a black population of 7,599 in 1910, a number that swelled to 38,894 by 1930. The following decade, the African American population of Los Angeles reached 63,774, a phenomenal increase in the space of three decades. In fact, more blacks lived in Los Angeles in 1940 than the combined black populations of every western state except Texas. Los Angeles offered African American migrants, many of whom had come to the City of Angels from southern states, the opportunity to work in a wide range of jobs and own their homes. Blacks also obtained employment on the railroads as laborers and Pullman porters in southern California, positions that carried prestige in the black community and offered black men economic stability.

Black urban communities grew slowly in other Pacific Coast cities such as San Diego, Sacramento, Portland, and Seattle prior to 1940. Many blacks viewed migration to a West Coast city, or even a city in the interior and Mountain West, as difficult and impractical because of the paucity of industrial jobs, the sheer distance of the migration, and the expense involved. Because these cities contained such small black populations, they lacked the types of social networks or migration clubs that southern blacks who had moved to northern cities such as Chicago and Detroit organized to acclimate recently arrived African Americans to urban life. Thus the black populations in western cities such as Phoenix, Tucson, Albuquerque, Oklahoma City, Wichita, and Denver also grew slowly prior to World War II. By 1940 only Houston's black community, which numbered 86,302, exceeded that of Los Angeles. Dallas' black population, which stood at 50,407, had more than doubled between 1920 and 1940. San Antonio's black population grew more slowly but increased nonetheless, to 19,235 by 1940, making it one of the four largest black communities in the West. The small size of these communities, although a defining feature, does not mean that their populations remained static. Quite the contrary, for the black populations in some western cities grew at a rate similar to or greater than that of many northern industrial centers.

Employment

Employment proved the most significant factor pulling African Americans to the urban West. African American migrants tended to move to cities in which economic opportunities beckoned and where established black communities existed, not unlike the case of European immigrants. Yet, no matter where African Americans settled in the urban West, finding gainful employment proved one of their greatest challenges. Between 1900 and 1940, the overwhelming majority of black westerners worked in unskilled, menial jobs. Whatever their level of education, prior experience, or skill, black men were principally hired as servants and unskilled workers; western black women, replicating the national pattern, typically worked in domestic service, the sector comprising more than 90 percent of all black female workers in some cities. The majority of western cities closed their doors to black males and females in the manufacturing and skilled sectors until World War II, when economic necessity compelled white employers to hire workers of any race or nationality. Only in Houston and Dallas did African American males succeed before the war, though not black women, in gaining a foothold in manufacturing jobs. By 1930, 40.7 percent of African American men in the Bayou City (Houston) worked in manufacturing, while 32.3 percent worked in such jobs in Dallas. West Coast cities as well as cities in the Mountain West hired African Americans selectively for industrial jobs, and labor unions in most western states barred blacks from joining them due to longstanding racial restrictions. The inability to gain union clearance effectively eliminated African American competition in numerous job categories, such as the building trades and positions as skilled artisans. Therefore, black workers had little choice in seeking less lucrative forms of non-union employment.

Along the Pacific Coast, African Americans had a long tenure as waterfront workers, working as seamen, longshoremen, and stevedores. In Seattle, Portland, Los Angeles, and San Francisco, African American longshoremen were recruited by local shipping companies on a non-union basis to load and unload incoming and departing ships; they were prohibited, as a result of longstanding custom and opposition from white workers, from joining the parent union. During the 1930s, however, with the influence of national labor organizations such as the emerging Congress of Industrial Organizations (CIO) and the rise of radical labor leaders like Harry Bridges, some longshoremen's unions began to recruit black workers on an integrated basis for the first time. Their numbers remained modest throughout the 1930s, but gaining membership in an integrated union represented an important breakthrough for western black workers who had been shunned previously by organized labor. Under Bridges' leadership, the International Longshoremen's Union (ILU) eliminated segregated work gangs and pay disparities based on race. The ILU also gradually elevated African Americans into union leadership. Other West Coast labor unions did not follow the progressive lead of the ILU, however, and even the CIO unions in Los Angeles, which organized Mexican workers in the manufacturing sector, did little to assist black workers. By the early 1930s, the president of San Francisco's NAACP chapter, Leland Hawkins, wrote despairingly that "labor unionism had frozen the Negro out of all work in this section of the country."

Employment opportunities for black women outside of personal service and domestic employment were severely restricted in the western states and territories by racial as well as gender prejudice among employers and unions. By 1930, 93.3 percent of black female wage earners in Dallas worked in domestic service. Black women in West Coast cities or in the Mountain West did not fare much better. In San Francisco, 88.9 percent of African American working women labored as domestics; in Los Angeles the figure was 86.7 percent. Only in Oakland, where 8.6 percent of black women worked manufacturing jobs, did black women make even the slightest bit of headway, even if 83.4 percent of black females in the East Bay City were also employed in domestic service. The experiences of Beatrice Greene and Kathryn Bogle illustrate the difficulties and the frustrations that African American women faced in gaining employment outside of domestic service. After graduating from Commerce High School in San Francisco with an accounting major, Greene was unable to get a job in that field, in large measure due to informal but pervasive racial restrictions on employing black women in white-collar or professional jobs. Like the majority of working black women in San Francisco, a disappointed Greene settled into domestic service, the only position that she could find. Kathryn Bogle, an African American high school graduate, faced a similar experience in Portland. She tried repeatedly to find employment in a variety of Portland offices, but potential employers told her that her skin color disqualified her for any position other than domestic work. Unlike white immigrant women, many of whom left domestic service to take jobs in manufacturing and industry, black women throughout the West found these jobs closed to them throughout the early part of the twentieth century.

Occasionally a black western woman did break through to find white-collar or professional employment, but as a group black women still lagged significantly behind the employment progress of either white or foreign-born workers. In the South, teaching positions had been widely available to African American women and men because of the segregated school districts, but black westerners faced great difficulty in obtaining teaching jobs. The smaller black population in the West meant that the majority of western school districts did not segregate their students by race. Prior to World War II, few school districts hired African American teachers, preferring white teachers for the white majority students. San Diego, a city with a multiracial population, did not hire its first African American teacher until 1942, and San Francisco followed two years later. In some other western cities, including Portland, Seattle, and Los Angeles, black residents fared somewhat better. Nonetheless, even those African Americans who sought work as typists, stenographers, sales clerks, and telephone operators found these jobs exceedingly difficult to obtain in western cities. Mary McCants Stewart, a graduate of the University of Minnesota and the Manning College of Music, Oratory, and Language, represented one of the fortunate few to find work as a clerk in a San Francisco pharmaceutical company during the prewar years. Although job opportunities improved for female workers in general between 1920 and 1930, African American women did not share in the progress.

Black, male white-collar workers in the West fared slightly better than their female counterparts, but racial restrictions hindered their opportunities, too. Every western state or territory contained a small number of black doctors, lawyers, nurses, and journalists. McCants Stewart, the eldest son of the eminent black southern leader T. McCants Stewart, relocated to Portland, Oregon, to establish a law practice after graduating from the University of Minnesota Law School in 1899. Stewart's practice struggled in Portland because of the unwillingness of whites to hire black attorneys and the small size of Portland's black community. In 1917, he relocated to San Francisco and joined the practice of the prominent black attorney and businessman Oscar Hudson. To his regret, Stewart found that San Francisco provided no more opportunities for his legal career than had Portland. Struggling to support his family and pay his debts, Stewart, at the age of forty-two, committed suicide, leaving behind a wife and daughter. Most black attorneys in other western states and territories never reached this level of despair, but their practices struggled in the majority of instances.

Despite the odds, some black attorneys thrived and maintained highly successful careers. Buck Colbert Franklin, born in the Oklahoma Indian Territory in 1879, whose father was a Chickasaw freedman, the former slave of a Chickasaw Indian family, and whose mother was one-fourth Choctaw Indian, maintained a successful legal practice in several Oklahoma communities, including Springer, Ardmore, Rentiesville, and Tulsa. Franklin established himself as a capable attorney and a community activist, challenging segregation laws in the state of Oklahoma and representing blacks and Native Americans in numerous legal matters such as oil leases and fraudulent land allotments under the Dawes Act. Loren Miller, a University of Southern California law school graduate, established a respected legal practice in Los Angeles for more than three decades. In 1963, the city of Los Angeles appointed him a municipal court judge. Thus, despite obstacles, a few African Americans cashed in on the promise of the West, exceptions to the racist rule, and inspired others to keep trying to follow their lead.

Black physicians and dentists also established their practices in western states, or relocated them there, with varying degrees of success. In so doing, each group ran the risk of been locked out of their profession or denied some privileges because of discrimination. Most local hospitals in the West refused to let black doctors work in them, a policy that undermined the doctors' reputations, limited their experience and training, and hurt them financially. Hospitals in the western states and territories were not, however, segregated, with the exception of those in Texas. Thus black doctors in the West, ironically, faced a disadvantage that their counterparts in the South, who worked in segregated medical facilities, did not. African American dentists fared somewhat better. Dr. Jack J. Kimbrough established his dental practice in San Diego in 1935 and became an important civil rights leader in that picturesque city. John Alexander Somerville, a Jamaican immigrant, graduated from the University of Southern California School of Dentistry and established a successful practice with his wife Vada in Los Angeles. Highly respected as a businessman and civil rights leader, Somerville served on the Los Angeles Chamber of Commerce and the Police Commission, both important breakthroughs for African Americans. Vada emerged as a leader in the black "clubwomen" movement in the western states.

Black ministers, perhaps the most prestigious members of the black professional class in the West, faced fewer racial restrictions because their churches served predominantly black congregations. Indeed, in San Francisco in 1930, the number of black ministers was exceeded only by the number of black musicians. Whether Baptist, Methodist, or Pentecostal, black western ministers catered almost exclusively to the black community to support their salaries and church-related activities. Black ministers embraced their activism and viewed themselves as natural leaders in the community. The Reverend Clayton Russell organized numerous programs to feed the hungry and the dispossessed from his pulpit at the People's Independent Church in Los Angeles during the Great Depression. Russell was also regarded by black Angelenos as one of the most significant crusaders for racial equality in the city. His was the typical path taken by black ministers in large urban areas in the West. Some of these individuals turned their churches into temporary shelters to house the homeless. In other instances, black ministers, because of their standing in the community, served as liaisons with whites and became political leaders in their quests to resolve problems.

The West always allowed for some exceptions, however, and several black ministers preached to mixed congregations, particularly among the Pentecostal movements that emerged among lower-class whites and blacks in various parts of the West in the early twentieth century. S. R. Martin, a minister in the Church of God in Christ, a brand of Christian Pentecostalism, ministered to westerners of all races in Cody, Wyoming, and Billings, Montana, before settling permanently in Monterey, California. Born in Texas and largely self-educated, Martin would rise to the rank of Bishop within the Church of God in Christ hierarchy. Men such as Russell and Martin believed in the liberating power of education to transform lives and improve race relations. Martin's case illustrates how black professionals might be required to move about and take chances before they could settle comfortably in a western community, generally following the pattern of other workers and professionals in the West.

The Entertainment Industry

African American musicians and actors worked independently in a way similar to clergy. Black musicians performed in every western city, most prominently in Los Angeles. The Central Avenue District of L.A. contained a vibrant and innovative jazz scene, one in which black musicians from across the nation migrated to practice their craft. These artists also organized Musicians Local 767, an all-black local, which represented almost all of Los Angeles' black musicians and served as their entree into regular gigs at clubs, parties, and Hollywood studios. Although Los Angeles remained the center of West Coast jazz, nearly every western city featured musicians who influenced the genre in important ways. African American musicians formed bands such as the Oklahoma City Blue Devils, which performed on a regular circuit of western states, including Kansas, Nebraska, Colorado, Texas, and New Mexico. Jazz and blues artists in numerous western communities crossed racial boundaries by playing before mixed audiences in night clubs and cabarets, several of which attracted such renowned jazz artists as Duke Ellington, Lionel Hampton, and the Count Basie.

Black motion picture actors, centered in Hollywood, emerged as important components of the black professional class and, until the emergence of black professional athletes, one of the most visible symbols of black achievement. Performers like Hattie McDaniel, Louise Beavers, Cab Calloway, and Lincoln Perry (known widely as Stepin Fetchit) entertained audiences of all races during the 1920s and 1930s. McDaniel would earn an academy award for best supporting actress for her memorable role as "Mammy" in *Gone with the Wind* (1939). Similarly, Louise Beavers, who starred in dozens of films during the 1920s and 1930s, is best known for her role as a beloved, albeit stereotypical mammy character in the 1934 film *Imitation of Life*. Cab Calloway was one of the premier jazz singers and band leaders of his era. He brought a new and rare energy to the big screen. Perhaps best known for his 1931 song "Minnie the Moocher," Calloway appeared in *International House*, a short film by Paramount Pictures in 1933.

Hollywood directors used Stepin Fetchit regularly, making him especially popular; he appeared in twenty-six films between 1929 and 1935. Like many black performers of this era, he portrayed African Americans in demeaning, stereotypical roles as lazy, superstitious, and dim-witted characters. Nonetheless, Fetchit commanded a wide following and earned considerable wealth before the NAACP, during the early 1930s, criticized his negative characterizations as demeaning. By this time, the NAACP had accelerated its civil rights campaign nationally to end discrimination. Stereotypical portraits of African Americans as dim-witted, shuffling, superstitious buffoons proved counterproductive to their efforts to cast Africans Americans in a more positive light. The majority of black actors, if they were lucky enough to find work at all in Hollywood, played parts as maids, servants, porters, and chauffeurs. With the exception of the black poet and writer Langston Hughes, almost no African Americans held writing jobs with a major studio, the majority of which also froze blacks out of technical jobs as well.

The black filmmaker Oscar Micheaux circumvented the narrow opportunities available for African Americans in Hollywood by producing his own films. Born in 1884 in Murphysboro, Illinois, and raised on a farm in Great Bend, Kansas, Micheaux eventually settled on the northern Great Plains, where he homesteaded in South Dakota. But Micheaux possessed a talent for writing and storytelling, and he produced several well-received fictional accounts of his life on the plains. He followed his first novel, *The Conquest* (1913) with *The Homesteader* (1917), a fictional account of his own experiences as a South Dakota farmer. In 1918, Micheaux, who was by this time living in Harlem, created the Micheaux Film and Book Company, which served as a vehicle to market and sell his books as well as produce films. Between 1919 and 1948, he produced forty-four full-length films and wrote seven more novels. Micheaux's independence from the Hollywood movie studios gave him the freedom to cast African Americans in roles other than the stereotypical and often demeaning. Micheaux also criticized the racism of established Hollywood directors such as D. W. Griffith, whose 1915 film *The Birth of a Nation* portrayed African Americans in the wake of slavery and during the era of Reconstruction as vicious, barbaric, and corrupt.

Entertainers and artists like Hattie McDaniel, Stepin Fetchit, Bill Pickett, and Oscar Micheaux thus carved out noteworthy careers in Hollywood, raising the profile of African Americans in the West and nationally. African American actors who starred in westerns, such as Bill Pickett and Micheaux, were especially popular. Even though they appeared on screen, making them seem successful, black actors also struggled with professional limitations, just as African American clergy and politicians did. Yet their presence in the industry increased western awareness of the African American population.

African American Businesses

African Americans also gained a degree of autonomy through the businesses they owned and operated, which by and large catered to a black clientele. Large western cities such as Houston or Dallas contained literally hundreds of black businesses, many of which had served the black community effectively since the end of slavery. In Texas alone in 1929, blacks owned 1,736 retails stores that employed over 3,000 persons. African American grocery stores, drug stores, restaurants, funeral homes, banks, and insurance companies dotted the western urban landscape, from Texas to California. The majority of these concerns were relatively small in size, for most African Americans lacked the capital or experience to expand their businesses beyond a local market. Yet some businessmen, such as Hobart Taylor, Sr., of Houston, who owned an insurance company as well as a taxicab business, became millionaires. Los Angeles served as the headquarters to the Golden State Mutual Life Insurance Company, the largest black-owned insurance company in the West, established in 1925 by Norman O. Houston, William L. Nickerson, and George A. Beavers, Jr. Some African American entrepreneurs, such as Dr. John Alexander Somerville, built hotels and office buildings, including the famous Somerville Hotel in Los Angeles, where the NAACP held its 1928 national convention. Yet most black businesses, particularly those in cities with small black populations, "struggled against intense competition from other people of color," as historian Quintard Taylor notes. This competition became especially intense in West Coast cities like Seattle, Los Angeles, and San Francisco, where large Asian communities existed, and where Chinese and Japanese businessmen welcomed African American customers.

Throughout the West, the black professional and business class proved far less successful than their counterparts in some ethnic minorities, the Japanese serving as one such example. In cities such as Seattle, the Japanese turned to forming their own businesses as a response to discrimination. The Japanese also relied on kinship networks to obtain employment and support their businesses. By 1930, for example, 402 Asian men operated retail stores in Seattle compared to only 15 for African Americans. The larger number of Japanese businesses allowed them to attract a more diverse clientele, including some African Americans who had patronized these businesses for many years. In Seattle, Japanese Americans also composed the city's largest racial minority group until World War II, one that competed with African Americans for many service-oriented jobs such as janitors, red caps, railroad porters, and domestics.

Housing

Despite their struggle throughout the West to improve employment opportunities and make inroads into skilled, white-collar, and professional jobs, a surprisingly large number of black westerners owned their homes. Home ownership rates, for example, exceeded 40 percent for blacks in Portland, 38.4 percent in Denver, 38.8 percent in Seattle, and 33.6 percent in Los Angeles in 1930. These rates of black home ownership exceeded by a significant margin the rates for African Americans in cities such as Chicago, (10.5 percent), or Detroit (15 percent). Los Angeles, which experienced a real estate boom in the early twentieth century, led all California cities, for it offered African Americans an opportunity to purchase attractive homes for modest prices. Indeed, Los Angeles' real estate boom served as a key ingredient in fueling the black population increase to Los Angeles and adjacent communities such as Watts, where African Americans made up 14 percent of the population in 1920.

Yet racial overtones tinged even the pride of home ownership in the West, as increasingly more cities and counties required black westerners to buy or rent their housing in established black neighborhoods, as opposed to buying or renting in white ones. Cities such as Houston and Dallas reinforced residential segregation through a state law passed in 1927. Predictably, the majority of African Americans resided in a handful of black neighborhoods such as Oak Cliff, South Dallas, and Deep Ellum in Dallas and the Fifth Ward in Houston. Houston's and Dallas' use of new housing laws to enforce segregated housing for African Americans reveals that some western cities had adopted the most restrictive racial patterns in the nation to separate blacks from whites. They also reveal that the West conformed during the 1920s to some of the worse racial practices of the nation. City fathers in virtually every western city put in place restrictive covenants, or agreements attached to individual houses to prevent African Americans and, in some cases, Jews, from buying them. Nor could Africans Americans, regardless of their economic status or occupation, rent or lease property with restrictive covenants. These legal vehicles guaranteed that African Americans would reside overwhelmingly in segregated communities, long after other groups such as immigrants, Asians, and Jews had been permitted to move into integrated neighborhoods. These covenants proved more effective in some areas than in others. The California Supreme Court in 1928 upheld these types of agreements when African Americans and others appealed their legality; incredibly, it ruled that even when blacks lived in white neighborhoods before local authorities established the restrictions, the law required them to vacate their own properties to conform with the covenants.

Racial housing covenants, established under the guise of protecting white property values, reinforced white supremacy as well as enforced residential segregation. As more African Americans moved into western cities, local laws and covenants increasingly forced them to crowd into existing black neighborhoods, placing many residential communities that housed native whites and white immigrants off-limits. Despite reporting the highest rate of black home ownership of any city in California, Los Angeles contained a well-defined black ghetto by 1930, as well as numerous neighborhoods where restrictive covenants prohibited African American occupancy. San Francisco, whose black population was considerably smaller than that of Los Angeles, also enforced restrictive housing covenants. Black residents in Phoenix experienced similar policies, with the majority of them living in the southwestern section of the city in wretched conditions. The prevalence of segregated and racially restrictive housing in the West spoke to a larger issue: the degree to which segregation would serve as an impediment to achieving racial equality. Residential segregation also brought into sharper focus whether the West was really any different than any other region of the nation when it came to the housing it offered to African Americans.

When the law and restrictive practices by banks and real estate agents did not suffice, the threat and reality of violence or arson sometimes made the point. The KKK was one such organization that terrorized African Americans, as well as foreigners, Roman Catholics, and Jews during the postwar years. This revival of the Klan restricted its membership to native-born white Protestants and grew rapidly, reaching a peak as high as 4 million members by the mid-1920s. The new Klan pledged to support "100 percent Americanism," a clear and derogatory reference to foreign immigrants. The KKK was especially prominent in western cities such as Los Angeles and Portland. As Josh Sides concluded in his discussion about housing discrimination in Los Angeles, "in communities where restrictive covenants had failed to restrict minorities, the Ku Klux Klan, which surfaced in Los Angeles during the 1920s, served a similar function, intimidating, threatening, and sometimes attacking blacks who moved into white neighborhoods." In this case, the West clearly followed national trends.

World War I

Black westerners supported the U.S. war effort as enthusiastically as did African Americans in any region of the nation. Like their counterparts in the South, East, and Midwest, black westerners purchased Liberty Bonds, held patriotic meetings, supported the Salvation

Army and Red Cross drives, and participated in food conservation programs. They also heeded the advice of W. E. B. Du Bois, editor of *The Crisis*, who urged blacks throughout the nation to "close ranks" in support of the American war effort and put aside their individual grievances throughout the duration of the war. Du Bois believed, perhaps naively, that African American patriotism and unity during World War I would hasten the day when whites would see blacks as true American citizens and grant them full equality. In Texas, African Americans provided a disproportionate number of the state's troops, contributing 25 percent of the 31,000 men who were called up from the Lone Star State to serve the nation in the "Great War," even though African Americans composed only 16 percent of the state's population.

Despite segregated and unequal conditions, African American had a long and proud tradition of military service. Historian Alwyn Barr also suggests that for some of these men, the military provided better food, housing, clothing, medical attention, and pay than they had known prior to their service. In other words, joining the military represented a form of upward mobility. An undetermined number of western black soldiers also succeeded in gaining admission to officers' training school after the military established a segregated school to train black officers in Des Moines, Iowa, in 1917. At Fort Des Moines, as the segregated camp for black officers was known, African American officer candidates learned to command men and earn the respect of their fellow soldiers. Such was the experience of Spencer Cornelius Dickerson of Austin, Texas, who served as a doctor in the army in 1916 at the rank of first lieutenant and later rose to the rank of brigadier general in 1934 in the Illinois National Guard, the first black Texan to achieve this rank. Similarly, Hugh McElroy of Houston, who had served in the Spanish-American War with General John J. Pershing, won the *Croix de Guerre* (Cross of War) for gallantry in action from French war minister Georges Clemenceau while attached to the French army during World War I. McElroy, who later stated that he was "always crazy about soldiering," also received the World War I Victory Medal, the Philippine Insurrection Service Medal, and the National Defense Medal, clear indicators of the esteem in which he has been held by the U.S. military.

A number of black Californians also achieved distinguished service during World War I, all of whom trained at the segregated camp in Des Moines. Aurelius P. Alberga, a resident of San Francisco since 1884 and a survivor of the cataclysmic 1906 earthquake that virtually destroyed the city, fought in France for nine months and achieved the rank of first lieutenant in the army. Following his discharge from the military, Alberga returned to San Francisco, where he received a warm welcome and established a career as a politician by allying with James Rolph, the city's mayor, and Republican Party leadership. Alberga later married Toni Stone, who in 1953 became the first woman to play professional baseball in the Negro American League.

Racial Tensions

African American soldiers and civilians experienced considerable discrimination in the military and on the home front. "They cheat us and mock us; they kill us and slay us; they deride our misery. When we plead for the naked protection of the law . . . they tell us to go to Hell!," echoed Du Bois in *The Crisis* in 1919, a statement in stark contrast to his optimism at the start of World War I. In many American cities, a combination of events such as the stress and dislocations of wartime, the sizeable migration of southern blacks to northern cities between 1916 and 1919 (commonly known as the "Great Migration"), and a series of strikes and labor problems led to widespread race riots. In 1919 alone, as many as twenty-five race riots erupted throughout the nation, prompting the writer, activist, and poet James Weldon Johnson to call this period the "Red Summer." Chicago, Illinois, experienced one of the most destructive race riots, resulting in the loss of thirty-eight lives, 537 injuries, and the displacement (left homeless) of more than a thousand families because of arson and the general destruction of property.

Although lynching and other forms of racial violence were far less common in the West than in the South, regrettably, black western-ers did not go unscathed, as intermittent displays of race-motivated violence broke out in the region during the first half of the twentieth century. The 1921 Tulsa Race Riot stands alone as the most serious racial violence perpetrated against African Americans in the early decades of the century. In June of 1921 rioting erupted in Tulsa, Okla-homa, ultimately claiming the lives of nine whites and twenty-one African Americans. Several hundred residents were also injured in the bloody conflict that would take four companies of National Guard troops to quell. The riot began after a black bootblack (shoeshine boy) stumbled as he stepped out of an elevator in a downtown office build-ing, accidently bumping into a young white woman who operated the elevator. Although the young man had committed no crime, he had violated one of the nation's revered traditions: engaging in unwelcome contact with a white woman. He was arrested on a charge of assault and taken to the local jail. When leaders in Tulsa's African American community heard rumors that he would be lynched, they marched down to the jail to protect him, where they confronted a white crowd estimated to be as large as two thousand people. An altercation erupted between blacks and whites near the jail and spread quickly to other parts of the city. In a short time, the entire city was under siege. White Tulsans looted, burned, beat, and killed African Americans at random. Dr. A. C. Jackson, widely regarded as one of the leading black surgeons in the nation, was murdered by whites after he surrendered to a group that had promised him protection. White rioters, who significantly outnumbered African Americans, also rode into Tulsa's black com-munity, known as the Greenwood District, and destroyed a four-block area valued at more than $1 million. In this instance, white westerners conformed to the heinous and unprovoked violence of whites in other parts of the nations who rioted during the Red Summer of 1919 and in the wake of World War I.

Despite these patterns of restriction and even violence in the West, many African Americans lived in mixed, rather than segregated, neighborhoods in the West and interacted with a broad spectrum of racial and ethnic groups. For example, blacks in cities like San Francisco, Seattle, San Diego, and Los Angeles interacted and resided in proximity to Japanese, Chinese, Mexican, and white working-class immigrants. San Francisco's small African American community bordered Japantown, a vibrant neighborhood of homes, apartments and businesses in the city's Western Addition. Black, white, Chinese, and Japanese children attended the same schools and shared similar public space such as parks, playgrounds, and community centers. Similarly, African Americans in Los Angeles and Seattle counted Japanese, Chinese, and Mexican persons as their neighbors, occasionally sharing rooms in the same apartments or renting out units to one another. The West contained numerous multiethnic neighborhoods during the post–World War I years, places where individuals of all races experienced periods of trust and cooperation as well as times of tension.

Struggles for Justice

African Americans united in their commitment to protest various forms of discrimination and racial equality in the American West. Protesting racial injustices signaled that they were not content with second-class citizenship, and it reminded recalcitrant whites that blacks would not sit passively by while their civil rights were being abridged. Although black protest took many forms in the West after 1910, numerous African American communities in the region joined their counterparts throughout the nation and organized chapters of the NAACP. A group of interracial Progressives, men and women who attempted to bring a greater measure of democracy to American society, and who rejected the racial accommodation of Booker T. Washington, founded the NAACP in 1909. The organization grew slowly during its formative years. By 1916, however, the organization's membership had soared to 8,785, with sixty-nine branches. By the conclusion of World War I, the NAACP's membership had grown to 50,000. Sparked by its uncompromising monthly journal, *The Crisis*, edited, as mentioned, by the Harvard-educated scholar W. E. B. Du Bois, the NAACP personified the "New Negro" who fought openly and militantly for civil rights.

In 1917 the NAACP hired as a full-time field secretary James Weldon Johnson, a man every bit as brilliant as the better-known Du Bois. A graduate of Atlanta University, the multitalented Johnson had taught school in Jacksonville, Florida, and served as a U.S. consul in Venezuela and Nicaragua. He also was part of a famous songwriting trio that wrote a number of successful Broadway tunes. Johnson composed his most enduring song, "Lift Every Voice and Sing," with his brother Rosamond. In 1919, the NAACP adopted this inspiring tune, which spoke to the hopes, aspirations, and struggles of African Americans, as the "Negro National Anthem." As the NAACP's national field secretary, Johnson played a major role in the organization's dramatic growth during its first two decades. His responsibilities included visiting far-flung communities throughout the nation and encouraging local leaders to establish NAACP branches, notably in diverse parts of the West.

Residents of Houston organized the earliest NAACP branch in the West in 1912, and in short order other branches appeared in Seattle, Portland, San Francisco, Los Angeles, Albuquerque, and Denver. Early western branches worked closely with the NAACP's national office in New York. One of their first efforts sought to ban screenings of the controversial film *The Birth of a Nation* (1915). The film, adapted from Thomas Dixon's novel *The Clansman*, depicted a view of the Civil War and Reconstruction that glorified southern whites as heroic victims doing their best to cope with their defeat in the war and the influx of corrupt and predatory northerners and blacks in *their* homeland. Produced by talented filmmaker and director D. W. Griffith, *The Birth of a Nation* was hailed by whites across the nation as a cinematic masterpiece. In sharp contrast, the nation's

African Americans hailed the film as vicious, inflammatory, and degrading. Under the leadership of branch president John Drake, for example, the Northern California NAACP branch rallied the black communities of San Francisco and Oakland in an attempt to ban further screenings of the controversial film locally. NAACP branches in other western cities, including Los Angeles, Seattle, Portland, Denver, and Wichita, also protested against the film, although there is little evidence that these collective protests had a substantial impact. NAACP branches in some cities did receive a partial victory when Griffith's film stopped playing in local theaters in the early 1920s, demonstrating a modest but real regional effect.

Despite limited resources, western branches of the NAACP waged numerous campaigns to achieve racial justice. In the majority of cases, western leaders addressed local or statewide matters by investigating and trying to bring to light such things as police brutality, employment discrimination, and discrimination in housing and public accommodations. Western NAACP branches also monitored national issues and supported national campaigns to attain justice in a southern courtroom, including an anti-lynching bill sponsored by L. C. Dyer, a Republican from Missouri in 1922, segregation cases in Louisville, Kentucky, and the struggle of nine young African Americans accused of raping two white women in 1931 in Scottsboro, Alabama (see below). In some instances, these western branches played a pivotal role in the success of the national office in winning justice. The NAACP's Oklahoma City branch, for example, assisted the national office in bringing a successful legal suit in *Guinn v. United States* (1915), which overturned Oklahoma's grandfather clause, a devise that numerous states had used successfully to deny African Americans their constitutionally guaranteed right to vote. The "grandfather clause" first appeared in Louisiana in 1898, and it retroactively established a permanent voter registration list that only included the names of all males whose fathers and grandfathers had been qualified to vote on January 1, 1867. Since no African Americans had been qualified to vote in Louisiana on that date, the legislature wrote this device into the Louisiana state constitution specifically to strip blacks of the right to vote. Grandfather clauses were remarkably effective in every state in which they appeared. In Louisiana, the number of black registered voters declined from 130,344 in 1896 to 5,320 in 1900, just two years after the state adopted this nefarious policy.

In Texas the NAACP fought for several decades to overturn the policy of the Texas Democratic Party that barred blacks from voting in the Democratic Party primary, or "White Primary," as Texans called it. While African Americans were allowed to vote in the general election, in a solidly one-party state such as Texas, the person who won the Democratic primary election almost always won the general election, with Republican candidates hardly ever succeeding after the end of Reconstruction in 1877. In 1923, the Texas legislature passed a law that prohibited African Americans from voting in Democratic primaries. When the law was challenged legally by African Americans in court, in *Nixon* v. *Herndon* (1927), the United States Supreme Court ruled that the white primary statute was unconstitutional because it violated the equal protection clause of the Fourteenth Amendment. At the same time, however, the Supreme Court left open the possibility that the Democratic Party, unlike the state, could still exclude certain groups from voting in its primary. In this way, the high court had upheld the policy by ruling that the party primary functioned like a private club. Outraged, the NAACP's national office and local NAACP branches supported black leaders in Texas for two decades through fund-raising and providing legal assistance in order to defeat this practice. In 1944, S. E. Allwright, a Houston judge, denied a Democratic Primary ballot to Dr. Lonnie Smith, a local black dentist. With the backing of the NAACP's national office and the leadership of attorney Thurgood Marshall, who would become the first black Supreme Court Justice in 1967, the U.S. Supreme Court ruled in *Smith* v. *Allwright* (1944) that the all-white primary was unconstitutional. This decision was not just a tremendous victory for black westerners and the NAACP, it resonated throughout the nation.

Western NAACP branches also supported national unions such

as the Brotherhood of Sleeping Car Porters, organized by A. Philip Randolph in 1925 to improve the wages and working conditions of black railroad porters. In many western cities, such as Oakland, Los Angeles, Seattle, Houston, Dallas, and Denver, Pullman porters composed an important segment of the black middle class. They also joined the NAACP in impressive numbers. Thus a black leader such as C. L. Dellums, a porter living in Oakland, served as president of the Oakland NAACP branch. In time, Dellums would emerge as one of the most powerful and respected leaders throughout the San Francisco Bay Area. Eventually, he led the West Coast Brotherhood of Sleeping Car Porters for three decades and wielded considerable influence as a trade unionist.

The gross miscarriage of justice that the Scottsboro Boys experienced in Alabama in 1931 also aroused western branches of the NAACP. Local authorities in Scottsboro, Alabama, imprisoned eight young men convicted by a typically all-white Southern jury of raping two white women (one boy, only twelve years old, was not convicted). Numerous western branches of the NAACP organized fund-raisers, rallies, and mass meetings to assist in their defense. Though the Alabama Supreme Court upheld the convictions of seven of the eight boys, one justice dissented, viewing the entire process of conviction and sentencing as biased. The cases were returned to lower courts and retried three times. The long process and ongoing protests revealed that black westerners felt an obligation to assist African Americans less fortunate than themselves. It also allowed black westerners to link and ally their own struggle for racial equality with the struggles of African American communities in other regions.

Western cities also established chapters of the National Urban League (NUL), the Universal Negro Improvement Association, political leagues, and women's clubs to challenge racial discrimination and give black westerners forums to state their grievances. The sizable influx of African American southern migrants after World War I into cities like Los Angeles made the NUL chapters particularly important. Founded in 1911, the NUL provided employment opportunities for African Americans through referrals, steered blacks toward affordable housing, and helped rural migrants adjust to the pace and sophistication of urban life. Although the NUL grew much slower in the West than did the NAACP, choosing instead to concentrate on those cities with sizable African American populations who worked in industrial jobs, four NUL affiliates organized in western cities prior to 1940. Omaha, Nebraska, established the first Urban League in the West in 1928. Two years later, activists founded NUL chapters in Los Angeles and Seattle. In 1931, Lincoln, Nebraska, leaders organized an affiliate. Rather than standing on the front lines and protesting an injustice, the Urban Leagues provided social services to their constituents. They helped black communities in several important ways, not the least of which were employment opportunities and a broad array of social services.

The Universal Negro Improvement Association (UNIA), founded in 1914 by the charismatic Jamaican leader Marcus Garvey, protested racial discrimination as vigorously as any organization in the West and had surprising strength. Los Angeles emerged as the center of the western wing of the Garvey movement, though supporters organized UNIA divisions in a total of nine western states. San Francisco and Oakland each had strong Garvey chapters; a local NAACP official in the San Francisco Bay Area reported, to his dismay, that the Garvey movement "is just reaching our section of the state and has much to do with retarding our progress." Even outlying communities in California with relatively few African Americans, such as Fresno and Bakersfield, reported UNIA activity. The state of Kansas had nine UNIA chapters. By 1926, virtually every major western city–including Kansas City, Denver, Dallas, Oklahoma City, and Phoenix–had UNIA chapters. Earl Little, whose son Malcolm X would become one of the most dynamic and influential African American leaders in the nation in the 1960s, headed the Omaha UNIA chapter. Garveyites promoted black nationalism, racial pride, and self help, values that resonated strongly with African Americans in western cities. When Marcus Garvey visited Los Angeles in 1922, the welcoming parade in his honor drew ten thousand people, a strong testament to his popularity. Garvey's imprisonment on charges of mail fraud in 1922, and his deportation as an undesirable alien in 1926, crippled the UNIA, but it did not kill the organization. The Los Angeles branch, which enrolled one thousand members, continued to function into the early 1930s, but did not survive the Great Depression.

The Great Depression

The Great Depression struck western cities with great ferocity, and African Americans, who typically held the most menial jobs, suffered the greatest hardships. African Americans from all economic classes either lost their jobs, when they disappeared or because whites now deigned to take them, or had to accept *any* available form of employment. Since the majority of African Americans in the West worked as unskilled laborers or domestics, companies and employers generally eliminated those positions first. Black westerners, therefore, had the highest rates of unemployment and the least opportunity to reenter the workforce as permanent workers. As the old saying goes, whenever times got tough blacks were the first to get fired and the last to get rehired. Although African Americans in every western state experienced high rates of unemployment, those in California were especially hard hit by the Great Depression. By 1934, five years after the stock market crash, one-fifth of all Californians received some form of public relief.

As the Depression deepened, many Americans continued to struggle, but black westerners suffered greater hardships than other racial or ethnic groups in the region. One-half of the black residents of Los Angeles suffered unemployment by 1934. By 1937, the black unemployment rate hovered at 15 percent in Oakland and nearly 14 percent in San Francisco. In many West Coast cities, blacks faced competition not only from white workers but from Asians and Hispanics seeking work as unskilled laborers and in service-industry jobs. In San Francisco alone, 35,000 members of other nonwhite races, primarily Asians, competed with 3,000 African Americans for employment. African Americans faced similar competition in Los Angeles and Seattle, other cities with large Asian communities. Western cities with large Hispanic populations, such as San Antonio, Houston, Phoenix, Albuquerque, and Los Angeles, also saw additional competition for African American workers.

Despite the odds, some black westerners proved resourceful, combining ingenuity with sacrifice to weather the harsh economic climate. Ersey O'Brien, a black worker in Depression-era Los Angeles, accompanied his mother two or three times a week to a local market where they gathered spoiled fruit that had been discarded to supplement the family's meager diet. Robert Flippin, one of the most respected black leaders in San Francisco by the early 1930s, waited tables at a San Francisco restaurant, despite having a college degree and status as a member of the black elite. William Pittman, a black dentist in Berkeley, California, worked as a chauffeur, while his wife, Tarea, though trained in social work and a college graduate, worked in a cannery briefly before losing that job. Tarea Pittman noted that even positions in domestic service were difficult for African Americans to find. Race compounded the economic difficulty faced by O'Brien, Flippin, and Pittman in finding employment during the Depression. As in the past, even when jobs were not so scarce, white employers favored white workers. In some instances, employers dismissed their entire African American workforce to open up jobs for whites. Nor did the organizing efforts of labor organizations such as the CIO, which began to recruit and organize unskilled and semi-skilled workers in the mass production industries after its founding in 1936, benefit most African Americans in western cities. Since black workers had been systematically excluded from most manufacturing jobs in the West, they reaped few of the rewards of increased union membership.

In the large urban centers of Texas, such as Austin, Dallas, and Houston, unemployment remained high and wages for black workers fell sharply. In Austin, African Americans composed 35.6 percent of the unemployed in 1931–32 and 33.5 percent in 1935. By 1937, African Americans composed 25 percent of all unemployed workers in the state, although they were but 14 percent of the population. As many as 90 percent of black farm workers in some areas of Texas could not find work in 1935. These dismal economic conditions in cities and rural areas motivated many African Americans to leave Texas during the 1930s to seek jobs in other states. Indeed, one of the long-term consequences of the Great Depression was that it set African Americans, as well as many poor white families, in motion, with many of them heading farther west.

The New Deal met the needs of African American workers unevenly in the West, but the aid provided by these federal programs reduced suffering and unemployment for African Americans in every state. In those western states in which segregation had been codified into law (as in the restrictive covenants) and racial practices proved more virulent (e.g., Texas and Oklahoma), black workers suffered greater deprivations. In Walker County, Texas, for example, only thirteen of the more than 1,300 black farm families received relief, suggesting that local authorities blocked federal relief. In Houston, African Americans received an average relief benefit of $12.67 per month, as compared to $16.86 per month for whites. In some instances, local administrators of programs discouraged black Texans from even applying to New Deal programs by spreading false rumors that only whites were eligible for these benefits.

Generally considered the most popular New Deal program, the Civilian Conservation Corps (CCC), established by Congress in March 1933, was designed to provide jobs and training to young, unmarried men between the ages of eighteen and twenty-five. This federal agency worked to reforest depleted lands, engage in soil conservation and flood-control projects, and improve the nation's parks. CCC workers also built the camps that housed each employee, and they were directed by foresters and army officers and labored under strict military discipline.

Officials initially told African Americans in Texas that the segregated Civilian Conservation Corps (CCC) camps were for whites only. In time, however, 400 black youths participated in the CCC, still less than .05 percent of the total number of people enrolled. African Americans, as well as whites who participated, received room and board and $30 a month, $25 of which was sent home to their families. CCC participants of all races also signed up for education courses and earned high school diplomas through the program.

African Americans in Texas also fared relatively well in other New Deal programs such as the National Youth Administration (NYA). In Texas, Lyndon B. Johnson, future president of the United States, administered this innovative federal program designed to put high school and college students back to work. Although the NYA remained segregated in Texas, Johnson appointed an all-black advisory board and established numerous programs that benefited capable African American students. Thus in Texas, African Americans, despite segregation, received a fair share of NYA jobs. In 1937, 40 percent of those who qualified for NYA employment were African American, a sign of the high rate of black youth unemployment and of Johnson's fairness in running the state program.

African Americans in other western states also succeeded in gaining NYA employment. The NYA hired African Americans in higher numbers than their proportion of the population in every western state except Wyoming. In 1941, black westerners worked in almost 21 percent of all NYA jobs. One can attribute this success in part to the leadership of Mary McLeod Bethune, one of the nation's most influential black leaders and the highest ranking African American in the New Deal. As head of the NYA's Division of Negro Affairs, Bethune worked closely with state advisors such as Vivian Osborne Marsh in California to ensure that African Americans were represented fairly. Black western leaders, including Marsh and C. L. Dellums, also hoped that NYA job training would serve as a bridge to permanent employment for African Americans, particularly in manufacturing and the skilled trades. As with housing and racial equality, the case of the NYA demonstrates that national trends could be reinforced or bucked by local authorities.

Most black westerners rejoiced when they obtained public relief jobs, no matter how meager the salary. Popular New Deal programs such as the CCC, NYA, Public Works Administration (PWA), and Works Progress Administration (WPA) employed African Americans in every western state. In some of these programs, blacks fared as well or better than their white counterparts, evidence of their greater hardship. Robert C. Weaver, a black advisor to Harold Ickes, who headed the PWA, remarked that New Deal programs like the WPA represented a "godsend" for African Americans. "It made us feel like there was something we could do in the scheme of things," affirmed one black worker. By 1937, Los Angeles reported 3,752 African American workers on New Deal relief projects, the largest number of any city in the state. In some instances, black workers succeeded in moving into skilled and semiskilled jobs. In San Francisco, 43 percent of African Americans worked in semiskilled jobs in 1937, a much higher percentage than reported in the 1930 census. Although most black westerners tolerated segregation within New Deal agencies, in part because they felt that they could command greater control over their affairs, some black western leaders attacked such segregation as unwise. C. L. Dellums was particularly vocal in denouncing the NYA's segregated program in California. NAACP officials also criticized segregation in the California CCC and the inability of African American workers to obtain employment in Nevada on the construction of the Hoover Dam. These protests uncovered a widespread pattern of segregation in the employment practices at Hoover Dam and resulted in the hiring of a small number of black workers, but segregation persisted in western New Deal programs.

Black farm families comprised a minority within the western farming community and benefitted the least from New Deal programs. The passage of the Agricultural Adjustment Act (AAA) in 1933 gave direct subsidies to farmers who took land out of production, an attempt to reduce the oversupply of specific farm commodities including cotton, wheat, corn, rice, dairy products, and hogs. Over the life of the program, the federal government paid almost $293 million to Texas farmers. Yet African American farmers and farm workers received few of these subsidy payments because the federal government paid them directly to farm owners whereas the majority of black Texans worked as tenants and farm hands on other people's land. The AAA farm programs also encouraged farm owners to take marginal lands out of production and reduce credit; both policies had the effect of driving black tenants off the land. The federal government paid the owners to stop farm production but the producers, black tenants, got nothing and lost their income. Like white tenant farmers, many black tenant farmers responded by migrating to cities, while others worked as day laborers and struggled to feed their families. In Texas alone, the number of African American tenant farmers declined by half, from 65,000 to 32,000 between 1930 and 1940. An additional 20,000 African Americans left the state to seek better job opportunities. The situation of black farmers in Oklahoma paralleled those in Texas. Between 1930 and 1940 more than 37,000 African Americans in the Sooner State left the farm, and the value of black farms in 1940 represented only about one-fourth of their value in 1920. In general, then, New Deal farm programs did little to address rural poverty in either the black or white community in the West, and they actually drove many blacks permanently out of farming and into urban areas.

Black leaders in the West believed that obtaining greater political power would improve the economic conditions of their communities and eliminate any remaining barriers to racial equality. Despite their small numbers in most western states, African Americans took a keen interest in politics during the 1930s. Black westerners joined their counterparts throughout the nation and shifted their political allegiance to the Democratic Party by 1936, breaking a political tie that had existed since the Reconstruction era. Perhaps naively, African Americans believed that the Democratic Party and the New Deal coalition that President Franklin D. Roosevelt (FDR) had forged by 1936 would be more responsive to their needs. They had seen evidence of this when FDR appointed the renowned black leader Mary McLeod Bethune to organize an informal group of black advisors dubbed the "black cabinet." The president had also appointed many other black advisors, including Bethune and Robert Weaver, a Harvard-trained Ph.D. in economics, to New Deal programs, and First Lady Eleanor Roosevelt spoke at numerous African American events and allowed herself to be photographed with black men and women. In a *Ladies Home Journal* column, Eleanor said that the federal government must act to promote racial equality, perhaps the boldest statement that a First Lady had every made in support of racial equality in American history.

Despite such support by the Roosevelts, only Los Angeles' black community was large enough to run a competitive candidate for political office prior to World War II. In 1934, Augustus F. Hawkins, a Louisiana migrant who grew up in Los Angeles' South Central neighborhood, defeated black Republican Frederick Roberts in the Sixty-second State Assembly District. A graduate of the University of California at Los Angeles, Hawkins convinced voters that he was prolabor and prowelfare, and would serve the interests of both African Americans and white middle-class voters. Young, intelligent, articulate, and progressive in his views, he personified the new black politician in the West. He remained the only African American in the state legislature until 1948, however, and no other major California city succeeded in electing an African American to even local office during the prewar years.

Not even Texas, with its large black communities in San Antonio, Dallas, and Houston, elected African Americans to political office. The prevalence of poll taxes, which discouraged black voters from registering, and the policy of electing candidates to at-large, rather than to single-member districts, worked to the disadvantage of black and minority group voters in general. Poll taxes, a small monetary fee that exacted a hardship against the poor of all races, but hit African Americans especially hard because of widespread poverty, significantly curtailed black voting wherever they were enacted. At-large districts had a similar effect, because they diluted the black vote, rather than permit African Americans and other minority voters who were concentrated in residential areas from electing candidates who might better represent their interests. In rare instances, black leaders formed successful alliances and encouraged progressive white politicians such as Maury Maverick, a congressman from San Antonio's Twelfth District, to support antilynching legislation and challenge the poll tax. But such alliances were rare, and not until 1966, with the election of Barbara Jordan to the Texas State Senate, did an African American win political office in Texas. So while the generally wholesale switch of African Americans from the "party of Lincoln" to the Democratic Party helped the latter party, it did little to further the political aspirations of African Americans in Texas.

This disenchantment with mainstream politics occasionally drove some black westerners to consider alliances with the Communist Party USA (CPUSA) or other radical organizations. In the West, African American communities had overwhelmingly supported the Scottsboro Boys in their quest for justice, with several black leaders openly criticizing the passivity of the NAACP for its initial refusal to take a strong public stand in this case. Attorney Loren Miller, for one, blasted the NAACP branch in Los Angeles for its silence as Alabama sentenced the eight young men to death for the alleged rape of two white women when all evidence pointed to the contrary. Communists, by contrast, had worked hard to support the boys and overturn their convictions. Miller himself would drift increasingly to the left, although he never formally joined the Communist Party. But, like many African Americans in both the West and throughout the nation during the 1930s, Miller found the Communist Party more receptive to the idea of racial equality than either the Democrats or the Republicans. He traveled to the Soviet Union in 1932 with the poet and writer Langston Hughes and a group of leftist African Americans at the request of the Soviet state to produce an ill-fated film on race relations in the American South. Upon his return, Miller gave numerous speeches in which he praised the Soviet way of life, particularly the absence of racial prejudice. John Pittman, the fiery editor of the San Francisco *Spokesman*, drifted even further to the left than Miller and embraced the Communist Party ideology by the mid-1930s. Pittman wrote that "the process of government as it now exists in this country is incomplete, undemocratic and chaotic." He, too, became ever more critical of the NAACP's moderate programs. Pittman resigned from the *Spokesman* and became one of the founders and executive editors of the *Daily People's World*, a left-wing political paper in San Francisco.

In general, however, the CPUSA made few inroads into African American communities in the West during the 1930s, attracting only a handful of loyal supporters. In no western city did the party approach the level of success it achieved in New York City, where more than 1,000 blacks in Harlem alone joined it. Most black westerners had good reason to be suspicious of the vague promises that Communist leaders made about improving the condition of all industrial workers and eradicating all forms of racial discrimination in light of the oppression that they saw and felt on a daily basis. The interracial meetings of the Communist Party became targets of police brutality and indiscriminate violence in western cities like Los Angeles, where the police chief encouraged his officers to disrupt any gathering of "suspected radicals." That only a small number of African Americans in the West joined the Communist Party, then, should not be surprising. Many more white immigrants who moved west, however, found the Communist Party's stance on equality among workers attractive and claimed active party membership.

The Great Depression thus exacted a heavy toll on black westerners, and no program established by any western state or the federal government did much to eliminate the massive unemployment and suffering the economic calamity wreaked. The New Deal did, however, put some black westerners back to work in many states and localities and provide a ray of hope, as did the appointment of several black advisors to New Deal agencies and the leadership of Mary McLeod Bethune, the first African American to head a federal agency. Indeed, the sensitivity of Franklin and Eleanor Roosevelt and many white New Deal officials to the plight of African Americans, and the employment of blacks in New Deal agencies, were perhaps the most significant reasons why African Americans in the West joined their counterparts throughout the country and shifted their vote to the Democratic Party ticket in the 1936 presidential election. Black westerners also increasingly turned to their own community institutions to provide social services and as forums to protest racial injustices. African Americans were especially effective in working toward relief and social services in their respective communities through an array of women's clubs, churches, community centers, and protest organizations such as the NAACP and the National Urban League. These organizations did little to relieve the high unemployment rates in western black communities, but collectively they provided comfort and limited but nonetheless valuable services, and they reassured many African Americans that they were not alone during these especially difficult years. The Great Depression tested the resolve of black westerners, but it did not break their spirit.

Conclusion

Over the course of the 1910s through the 1930s, black westerners took two steps forward and one step back as they fought for recognition and their rights. Though they fared better than their counterparts in the South and East when it came to housing and local rights, they, too, suffered from national trends such as lynching, restrictive housing covenants, and poll taxes. For many African Americans, the Great Depression took more away than it did from many whites, Hispanics, Asians, and others, leaving African American communities more centralized in urban areas, and with less property and power. As for the other groups, however, the onset of World War II at the end of the decade would provide African Americans new opportunities for employment and encourage more westward migration in the quest for work and a better life. For African Americans and other racial minorities, the World War II years would replay familiar racial inequities, but they would also hold out new reasons to hope that one day they would achieve their full civil rights as American citizens.

Suggested Readings

Bogle, Don. *Bright Boulevards, Bold Dreams: The Story of Black Hollywood.* New York: Random House, 2006.

Botson, Michael R., Jr. *Labor, Civil Rights, and the Hughes Tool Company.* College Station: Texas A&M University Press, 2005.

Bourgeois, Christi L. "Stepping over the Lines: Lyndon Johnson, Black Texans, and the National Youth Administration, 1935–1937." *Southwestern Historical Quarterly* 91 (October 1987): 149–172.

Broussard, Albert S. "The Worst of Times: African Americans in the Great Depression" Hamilton Cravens, ed. *The Great Depression: People and Perspectives*, Santa Barbara: ABC-Clio, 2009.

DjeDje, Jacqueline C. and Eddie S. Meadows, eds. *California Souls: Music of African Americans in the West.* Berkeley: University of California Press, 1998.

Cox, Thomas C. *Blacks in Topeka, Kansas: 1865–1915.* Baton Rouge: Louisiana State University Press, 1982.

Cripps, Thomas. "The Reaction of the Negro to the Motion Picture *Birth of a Nation*." August Meier and Elliott Rudwick, eds. *The Making of Black America: Essays in Negro Life and History.* New York: Atheneum Press, 1969.

Crouchett, Lawrence, Lonnie Bunch, and Martha Kendall Winnacker. *Visions Toward Tomorrow: The History of the East Bay Afro-American Community, 1852–1977.* Oakland: Northern California Center for Afro-American History and Life, 1989.

Daniels, Douglas Henry. *One O' Clock Jump: The Unforgettable History of the Oklahoma City Blue Devils.* Boston: Beacon Press, 2007.

de Graaf, Lawrence. "The City of Black Angels: The Emergence of the Los Angeles Ghetto, 1890–1930." *Pacific Historical Review* 39 (August 1970): 323–52.

Flamming, Douglas. *Bound for Freedom: Black Los Angeles in Jim Crow America.* Berkeley and Los Angeles: University of California Press, 2005.

Gower, Calvin. "The Struggle of Blacks for Leadership in the Civilian Conservation Corps." *Journal of Negro History* 61 (April 1976): 123–35.

Hine, Darlene Clark. *Black Victory: The Rise and Fall of the White Primary in Texas.* Columbia: University of Missouri Press, 2003.

Mihelich, Dennis. "The Lincoln Urban League: The Travail of Depression and War." *Nebraska History* 70 (Winter 1989): 303–16.

Sides, Josh. *L.A. City Limits: African Americans from the Great Depression to the Present.* Berkeley: University of California Press, 2003.

SoRelle, James M. "The Emergence of Black Business in Houston, Texas: A Study of Race and Ideology." Howard Beeth and Cary D. Wintz, eds. *Black Dixie: Afro-Texans' History and Culture in Houston.* College Station: Texas A&M University Press, 1992.

Taylor, Quintard. *The Forging of a Black Community: Seattle's Central District from 1870 through the Civil Rights Era.* Seattle: University of Washington Press, 1994.

Tolbert, Emory J. *The U.N.I.A. and Black Los Angeles: Ideology and Community in the American Garvey Movement.* Los Angeles: University of California Press, 1980.

Whitaker, Matthew. *Race Work: The Rise of Civil Rights in the Urban West.* Lincoln: University of Nebraska Press, 2005.

Wild, Mark. *Street Meeting: Multiethnic Neighborhoods in Early Twentieth-Century Los Angeles.* Berkeley: University of California Press, 2008.

CHAPTER FOUR

World War II

World War II had a more dramatic impact on the American West than any single event in the first half of the twentieth century, even the Great Depression. The mobilization of U.S. troops and the multitude of defense industries and shipyards pulled the nation out of the Depression and transformed the western states and territories in ways that few could have imagined. The far western states—in particular, California, Oregon, and Washington, because of their proximity to major ports—received hundreds of thousands of military personnel and defense-industry workers of all races. Even the distant territories of Alaska and Hawaii, both considered strategic locations in the fight against Japan in the Pacific, attracted a sizable influx of U.S. military personnel. The war also brought new hope to African Americans and their supporters that racial equality loomed within reach. President Franklin D. Roosevelt's Executive Order 8802, which prohibited discrimination in the nation's defense industries, emboldened them. That decision, and the increasingly militant insistence of African American leaders that the federal government should act to eradicate discrimination and Nazi-style racism at home as well as abroad, led black westerners and African Americans in all regions of the nation to believe that the war would improve their collective status. They often referred to this hope as the "Double-V campaign," a phrase coined in 1942 by the *Pittsburgh*

Courier, an influential black newspaper, for victory over racism at home as well as over racist dictatorships overseas. If nothing else, the millions of American men overseas in the armed forces meant that African Americans, along with other racial minorities and women would, of necessity, have new opportunities to find jobs in fields from which they previously had been barred. They felt, moreover, that their loyalty and patriotism, combined with persistent agitation, would construct a new racial framework. After the setbacks of the 1930s, black westerners saw the World War II years as a time of new opportunities—economically, socially, and politically.

On the Move, In Search of Work

The African American population in the West grew dramatically during the 1940s. In sharp contrast to the first four decades of the twentieth century, nearly every major urban community in the West experienced a large in-migration of African Americans. The new lure of high-paying jobs in the defense industries and the old promise of a chance for a better life attracted African American migrants from all regions of the nation. As historian Quintard Taylor writes, "the region's black population grew by 443,000 (33 percent) during the forties and redistributed itself toward the West Coast." Black wartime migrants, however, targeted a select number of metropolitan regions, notably the San Francisco Bay Area, San Diego, Los Angeles–Long Beach, Seattle-Tacoma, and Portland. Yet even cities like Las Vegas, Nevada, Phoenix, Arizona, Denver, and Honolulu saw significant increases in their black populations. Black and white migrants alike equated these cities and metropolitan areas with jobs. This dramatic increase of black migrants exemplifies the general movement of people to the West. About 8 million people moved west of the Mississippi during the 1940s, and roughly 3.5 million of these sojourners came to California alone. Indeed, the total population of the West grew by 26 percent during the 1940s, with people of all races seeking new opportunities during these years.

Black population increases proved significant for several reasons. The relative number of African Americans who had resided in the West during the prewar years had been small. Race and ethnicity, particularly dark skin, had served as barriers to many African Americans, but also for Mexican, Japanese, and Chinese westerners. And while some native-born white westerners, such as Portland mayor Earl Riley, resented newcomers of any racial stripe, in their eyes African Americans represented the most undesirable of all migrants. "Undesirables—white or colored—are not wanted and if they fail to obey our laws, will be unceremoniously dealt with," Riley stated. Some white westerners also feared the potential for an outbreak of racial violence with a sharp increase of African Americans in their communities. Yet others, including many city officials in Seattle and San Francisco, embraced black newcomers, even forming committees to work toward their peaceful transition into the community.

California held the greatest appeal to African American migrants, as it did with all migrants. Despite the Golden State's considerable distance from the southern states, many black southerners pulled up stakes and temporarily severed family ties to make the long journey there. That these resilient migrants had just endured more than a decade of economic depression did not deter them in the least. The major shipyards in the San Francisco Bay Area, like the Kaiser Shipyards and Marinship, actively recruited some of the new arrivals. Other African Americans headed west solely on the recommendation of friends, relatives, or strangers that jobs existed in California shipyards for anyone, irrespective of race or gender, willing to work. In a short time, according to the San Francisco Chamber of Commerce, the Bay Area became the largest shipbuilding center in the world. Kaiser Shipyards alone employed 90,000 workers at the height of wartime production, of which about one in five was African American. Yet Kaiser was just one of seven Bay Area shipyards, and African Americans found employment in each.

The Los Angeles–Long Beach and San Diego metropolitan areas also served as important destinations for potential defense-industry employees, and jobs in shipbuilding and aircraft production attracted African Americans. Unlike the Bay Area cities of northern California—San Francisco, Oakland, Alameda, or Richmond—which contained small pre–World War II black communities, Los Angeles's black population had reached 64,000 in 1940. Black migrants from Texas, Louisiana, Mississippi, and Oklahoma poured into L.A. between 1942 and 1945 in search of work. California Ship (more widely known as Cal Ship) employed about 7,000 black workers in 1944, approximately 15 percent of its workforce. After initial resistance by white employees and supervisors, who opposed hiring black workers on racial grounds, broke down due to wartime contingencies, African Americans also made impressive gains in finding jobs at aircraft companies like Consolidated-Vultee, Douglas, Lockheed-Vega, and Boeing. San Diego's defense contractors, likewise, slowly began to hire black aircraft workers after first putting up considerable resistance. One company, Consolidated Aircraft, employed 1,000 black aircraft employees by 1945. In short, it had become unpatriotic to discriminate; to do so in the face of a shortage of workers would hurt production, and thereby the war effort.

For the first time in the twentieth century, blacks had made inroads into industries that traditionally had been closed to them. Racism had confined San Diego's small pre–World War II black community (a mere 4,143 residents out of a total population of 203,341 in 1940) to service jobs and unskilled menial labor, with few exceptions. In addition, the sheer number of black workers who gained employment in shipbuilding, aircraft construction, and related defense industries often was larger than the percentage of African Americans in the total population of West Coast cities, an indication that defense industries aggressively pursued black workers. Black shipyard workers in Portland, Oregon, serve as a case in point. The Portland area shipyards employed more than 7,000 black workers in 1944, about 9 percent of the total workforce, yet a staggering 96 percent of all black workers in the city. African Americans gained employment in semiskilled and skilled positions for the first time in many of these industries. These breakthroughs, which seemed modest at first glance, opened the door to more lucrative jobs for African Americans in the future.

African American migrants showed remarkable tenacity and ingenuity in making the westward journey during World War II. The states of Texas, Louisiana, Arkansas, and Oklahoma contributed the lion's share of these new westerners. Black migrants to western cities were as likely to be women as men, and many of them came as families. Some, like Sarah Hastings, who left Kansas City, Missouri, in 1942 and moved to Los Angeles to work in the shipyards, came by train. A widow raising two children, Hastings had worked as a domestic her entire life. She learned from a friend and from flyers posted in her neighborhood that West Coast industries had a great demand for workers of all races and genders and paid wages considerably higher than domestic service. The defense industries did indeed use flyers and handbills to advertise jobs in western cities, but news of employment opportunities also spread by word of mouth among workers of all races. Word of jobs also spread via black churches, barbershops, beauty salons, taverns, and community centers. An enterprising woman like Hastings believed that she had little to lose. She took a welding class in the evening, after working a long day, in order to prepare for shipyard employment, then quit her job as a maid and headed to California. Yet train travel was difficult because troops filled almost every available space, and the journey took between three to four days in hot, crowded surroundings. To add to the discomfort of overcrowding, trains originating in southern states were segregated. Hastings would have agreed with the blunt assessment of Fanny Christina Hill, a black migrant who in 1942 moved from Tyler, Texas, to Los Angeles and found work at the North American Aviation Company. "It was Hitler who got us out of the white folk's kitchens," she explained. In this instance, World War II opened up wholly new job opportunities for black women.

Other migrants, black and white, arrived west by automobile, many of them traveling along Route 66, the same highway that so many Dust Bowl migrants had taken west during the 1930s. Once blacks arrived, they settled into one of the established black neighborhoods in the cities, most of which had already grown crowded in the wake of new housing covenants that kept blacks out of white parts of town. With the tremendous demand for lodging, black communities quickly became overburdened. In 1942, S. R. Martin, a pastor in the Church of God in Christ, moved his family from Billings, Montana, to San Francisco and crowded into the city's Fillmore District, which had grown tremendously during the war. The Martins shared an apartment with two families and rented a room to another young couple who sought scarce lodging. Rudy Martin, one of Reverend Martin's two young sons, described the neighborhood's hustle and bustle vividly: "A black USO operated around the corner from us on Buchanan Street, and the Fillmore District was full of more black people than I had ever seen—service people, deliverymen, air raid wardens, military and civilian police, and other residents as crammed together as we were. People sang, danced, laughed, wept, bellowed, and fought in delight, desperation, and despair near the USO and the bars and cafes in the neighborhood." The remarkable number of black migrants who came West between 1942 and 1945 alone reveals that these individuals made whatever sacrifices required to reach California and other Pacific Coast states with plentiful defense-industry jobs.

In some western communities the dramatic increase in the African American population realigned the percentage of blacks relative to other minority groups. In San Francisco, for example, African Americans had composed only 15.2 percent of the total non-white population in 1940. Just five years later, in 1945, African Americans composed 53.1 percent of the city's nonwhite population, for 27,155 black migrants moved to San Francisco during this period. The federal government's internment of foreign-born Japanese immigrants as well as native-born Japanese Americans during the war certainly accounted for part of the relative decline in other nonwhite minority groups in San Francisco, yet the Asian percentage of the population continued to shrink relative to African Americans for several more decades. Sadly, it was the relocation and internment of Japanese Americans from San Francisco, Los Angeles, and other West Coast cities that provided African Americans with sorely needed additional housing, recreational space, and community centers. Black migrants from the South streamed into the housing vacuum created when the federal government forced the Japanese to leave their homes and businesses on short notice and enter relocation camps. The rapid growth of the Hispanic population, composed primarily of Mexican immigrants, occurred principally in southern California. Fighting the war at home thus changed the racial landscape, not just for African Americans but for various non-white groups in relation to each other.

Some interior western states also attracted black migrants during the war. Las Vegas, Nevada, proved an especially attractive locale to black men and women from southern cities like Fordyce, Arkansas, a segregated rural community that offered few employment opportunities for African Americans. Nevada and the three Pacific Coast states–California, Oregon, and Washington–led the nation in the percentage of black population growth, expanding 548 percent between 1940 and 1950. Between 1940 and 1950, Nevada's black population grew from 178 to 2,888. The demand for war workers in Nevada's defense industry and the need for labor in the fledgling Las Vegas hotels and casinos helped fuel this dramatic growth. These jobs in particular attracted black women, and southern migrants established a grapevine, an informal cross-country network of communication, to alert African Americans in rural communities that job opportunities were readily available "out West" and that these positions paid high wages. As one black woman explained to a prospective recruit, "I can make $10 a day and work in the shade." The growth of Nevada's black population during World War II, while unusual in scale, represents a broader trend in interior western states.

This growth was nearly as dramatic in other western cities that offered defense-industry jobs. Tacoma, Washington, for example, experienced a black population increase of 393 percent, while Denver's black community grew 94.1 percent in the course of a decade. Less dramatic though still significant gains were registered in Salt Lake City, Utah, (63.5 percent), San Antonio, Texas, (48.1 percent), Houston, Texas, (44.5 percent), Fort Worth, Texas, (42.1 percent), and Wichita, Kansas (39.3 percent). The modest increases registered in Texas and Oklahoma, including in the large urban centers where the black population barely grew or remained static during the 1940s, reflected the assertiveness and pragmatism of African American migrants. Clearly these black people were voting with their feet—following one another, seeking out opportunities not barred by race, and rejecting racist limitations in their current workplaces.

Despite acute labor shortages in Dallas, Fort Worth, and Houston, for example, numerous defense contractors and war industries in Texas typically refused to hire black workers. The *Dallas Express*, an African American newspaper, reported as late as May 1943 that at least twenty-six defense plants in Dallas refused to hire blacks in skilled jobs. Houston was no better. In that city, only the Hughes Tool Company, which had a longstanding policy of hiring skilled black workers, deviated from this policy of racial exclusion. The Houston Shipbuilding Company, the city's largest employer, refused to hire skilled black workers in 1942. Even a shortage of workers in their industry failed to convince the company to change its discriminatory policy, noted the *Houston Informer*, an African American newspaper. Discriminatory racial policies like these in the face of job shortages stimulated the out-migration of African Americans from Texas to West Coast cities. They also demonstrated the deep-seated traditions of racism and racial exclusion in Texas. The difficulty that some African Americans faced in securing jobs in wartime industries because of racial discrimination also reveals that some cities in the West failed to enforce FDR's Executive Order 8802, which prohibited discrimination in hiring in these industries based on race. In Texas and Oklahoma, racial discrimination flourished in wartime factories, despite an acute shortage of labor, and black workers waged numerous complaints with the Fair Employment Practices Committee (FEPC) attesting to that fact.

The World War II migration also brought the first significant black populations into the western territories of Hawaii and Alaska. Blacks had migrated to Hawaii in modest numbers prior to 1940, as the distance from the mainland states, the expense involved, and the unfamiliarity of the islands made it a difficult place for most black migrants to reach. The sheer distance from the southern states to Hawaii was considerably beyond the means of most westward-bound black southerners, the majority of whom worked as sharecroppers, tenant farmers, domestics, and unskilled laborers. In 1940, only 255 African Americans lived in Hawaii, where they represented a mere 0.2 percent of the total population. World War II changed the racial and the demographic landscape of Hawaii in profound ways. During the war roughly 30,000 African Americans came to Hawaii, the majority as soldiers, sailors, and marines. These men and women, wrote historians David Farber and Beth Bailey, "found themselves in a racial hothouse." Unlike black migrants who worked in West Coast shipyards and defense industries, most African Americans in Hawaii during the early 1940s served in the U.S. military. The relatively tolerant and tranquil racial atmosphere of the islands changed dramatically with the importation of unprecedented numbers of U.S. military personnel. African Americans had always experienced a degree of racial discrimination in Hawaii, but the war greatly accelerated this tendency. In the crowded military bases, white servicemen and their commanding officers attempted to recreate the segregated policies that had existed on the mainland for nearly a century. In effect, they imported their bigotry and discrimination from the Mainland to Hawaii. They spread vicious rumors regarding the alleged criminal tendencies of black servicemen, portraying them in the public mind as a race to be feared. African American servicemen also faced a widespread pattern of segregation in hotels, dance halls, and public accommodations, all of which stoked racial tension and, not surprisingly, greater militancy on the part of black military personnel. The situation convinced the NAACP's national office in 1945 to charter a branch in Hawaii, the first one outside of the continental United States.

The black presence in Alaska mirrored that in Hawaii in several respects. Few African Americans lived in Alaska prior to World War II, and blacks viewed the territory prior to statehood in 1959 as a remote locale with few economic opportunities and an inhospitable climate. Like other migrants, African Americans traditionally relied on the advice and support of family and friends for employment and housing information when they came west or north. The absence of extended kinship networks and relatives who could potentially help acclimate new migrants to the rigors of life in this still frontier-like territory also discouraged sizable black migration. Only 168 African Americans resided in the entire territory at the turn of the twentieth century, and a mere 139 lived there in 1939.

World War II thus had a great deal to do with changing African Americans' perception of Alaska as a place in which they could advance. It brought new opportunities and new possibilities, and the military led the way, stationing African American soldiers in Alaska as laborers and engineers. For example, troops from the 93rd, 95th, 97th, and 388th engineers regiments contributed to the building of the Alcan (Alaska) Highway through Alaska and the Canadian Northwest to reach the "lower forty-eight." Optimistic about the unlimited possibilities that Alaska had to offer, in large measure due to the abundance of cheap land, some black soldiers returned there after the war, taking up homesteads. These early African American settlements in Alaska, primarily military personnel and their families, in short order organized churches, lodges, fraternal societies, and started a weekly newspaper, *The Alaska Spotlight*, which became an importance voice in the community.

The effect World War II had on migration to Alaska did not unfold overnight. In 1950, a census taker apparently still thought it a waste of time even to list African Americans separately from other nonwhite races. By 1960, however, a sizable African American community had moved into the state (like Hawaii, Alaska had gained statehood in 1959), with the majority residing in Anchorage, Alaska's largest city. The 1960 census reported 6,758 African American residents, a staggering increase from the 139 just twenty-one years earlier. Anchorage had experienced a general population boom of 293.1 percent between 1950 and 1960. Similarly, Fairbanks' total African American population had increased 130.7 percent, Kodiak's 53.7 percent, and Juneau's, Alaska's capital, 14.1 percent. Clearly, not only Anchorage but every major city in Alaska saw a rapid and sizeable increase in its black population in the wake of statehood.

Civil Rights and the Military

Beyond encouraging African Americans to move to new territories, the war also triggered a new militancy among African American men and women in all branches of the military. Black soldiers often took the lead in establishing local NAACP chapters in remote locales, for example, such as Hawaii and Alaska. They also demanded better treatment in a still segregated military apparatus, as well as fair treatment in the local communities in which they served or trained, insisting that local businesses cease discriminating in public places. Black soldiers and sailors in Hawaii protested a widespread pattern of discrimination in hotels, dance halls, and public accommodations. They also denounced the local press' depiction of African American men as thieves, rapists, murders, criminals, and a disease-ridden lot. Their counterparts stationed at Fort Lawton, in Seattle, Washington, expressed their frustration more dramatically, staging a riot when they were excluded from clubs that served Italian prisoners of war but excluded African American soldiers. This incident drove home to African American servicemen that despite their patriotic actions, society still saw them as beneath the peoples of European descent, even the enemy in time of war.

Black servicemen occasionally spoke out against military policies that they deemed unfair, although they generally were measured in their criticism because they ran the risk of facing a court-martial and incarceration for insubordination. The case of Jackie Robinson serves as an excellent example. In 1942, Robinson, who had lettered in four sports at the University of California at Los Angeles, entered the U.S. Army. Assigned initially to Fort Riley, Kansas, Robinson distinguished himself on the firing range and gained promotion to corporal. When Robinson, who had completed three years of college, tried to enter officers' training school, the army initially denied him the opportunity. Only after Joe Louis, the heavyweight boxing champion of the world, who also served in the military, intervened in his behalf was Robinson permitted to enroll. In 1943, Robinson became a commissioned officer with the rank of second lieutenant and was appointed acting morale officer for a black company at Fort Riley. By all accounts, the young African American officer made an excellent platoon leader who was highly respected by his fellow soldiers. But Robinson refused to accept quietly the second-class and inferior status expected of black soldiers and officers by the army and other armed services. Foreshadowing his future role in desegregating major league baseball after the war, he protested his omission from the Fort Riley baseball team because of his race. Robinson waged his protest by refusing to play for the camp's football team, which earned him a stern reprimand from his commanding officer.

In 1944, the army assigned Robinson to Camp Hood (now Fort Hood), a large military base in Killeen, Texas. There, Second Lieutenant Robinson was attached to the 761st Tank Battalion, a black unit that would distinguish itself later that year at the pivotal Battle of the Bulge. Camp Hood and the surrounding communities of Temple and Killeen had well-deserved reputations as bastions of segregation and white supremacy. One of Robinson's fellow African American soldiers, Harry Duplessis, observed "Camp Hood was frightening. . . . Segregation there was so complete that I even saw outhouses marked White, Colored, and Mexican." While there, Robinson failed to observe a common racial practice by refusing to move to the back of one of the military post's busses. Fully aware that the federal government had recently issued a policy that disallowed segregated buses on military bases, Robinson, when someone ordered him to move to the back of the bus while en route to a military hospital, simply refused to do so, remaining quietly in the seat in which he was already sitting. This breach of racial etiquette ultimately led to a court-martial trial for Robinson in 1944.

Robinson's defiance of segregation at Camp Hood and the sequence of events that led to his court-martial trial were strongly influenced by the growing militancy of African Americans throughout the nation. Black soldiers in particular were defying Jim Crow laws and customs in southern towns and military bases because they viewed them as hypocritical to the professed aims of the U.S. government during World War II. The *Pittsburgh Courier* reported that it had received numerous complaints from black soldiers, and "frustrations on buses in the South was one of the most fruitful sources of trouble for negro soldiers." In one particularly gruesome incident, a white bus driver in Durham, North Carolina, shot and killed a black soldier who had refused his order to move to the back of the bus. Yet Robinson stated in his autobiography, *I Never Had it Made* (1972), published nearly three decades after the incident, that the African American boxers Joe Louis and Ray Robinson, both world champions in their respective weight divisions, had also influenced his militant stand against segregation by their own recent refusals to comply passively with segregated bus regulations in Alabama.

Robinson's bold act placed the army in a difficult position, for it could not logically prosecute him for refusing to move to the back of the bus since the military had only recently issued orders eliminating segregated buses on military posts. Instead, Robinson was charged with insubordination, disturbing the peace, drunkenness, conduct unbecoming an officer, insulting a civilian woman, and refusing to obey the lawful orders of a superior officer. Although Robinson had not committed any of these alleged offenses, he was convinced that military officials at Camp Hood viewed him as "uppity," a term that many whites reserved for African Americans who challenged white authority, and that they had conspired to court-martial him so he would be dishonorably discharged from the armed forces. This fear was not as far-fetched as it sounds. As historian Jack D. Foner writes, "many black soldiers were unjustly convicted by court-martial, either because their officers assumed their guilt regardless of the evidence or because they wanted to 'set an example' for other black soldiers." Perhaps sensing its case against Robinson lacked merit, but still attempting to save face, the army dropped all charges stemming from the bus incident, although Robinson still faced a court-martial on two lesser charges of insubordination stemming from his behavior following his detention in the guardhouse.

Following the episode on the bus, Robinson had been escorted by the MPs to their headquarters, where Robinson confronted a white private who referred to him as a "nigger lieutenant." Robinson also challenged the veracity of several statements regarding the episode, and he corrected a white female stenographer who consistently interrupted his version of events and chided him for his breaches of racial etiquette in Texas.

At trial Robinson received an excellent defense from Lieutenant William Cline, a young, white lawyer from the Midwest. Unlike the majority of court-martial cases involving African Americans, Robinson's drew national attention from leading black newspapers such as the *Chicago Defender* and the *Pittsburgh Courier*. The national office of the NAACP also learned about the case and Robinson specifically asked the pioneering civil rights organization for its assistance, but they refused to provide him with legal assistance because of the flood of complaints they had already received from other black soldiers. After hearing the evidence from all parties, the military court-martial board found Robinson not guilty on all remaining charges. Honorably discharged from the military in November 1944, Robinson would draw upon this indomitable fighting spirit often as he integrated the Brooklyn Dodgers in 1947 to become the first African American to play major league baseball. Robinson's career in the Army represented typical patterns of discrimination throughout the military during World War II, even as his fame in baseball makes him stand out historically.

In rare cases, African American military personnel collectively protested unjust policies. The most dramatic example, known as the Port Chicago mutiny, occurred in the wake of a military tragedy. On July 17, 1944, at the Port Chicago Naval Base, some thirty-five miles from San Francisco, a massive explosion occurred that could be seen for more than twenty miles. As black and white stevedores loaded two ammunition ships, the *Quinalt Victory* and the *E. A. Bryan*, an explosion of undetermined origin destroyed both ships and killed 320 men, including 202 African Americans. Black stevedores dominated the labor force at this naval facility, and they had complained frequently that their white superiors and officers assigned them to dangerous work details without proper training. They also asserted that these same officers assigned only black sailors to load ammunition on ships. Both practices suggest that the white officers considered the lives of the black sailors as expendable.

Several weeks after the horrific accident at Port Chicago, officers ordered 328 black stevedores to load ammunition ships at Mare Island in the San Francisco Bay. At first, all of the men refused to obey the order. Naval officials eventually convinced the majority of them to comply, but fifty of the black sailors still refused. After the arrest of the sailors by military police, a military tribunal tried the men for mutiny in what became the longest and largest such trial in naval history. The tribunal found all fifty sailors guilty and sentenced them to fifteen years detention and dishonorable discharges. President Harry Truman, perhaps sensitive to the racial overtones of the case, as well as the need for national unity, pardoned most of these men. In January 1946, the government released all of them from prison but required that they remain in the Navy, which sent them overseas to the South Pacific. These two cases demonstrate the tensions over race that existed within World War II America: the white naval officers saw blacks as expendable and assigned them dangerous jobs in the states; for its part, the federal government was anxious about the appearance of racism but nonetheless sent the black men it had "pardoned" into dangerous jobs abroad.

The experiences of African American soldiers in the West during World War II resemble those of Mexican Americans and American Indians in several respects, but they also differ in significant ways. Each group served the United States in large numbers despite the second-class treatment it received from the white majority. Approximately 750,000 Mexican Americans served in the military during the war, seventeen of whom earned the Congressional Medal of Honor, including five from Texas. Similarly, over 25,000 Native American men served in World War II, and they, too, distinguished themselves on the battlefield. One of the most notable contributions of Native Americans to the American war effort was their role as "code talkers," using their native languages to encode and decipher messages. Native American and Mexican American women, like black western women, also worked in defense plants, and a small number of them volunteered as military nurses. Mexican American and Native American leaders believed that the call for patriotism and national unity should take precedence over specific grievances that their groups might have against the U.S. government for past mistreatment. Unlike African Americans soldiers, however, Mexican American and Native American soldiers fought, with few exceptions, in integrated units led by white officers. Although racial tensions existed in some of these units, neither group faced the stigma of serving in a Jim Crow army.

Black westerners also contributed to the war effort as soldiers, sailors, and aviators. At least one black westerner, Lincoln Ragsdale of Phoenix, Arizona, served as a member of the famed Tuskegee Airmen, who collectively performed distinguished service escorting American bombers during the conflict. Doris Miller, a native of Waco, Texas, received a Navy Cross for manning a .50 caliber Browning anti-aircraft machine gun during the Japanese attack of Pearl Harbor until he ran out of ammunition and was ordered to abandon ship. Because of segregated military regulations, Miller served as a mess attendant or cook, and had received no prior training to operate a machine gun. Chester W. Nimitz, the commander-in-chief of the Pacific Fleet, personally presented the Navy Cross to Miller, the black messman's extraordinary act of courage in battle leading Nimitz to remark at the award ceremony: "This marks the first time in this conflict that such high tribute has been made in the Pacific Fleet to a member of his race and I'm sure that the future will see others similarly honored for brave acts." Miller served in the Pacific Theater of war until November 1943, when his ship was struck by a torpedo fired from a Japanese submarine. The American warship on which Miller served sank within minutes, and Miller, one of the heroes of Pearl Harbor, was listed among 646 fatalities. The United States Postal Service recognized Miller in 2010 by issuing a stamp in his honor that paid tribute to distinguished American sailors. In 1973, the United States Navy commissioned the USS *Miller*, a Knox-class frigate, in honor of Doris Miller, and a bronze commemorative plaque of Miller is located at the Miller Family Park on the U.S. Naval Base, Pearl Harbor.

Yet no matter how well sailors like Miller and many other blacks in the Navy and the other arms of the military performed in battle, not a single African American received the Medal of Honor, the nation's highest honor for bravery and valor in combat, during World War II. The U.S. War Department did, however, attempt to correct this omission more than a half-century following the conclusion of the war when it investigated exceptional acts of heroism performed by African Americans during the conflict. Acting on their recommendation, Vernon Baker and seven other black soldiers were nominated in 1996 to receive the Congressional Medal of Honor. The following year Baker, born in Cheyenne, Wyoming, and a career soldier, became the first and only living African American to receive this prestigious award, the seven other recipients receiving it posthumously. The Department of the Army concluded that a "climate of racism prevented proper recognition of the extraordinary heroism of some black fighters." At the time, recognizing the valor of black soldiers would have challenged white supremacy. Nevertheless, the able performance of many black servicemen proved to all who witnessed it that African Americans could serve their nation ably, not only as messmen but, like white soldiers, in positions of leadership and authority.

Vernon Baker's World War II service proved this point convincingly. On April 5, 1945, Lieutenant Baker advanced at the head of his weapons platoon, supported by three rifle platoons, toward a German mountain stronghold known as Castle Aghinolfi. As these soldiers neared the castle, Baker noticed two cylindrical objects sticking out of an undercut in the hill. Baker crawled under the opening and stuck his rifle into the slit, emptying his clip. In doing so, Baker killed the observation post's two occupants and then immediately moved into another position, in which he located and advanced upon a camouflaged machine-gun nest, shooting and killing two German soldiers there who had paused to eat breakfast. As Baker's company commander joined Baker and the small group of black soldiers he was with, a German soldier suddenly appeared, hurling a hand grenade, which failed to explode. Lieutenant Baker shot the soldier twice as he attempted to flee, then, acting alone, he blasted open the concealed entrance of a dugout with a hand grenade, after which he shot another German soldier who emerged from it. Now Baker tossed another grenade into the dugout and entered the dangerous area, firing his sub-machine gun as he went, killing two more Germans. At this point, Baker's captain ordered a withdrawal, as he and his fellow soldiers were under heavy fire. But even under these circumstances, Baker pushed on, destroying two more enemy machine-gun positions. It was this type of action that earned Baker the highest honor that the United States can bestow on a soldier.

By 1945, numerous African American soldiers had trained or served on bases in western communities, with one of the largest concentrations of black soldiers stationed at Fort Huachuca in southern Arizona, a state whose black population had grown slowly before 1940 but mushroomed during the war. Fort Huachuca, the former home of the Tenth Cavalry, the Buffalo Soldiers, housed approximately14,000 black soldiers during World War II. The fort trained the Ninety-second and Ninety-third divisions of the U.S. Army, the only two all-black divisions that served in the war. Colonel Edwin N. Hardy commanded Fort Huachuca during the war, and the majority of the black soldiers judged him a fair man. Because army regulations required segregation, all facilities on the base were built in duplicate, including chapels, officers' clubs, and hospitals. At the time, Fort Huachuca housed the largest African American hospital in the United States, with 946 beds and staffed by African Americans. Since the fort was relatively isolated from major towns and urban centers in Arizona, black soldiers there experienced none of the major conflicts their counterparts faced with hostile whites or Hispanics in bases located in other parts of the West. Traveling USO shows performed at the fort's theater, and such famous entertainers as Louis Armstrong, Hattie McDaniel, Lena Horne, Dinah Shore, and Pearl Bailey, visited the fort to entertain the troops. Horne, a striking beauty as well as a talented entertainer, was voted "Sweetheart of the 92nd" after her visit in 1942. Horne endeared herself to the black troops in another important way. After learning that she was about to perform in a theater in which German POWs were seated in front of black soldiers, Horne left the stage and sang instead from the rear of the theater, her back facing the German soldiers. This small act of protest, although symbolic, dealt a blow to Jim Crow in the military.

In addition to Fort Huachuca, black soldiers and sailors were stationed at Fort Lewis near Tacoma, Washington, at Fort Lawton in Seattle, and at military bases in Denver, San Antonio, and Los Angeles. In some communities, such as Hastings, Nebraska, black soldiers patrolled ammunition depots. African American women, some of whom joined the Women's Army Corps (WAC) in 1942 at the encouragement of the African American leader Mary McLeod Bethune, also supported the war effort as typists, postal clerks, and truck drivers. Two units of the Women's Army Corps were stationed at Fort Huachuca. By law, all women were prohibited from serving in combat areas. Yet the military provided a means for African American women to demonstrate their patriotism and learn new skills.

Challenging Discrimination on the Job

Despite a wide breadth of employment opportunities in West Coast defense industries and a presidential executive order to cease discrimination on the basis of race, nationality, religion, or ethnicity, numerous companies in the West continued to discriminate against African American workers. But even those blacks who found work in defense industries often faced racial barriers. African American workers learned quickly that landing a job was no guarantee of equality in the workplace.

African American workers in every western city faced varying degrees of employment discrimination. Some in the defense industry found themselves restricted to a narrow and proscribed range of jobs. Others, though well qualified to perform skilled tasks, found themselves barred from these positions in order to preserve an unspoken racial hierarchy within the shipyards or the aircraft industry. Companies never permitted black workers to supervise white shipyard personnel, no matter how qualified. "We wouldn't ask white people to work under a Negro and we shouldn't expect them to," stated one white shipyard personnel director in California, when questioned about his company's employment policies. Herein lay a crucial distinction between African Americans and white immigrants who came west. White immigrants, including the Dust Bowl migrants of the 1930s whom long-settled whites on the West Coast disparaged as "Okies" or "Arkies," also struggled initially to find jobs in western communities, and some did indeed face discrimination because their speech, customs, or culture did not readily conform to the dominant culture. But African Americans also faced rampant discrimination, despite their education or qualifications, solely because of their skin color and the widespread perception that blacks comprised an inferior and despised race.

White racial attitudes, however, proved to be only part of the problem. Wartime industries required African Americans to be members of local unions, many of which had excluded both blacks and women prior to World War II. Only the Industrial Union of Marine and Shipbuilding, a CIO-affiliated union, was racially integrated. The International Brotherhood of Boilermakers, which represented the majority of shipyard workers, between 1941 and 1942 negotiated closed-shop agreements with the Kaiser Company and other major West Coast shipyards. Closed-shop agreements required that workers must first be dues-paying members of a union before they could gain employment. In 1937, however, the Boilermakers, in anticipation of a rapid growth in U.S. shipyards during wartime, established segregated auxiliary unions for African Americans. By 1944, the union had established forty-four such associations throughout the nation, three of them in the San Francisco Bay Area. The Boilermakers had jurisdiction over two-thirds of all U.S. shipyard workers, virtually all of whom were employed on the West Coast. Seattle was the lone exception.

African Americans argued that membership in the segregated auxiliary unions placed them at a grave disadvantage relative to white workers. Though employment in West Coast shipyards required union clearance, membership in an auxiliary union reinforced the idea of African American workers as second-class citizens. It denied them the same seniority or job protection as white union workers and took away access to better jobs. Black workers also faced far greater risks of being laid off or terminated than did whites. Moreover, at any time the parent union could abolish the auxiliary unions, unlike a regular union.

Unhappy with the segregated auxiliary, black shipyard workers along the entire West Coast worked toward its abolition. In 1943, Joseph James, a recent migrant to San Francisco and a welder at Marinship, organized a broad coalition of interracial opposition to the auxiliary. As the president of his newly organized Committee against Segregation and Discrimination, James urged black shipyard workers to demand equality with white union members and brook no compromise. In cities like Portland and Los Angeles, African Americans appealed to the FEPC, which, after investigating these allegations, urged the Boilermakers and shipbuilders to cease discrimination and abolish auxiliary unions. The Boilermakers refused to comply. Now the black shipyard workers, in following James' directive not to compromise, ran the risk of losing their jobs if they continued to protest or refused to pay membership dues to the auxiliaries. In some instances, black shipyard workers did refuse to pay their dues, resulting in the dismissal of nearly one thousand workers at West Coast shipyards, including James himself, who also had served as the San Francisco NAACP's branch president.

The Boilermakers' recalcitrance forced the hand of black shipyard workers. Joseph James ultimately chose to file a lawsuit against the Boilermakers to halt the dismissal of African Americans who refused to pay dues to the segregated auxiliary. Supported by the local branch of the NAACP and Harry Kingman, a prominent white liberal who headed the West Coast regional office of the FEPC, James pressed on, his case against Marinship reaching the California Supreme Court in *James* v. *Marinship* (1944). The state's highest court ruled that "an arbitrarily closed or partially closed union is incompatible with a closed shop." The court ruled further that African Americans "must be admitted to membership under the same terms and conditions applicable to non-Negroes unless the union and the employer refrain from enforcing the closed-shop agreement against them." This unanimous decision reverberated throughout the West. A U.S. District Court in Portland made a similar ruling, and in 1946 the California Supreme Court reaffirmed the opinion in *James*. By 1946, the Boilermakers announced that they had dismantled the auxiliary unions, yet they retained other discriminatory practices. The Boilermakers' decision to continue to practice some forms of segregation within their unions essentially became moot at the conclusion of World War II. As many black leaders had predicted, the transition to a peacetime economy resulted in massive layoffs of black defense workers. Nonetheless, the presence of African American wartime workers in the western labor force had led to radical changes in many western cities.

For the first time, black workers had broken long-standing racial barriers in many western industries and made modest inroads into occupations beyond menial employment. In some West Coast cities, African Americans had competed with white workers for semiskilled and skilled positions, as well as for professional and white-collar jobs. Some western cities like San Francisco hired their first African American public school teachers and bus drivers during World War II. Others such as Portland, Seattle, and Phoenix expanded the number of African Americans in the professions or as managers, supervisors, and skilled technicians. World War II improved race relations in the West in some important respects, but most important, it opened many new doors for African Americans.

Fighting Discrimination in Housing

Despite the noteworthy changes in employment practices, other doors stayed firmly closed to African Americans. Finding housing represented one of the greatest challenges for wartime migrants of any race or nationality. Thanks to migration during the war, the housing supply remained critically short in every West Coast city. The modest incomes of African Americans and local restrictions that limited blacks to certain neighborhoods compounded the problem. Although few cities had formed black ghettos by 1940, residential segregation remained widespread throughout the West, and in many cities the black population was already concentrated in a handful of neighborhoods. Restrictive covenants in many cities barred blacks and other nonwhites such as Hispanics and Asians from buying, renting, or leasing property in most white neighborhoods. In San Francisco, the Board of Supervisors (similar to a city council) conducted a series of open hearings in 1943 and discovered that restrictive covenants were widespread. The situation was even more dire in Los Angeles, which had formed a black ghetto by 1930 and where white residents used the law and intimidation to enforce restrictive covenants widely throughout the city.

Because African Americans in many parts of the wartime West experienced discrimination in housing, they faced severe overcrowding in their neighborhoods. West Coast cities fared the worst of all, because the number of black migrants who flocked to them was the greatest. San Francisco represents a case in point. Between 1940 and 1945, a special wartime census revealed that the city's black population increased by 500 percent, growing from 4,800 to 32,000. Most of these migrants arrived between 1942 and 1945, placing a tremendous strain on available housing in established black neighborhoods. Many of these black defense workers crowded into the Fillmore District, while others occupied nearby Japantown, which had emptied in 1942 when the government interned its residents in relocation camps. Other black migrants occupied any physical space suitable for human habitation, crowding into apartments and boardinghouses in numbers that placed an enormous physical strain on the facilities. Because the sky-high demand made lodging a profitable enterprise, many established residents took in lodgers. Some even rented "hot beds," rooms where migrants slept for periods of eight to ten hours, after which they vacated the space so someone else could sleep in it.

Other West Coast cities, such as Los Angeles, Portland, Seattle, and Oakland, experienced similar problems. Los Angeles' Central Avenue District, which housed about two-thirds of the city's prewar African American population, absorbed the majority of black migrants. Central Avenue soon expanded its geographical boundaries south towards Watts and north toward Little Tokyo, Los Angeles' Japanese community. Little Tokyo experienced a sizable influx of African American wartime migrants, as blacks flooded into the houses and occupied many of the businesses and storefronts that the

Japanese in Los Angeles left behind when the government forcibly removed them from the West Coast and imprisoned them in camps in the interior West. In both San Francisco and Los Angeles, these large black migrant populations faced markedly strained race relations in the postwar years with Japanese residents, a relationship that had been cordial prior to 1940. The Japanese concluded that black migrants had taken advantage of their misfortune by moving into their community and occupying their businesses. They also assumed, incorrectly, that these black wartime migrants would vacant their old neighborhoods at the conclusion of the war.

Portland's black community also increased rapidly during World War II, having grown to nearly 20,000 from less than 2,000 in 1940. Attracted by high-paying defense-industry jobs, the majority of these defense workers moved into the Albina neighborhood, which had housed about half of Portland's prewar black community. Black workers also crowded into segregated sections of defense housing constructed in the Vanport and Guild's Lake sections of Portland. Vanport was considered the largest wartime development in the nation, and housing in Portland, as in every West Coast city, remained in critically short supply. The rapid influx of African American war workers into the Albina District prompted whites to flee the neighborhood for the suburbs or surrounding neighborhoods at the earliest opportunity. As more war workers arrived, the neighborhood quickly became overcrowded and rundown.

Both Seattle and San Diego experienced housing shortages, but the black wartime influx, although sizable, did not cause these cities problems as severe as those that San Francisco, Oakland, Portland, and Los Angeles faced. Seattle and San Diego remained racially integrated, and blacks lived and interacted with Asians, Hispanics, and working-class whites. The various races also shared public space. Before the government relocated them, for example, Japanese baseball teams in Seattle had competed not only against fellow Asians but African Americans. During the war, Seattle's Central District successfully absorbed the majority of African American newcomers.

Similarly, San Diego had little difficulty integrating black migrants into its broader community, although racial concentration in older black neighborhoods became much more pronounced. Because San Diego's Mexican population also expanded rapidly during the war years, fierce competition for housing plagued the city's older black neighborhoods. West Coast cities thus saw an influx of black workers generally during the war, and housing remained critical to absorbing this influx, but each city handled the challenges that followed in a unique way, setting each of them up for their own problems after the war.

The practical challenges of finding housing for existing residents and wartime migrations often pitted white and black residents against each other, and led to a legal struggle over civil rights in housing. White westerners feared the prospect of having African Americans as their neighbors as much as did their counterparts in other regions of the country, and they organized to keep blacks out of their neighborhoods. In only a small number of western cities did whites resort to violence, however, and in no instance did they organize massive demonstrations on the scale of those that broke out in wartime Detroit, where local officials summoned thousands of local and state police to move African American families into a public housing project. White westerners resorted to enforcing restrictive covenants rather than engaging in violence, although in at least one instance an African American family in Fontana, California, a working-class community near L.A., had its property destroyed in a fire, resulting in a fatality. Southern California newspapers such as the *Maywood-Bell Southeast Herald* encouraged city leaders in 1942 to write more-effective restrictive covenants to keep blacks out of established white neighborhoods. These housing restrictions based on race, ethnicity, and nationality also hampered Asians and Hispanics.

In response, black westerners turned increasingly to the NAACP for help in fighting restrictive covenants. Los Angeles, where an estimated 95 percent of World War II housing proved unavailable to African Americans, served as a focal point. Loren Miller, a respected

NAACP attorney and racial activist, filed numerous lawsuits in L.A. challenging the legality of restrictive covenants. A strong NAACP branch and a thriving black middle class who could afford to support these lawsuits buttressed his efforts. However, neither Miller nor black leaders in other western cities succeeded during the war years in eliminating housing restrictions against African Americans. Miller's efforts to ban restrictive covenants would come to fruition during the postwar era.

Western cities such as Phoenix, San Francisco, Oakland, and Berkeley also enforced restrictive covenants to keep African Americans and other racial minorities out of white neighborhoods (as did many cities in the South, Midwest, and Northeast). Consequently, housing opportunities in many western cities grew more instead of less restricted as World War II drew to a close. Overcrowding and increased racial segregation accelerated the creation of black ghettos in many cities as well as tensions between the various communities in each distinct city. They also contributed to an increasing concentration of African Americans in their own neighborhoods, limiting social and political interaction between diverse groups that had lived together peacefully for many decades previously.

Despite the efforts of black leaders and some whites to promote unity and interracial harmony, violence between the two races flared up occasionally in some western communities. Most of these clashes were relatively small and localized, like the confrontations between black and white soldiers in Honolulu, Fort Bliss, Texas, and Camp Phillips, at Fort Riley, Kansas. In 1943 a major riot did, however, erupt in the Gulf port city of Beaumont, Texas, arguably one of the most violent racial clashes in the nation, and the most serious wartime race riot in the American West. A major war production center, Beaumont's population grew rapidly in the early 1940s, and blacks as well as whites flocked to the city's shipyards in search of work. When the wife of a white shipyard worker reported that she had been raped by an African American, white shipyard workers raced to the city's black neighborhoods, an act reminiscent of the destructive Tulsa, Oklahoma, race riot of 1921. The enraged whites proceeded to vandalize and loot indiscriminately and with impunity. Their rampage destroyed dozens of black businesses and homes and resulted in the loss of four lives. An estimated twenty-five hundred African Americans fled Beaumont in the wake of the incident, a clear-cut indication that many of them feared for their lives. An investigation revealed later that the riot's catalyst, the alleged rape of a white woman by a black man, was a hoax. The violent response and swift retribution nonetheless had exposed the intensity of the racial tensions that existed in some western cities during World War II, and that many whites held little regard for either the lives or property of blacks.

Wartime tensions existed in every western city, as overcrowding, wartime dislocation, and the integration of tens of thousands of southern black migrants into the many communities produced short tempers. Hostility toward the newly arrived black southerners sometimes cut across racial and class lines, as some African American residents disapproved of the lifestyle and folkways of southern blacks as readily as did whites. C. L. Dellums, the aforementioned African American labor leader and himself a migrant from Texas, wondered why migrant defense workers and their families seemingly made undesirable new westerners. In a letter he penned in 1942 he opined, "Unfortunately thousands of the worst type and most ignorant are leaving the South, but those who are a credit to the race and can make a contribution still toward its progress aren't coming out fast enough." A number of long-established black westerners, some of whom had family members in southern states, likewise portrayed recent black migrants as unsophisticated, uneducated, uncouth— "country." Others found the outward signs of southern culture such as regional speech patterns, conversing loudly in public, and lounging on street corners embarrassing. They expected black migrants to leave their cultural baggage back in the South when they moved to western cities. Despite occasional bigotry of this sort, African American migrants helped integrate black southern culture into West Coast cities. Proudly displaying their southern roots and home-grown folk-ways, black southern migrants established new churches, clubs, and community organizations with a decidedly southern bent, eventually changing black western culture. Black women in cities like Oakland and Richmond, for example, formed blues clubs. Other migrants planted gardens, practiced herbal medicine or folk remedies peculiar to the South, and opened restaurants or small cafes that specialized in traditional southern foods such as fried okra and barbecue. These cultural practices, however, were not unique to the West Coast, for the influx of southern migrant culture significantly influenced interior western cities like Las Vegas, Denver, and Phoenix. In similar fashion, white southern migrants often received a similarly hostile welcome from establish whites in the West and the North, but they, too, stubbornly transplanted their religious traditions and folkways, also contributing to a southernization of the nation in the postwar era.

World War II also accelerated interracial and multiracial alliances and cooperation between African Americans and other groups in the West. The urgency of the war prompted numerous city officials to collaborate with African American leaders and representatives from other nonwhite races to work toward racial peace and harmony. Cities like Los Angeles and Seattle created civic unity councils, part of a nationwide movement to prevent racial violence and promote racial unity. Phoenix would create its council in 1948. Other western cities established ad hoc committees comprised of their leading citizens of all races to address specific concerns before they reached a critical stage. In Los Angeles and San Diego, African Americans reached across the cultural divide and supported Hispanics and Asians in their attempt to integrate defense industries. African Americans also spoke out against police brutality toward Hispanics in the infamous Zoot Suit riots in June of 1943. U.S. Navy officers had instigated these riots when they entered Mexican neighborhoods in Los Angeles and indiscriminately beat and attacked Hispanic youth, in many instances tearing off the popular clothing, or zoot suits—long sports coats, baggy pants, a pork-pie hat, and an overly long pocket-watch chain—that the Hispanic youth of the day liked to wear. The Los Angeles NAACP's local president, Thomas L. Griffith, wrote both Governor Earl Warren and President Roosevelt to express the branch's disapproval of this malicious racial violence and ask each leader to halt the violence. Though the riots did not affect the black community directly, its leaders still demanded justice for those who had been victimized.

Some black leaders established community institutions specifically designed to foster racial harmony. Howard Thurman, the former Dean of the Chapel at Howard University, moved from Washington, D.C., to San Francisco in 1943 at the invitation of Dr. Alfred G. Fisk, a professor at San Francisco State College and a Presbyterian clergyman. Thurman helped establish The Church for the Fellowship of All Peoples, an integrated, non-denominational community of all races and ethnicities. Thurman was a prolific scholar, and many religious leaders at the time regarded him as one of the leading African American ministers in the nation by the early 1950s. Through Thurman's leadership, and the dedicated service of his wife, Sue Bailey Thurman, a prominent clubwoman, Fellowship Church developed numerous multicultural programs such as workshops, forums, and intercultural exchanges, programs that gave church members, as well as the broader San Francisco community, an opportunity to become acquainted with people of all races. Howard Thurman believed that these experiences were critical if people were to learn to respect each other as human beings. These efforts rose out of the morass of racial segregation that grew during the war years. The efforts of leaders like Thurman in promoting racial harmony and civil rights for African Americans, along with the growth of the African American population in many parts of the West, would promote growing political influence during and after the war.

Black westerners, although neither disinterested nor disengaged from politics, had played only a marginal role in the two major political parties prior to 1940. Their relatively small local populations placed them at a severe disadvantage relative to larger and more powerful political groups. Before World War II, only Los Angeles, which contained one of the largest black populations of any western city, elected African Americans to political office. The war changed the political calculus in many western cities, however, as white politicians gradually began to pay greater attention to and court the black vote. By 1943, a black Coloradan, Earl Mann of Denver, was elected to the Colorado legislature. Californians followed suit and elected William Byron Rumford, a Bay Area black pharmacist, to the California State Assembly in 1948. Two years later, Charles Stokes from Seattle won a seat in the state legislature in Washington. The election of these early black politicians in the 1940s set the stage for an upsurge in black office holding in the western states between 1965 and 2000.

Conclusion

World War II proved to be a critical event and a pivotal moment for black westerners. For the first time in the region's history, a sizable number of African Americans migrated to the West in pursuit of jobs and better lives. As a direct consequence of the war and the critical need for laborers of all races, many jobs in both the public and private sectors began to open their doors to black men and women for the first time. Mandated by the courts to cease discrimination, labor unions gradually, if grudgingly, admitted African Americans to membership on an equal basis. The entry into union membership opened numerous doors for black workers during the postwar era. The large wartime migration also spread many aspects of black southern culture to western cities, as black southerners left their imprint and their cultural stamp wherever they settled, often to the displeasure of whites as well as long-standing black residents. Finally, World War II triggered much greater racial activism by black westerners and their white allies, who collectively sought to break down existing racial barriers and provide new opportunities to African Americans and other nonwhite races. African Americans in the West, therefore, personified the Double-V campaign as much as did their counterparts in other regions of the nation. In their eyes, World War II was fought not only to defeat Nazi racism and Japanese imperialism abroad but also to defeat racism at home. World War II, therefore, served as an important benchmark for racial progress. Although it did not eliminate all racial barriers in the West, the war did lay the foundation for the modern civil rights movement, setting the stage for mass protest in western cities during the 1950s and 1960s.

Suggested Readings

Allen, Robert L. *The Port Chicago Mutiny.* New York: Heyday Books, 1993.

Anderson, Karen Tucker. "Last Hired, First Fired: Black Women Workers during World War II." *Journal of American History* 69 (June 1982): 82–97.

Bailey, Beth and David Farber. *The First Strange Place: The Alchemy of Race and Sex in World War II Hawaii.* New York: Free Press, 1992.

Broussard, Albert S. "The Honolulu NAACP and Race Relations in Hawaii." *Hawaiian Journal of History* 39 (2005): 115–33.

Burran, James A. "Violence in an 'Arsenal of Democracy': The Beaumont Race Riot, 1943." *East Texas Historical Review* 14 (Spring 1976): 39–51.

Buchanan, Russell A. *Black Americans and World War II.* Santa Barbara: ABC-Clio, 1977.

Fluger, Walter and Catherine Tumber, eds. *A Strange Freedom: The Best of Howard Thurman on Religious Experience and Public Life.* Boston: Beacon Press, 1999.

Gibson, Karen J. "Bleeding Albina: A History of Community Disinvestment, 1940–2000." *Transforming Anthropology* 15 (2007): 3–25.

Johnson, Marilynn S. *The Second Gold Rush: Oakland and the East Bay in World War II.* Berkeley: University of California, 1993.

Kurashige, Scott. *The Shifting Ground of Race: Black and Japanese Americans in the Making of Multiethnic Los Angeles.* Princeton: Princeton University Press, 2008.

Leonard, Kevin Allen. *The Battle for Los Angeles: Racial Ideology and World War II.* Albuquerque: University of New Mexico Press, 2006.

McElderry, Stuart. "Building a West Coast Ghetto: African-American Housing in Portland, 1910–1960." *Pacific Northwest Quarterly* 92 (2001): 137–148.

Morgan, Lael. "Writing Minorities Out of History: Black Builders of the Alcan Highway." *Alaska History* 7 (Fall 1992): 1–13.

Pruitt, Bernadette. "For the Advancement of the Race: African-American Migration to Houston, 1914–1940." *Journal of Urban History* 31 (May 2005): 435–478.

Sonenshein, Raphael J. *Politics in Black and White: Race and Politics in Los Angeles.* Princeton: Princeton University Press, 1993.

Sides, Josh. "Battle on the Home Front: African American Shipyard Workers in World War II Los Angeles." *California History* 75 (Fall 1996): 250–263.

Taylor, Quintard. "The Great Migration: The Afro-American Communities of Seattle and Portland during the 1940s." *Arizona and the West* 23 (Summer 1981): 109–26.

Verge, Arthur C. *Paradise Transformed: Los Angeles during the Second World War.* Dubuque: Kendall Hunt Publishing Company, 1993.

Vose, Clement. *Caucasians Only: The Supreme Court, the NAACP and the Restrictive Covenant Cases.* Berkeley: University of California Press, 1967.

Wollenberg, Charles. "Blacks vs. Navy Blue: The Mare Island Mutiny Court Martial." *California History* 58 ((Spring 1979): 62–75.

Wollenberg, Charles. *Marinship at War: Shipbuilding and Social Change in Wartime Sausalito.* Berkeley: Western Heritage Press, 1990.

CHAPTER FIVE

New Expectations, New Frustrations, 1945–1970

The vast majority of African Americans living in the West remained there after the end of World War II, naturally preferring the region's better opportunities for decent jobs, education, housing, and the right to vote over the stifling racism and brutality of the South, whence many westerners, black and white, had come. Therefore, in spite of varying degrees of racial discrimination in the western states and territories, the benefits outweighed the familiarity of living with old friends and family in the South. Emboldened by the profound changes they had experienced during the war years and the economic success many of them had achieved in defense industries, most black westerners settled comfortably into their respective communities and attempted to build on their wartime progress. Indeed, black westerners continued to break new ground in finding jobs in the building trades, the food and clothing industries, metal and machinery shops, and civil service work, convincing many individuals that western cities were the best places to live. But even if many of them thought the future looked promising, black westerners realized that they would have to continue to fight and struggle in order to secure many of their newly won gains.

Postwar Opportunity

Rather than experiencing an out-migration following World War II, many western cities continued to attract black migrants. The black population of Los Angeles, for example, grew from 63,774 in 1940 to 171,209 in 1950. Nearly 40,000 African Americans had come to Los Angeles in the five-year interval between 1945 and 1950 alone, one indicator that the city continued to offer blacks a much better chance to find a good job and purchase an inexpensive home than did many southern cities. Black Angelenos could also vote without fear of losing their lives or their livelihood, a right still denied to African Americans in most southern states. Furthermore, Los Angeles schools far out performed schools in even the most progressive southern cities, and in California, African Americans had an opportunity to attend integrated colleges and universities.

San Francisco, San Diego, Oakland, Richmond, Portland, and Seattle experienced similar gains, with the San Francisco Bay Area registering the most dramatic population increases. By 1950, Oakland's black population had soared to 47,562, as compared to only 8,462 in Oakland in 1940. San Francisco's black population recorded an even greater increase, jumping from 4,806 in 1940 to 43,460 in 1950. The San Francisco Urban League's executive director, Seaton Manning, was so struck by the number of black migrants who continued to stream into the city he remarked, "I find it hard to believe that there are any Negroes left in Texas and Louisiana." The interior cities in the West grew at a much slower pace, although some urban centers registered impressive growth. In Wichita, Kansas, which had benefitted from defense industry employment, the black population grew from 5,686 to 7,925 over the decade, a 39.3 percent increase. The black population in Kansas City grew from 21,033 in 1940 to 26,590 in 1950, a gain of 26.4 percent. Denver registered an even sharper gain in its black community, which rose from 7,836 in 1940 to 15,214 in 1950, an increase of 94.1 percent.

The success that African Americans experienced in obtaining

defense-industry jobs and other industrial employment in western cities during the war fueled a postwar optimism. African American women, in particular, hoped that the gains they had made in raising their low wages and their status during wartime would continue. Indeed, black women slowly started to shed domestic service; while more than half (52 percent) of all black females in the San Francisco–Oakland metropolitan area were classified as servants in 1950, this was down dramatically from a whopping 90 percent in 1930 and 66 percent in 1940. Many western cities also began to hire black women as teachers for the first time, such as San Francisco in 1944. Oakland, Los Angeles, Portland, and Seattle also expanded their number of black teachers, with some school districts hiring black principals and administrators. These cities differed from southern cities in an important respect: they already had integrated schools, something the solidly segregated South would continue to fight for another decade. Indeed, at the conclusion of World War II, the vast majority of black children in the West attended integrated schools, institutions staffed by both black and white teachers, and their classmates comprised children of all races and nationalities, including Japanese, Chinese, Filipino, and Mexican American. Establishing separate schools for black children in most western states had been impractical because of their small numbers in most locales, with the exception of Texas, which had a long tradition of segregation and racial exclusion. In any event, many western states had abolished segregated schools for African Americans back in the nineteenth century, in some cases under pressure of the African American population.

Black policeman and fireman also found employment in more western cities after 1945, and black nurses, physicians, dentists, and attorneys, many of them wartime migrants, worked and practiced with greater frequency. For black doctors and nurses, in particular, these were monumental achievements, for even gaining access to nurse-training programs in cities like San Francisco and San Diego had proven exceedingly difficult before 1940. Black physicians also increased in number, although some faced entrenched racist practices in western hospitals that denied them the same set of privileges enjoyed by their white counterparts. This growing professional class of African Americans served as a role model for other black men and women who sought to enter professional employment. They also provided leadership within African American communities as well as in the major civil rights organizations in the West. Some of these African American professionals, as well as other members of the expanding black middle class, had benefited directly from the G.I. Bill of Rights, federal legislation that made available to veterans a government subsidy to pursue higher education. Like many white and Mexican American veterans throughout the nation who also took advantage of this provision, the growth of the black professional and middle class was fueled in part by this novel government program.

Civil Rights

Black doctors, dentists, and medical workers played important roles in expanding civil rights and breaking down racial barriers in the postwar West. Some of these men and women worked through long-standing community institutions such as local chapters of the NAACP, National Urban League (NUL), black churches, and the National Council of Negro Women (NCNW). Dr. Jack J. Kimbrough, a San Diego dentist, served briefly as president of the San Diego NAACP branch and became the driving force behind establishing a San Diego branch of the NUL. One of the most active members of San Diego's black professional class, Kimbrough sought to end discrimination in employment and public accommodations, as well as restrictive housing covenants. Kimbrough also used his connections in San Diego's African American community to forge effective coalitions between local business leaders and politicians.

African American professionals in San Francisco played similar roles in leading civil rights organizations. William McKinley Thomas, a black migrant from Bryan, Texas, had served as a physician in the U.S. Army during World War II before relocating to San Francisco, where he became a respected community leader. A graduate of Meharry Medical School in Nashville, Tennessee, and the Harvard School of Public Health, Thomas served as a housing authority commissioner from 1946 to 1950, the first African American in San Francisco to hold this prestigious position. The black physician Carlton B. Goodlett also became a significant voice for racial equality in the Bay Area, chiefly through the publication of his weekly newspaper, the *Sun-Reporter*. Though ministers and teachers actively participated in civil rights movements, doctors often assumed a leading role in the West.

African American professionals also took an important role in forming urban leagues, fraternal organizations, sororities, and women's clubs in the postwar West. Compared to their prewar predecessors, they had greater strength in numbers and pushed for civil rights and racial equality with more fervor and militancy. Western black professionals were also far less isolated than their prewar counterparts and enjoyed a greater sense of community, a factor that spurred them to push for equality in new directions and to embrace a new set of challenges. Many of these leaders had migrated from other states and locales to the West, where they found that segregation proved less virulent and African Americans occupied a broad range of leadership positions. Furthermore, this new western professional class comprised a broader range of professional occupations than that in the South, where black ministers dominated the cadre and frequently headed civil rights organizations.

Sue Bailey Thurman, the aforementioned wife of black theologian Howard Thurman, serves as a case in point of the possibilities for black women. As noted in the previous chapter, the Thurmans had moved to San Francisco during the war. A protégée of Mary McLeod Bethune, Sue Bailey became a leading figure in the National Council of Negro Women (NCNW). When she arrived in San Francisco, Sue Bailey organized a local chapter of the NCNW, directed the intercultural programs of Fellowship Church, where Howard served as the pastor, and traveled extensively. In 1947, she served as a delegate to the first Inter-American Congress of Women in Guatemala. Two years later, she led a delegation to a conference in Paris sponsored by the United Nations Educational, Scientific, and Cultural Organization. Sue Bailey's activism showed that African American women could serve in the black professional leadership class, and in important positions.

Unlike Thurman, most of the black professional women who played important leadership roles in the postwar West generally worked within traditional black women's organizations such as sororities, churches, the YWCA, and women's clubs. Here, black women mirrored the activism of white professional women in the West, who often excluded African American women from their clubs and professional organizations. Nonetheless, these gendered organizations offered black and white women opportunities to develop confidence and leadership skills outside of the purview of male leaders. They also allowed African American women to address problems in their communities, where women of all races traditionally had taken the lead in pushing for reform. Herein lay a crucial distinction between black and white female organizations: black professional women did not possess the luxury of ignoring race and segregation—it was always intimately linked with reforming and improving their community, and the advancement of African Americans, irrespective of class or region, depended on black professional women grappling with race and segregation in some form or fashion. Because black professional women, or clubwomen, as they were commonly known, were generally the most educated women in the African American community, white leaders, both male and female, were more inclined to take their grievances seriously. Thus, two prominent black female leaders, Vada Somerville and Vivian Osborne Marsh, each served as president of California chapters of the NCNW and organized other women to challenge racial inequality in a multitude of ways. Marsh, who had obtained an important position during the New Deal as head of the segregated California section of the National Youth Administration, would also serve as national president of Delta Sigma Theta sorority, providing her with a wider base of support and influence than perhaps any western woman until the 1960s.

Delta Sigma Theta (DST) formed on the campus of Howard University in 1913, and it defined the level of activism and commitment that the black community would come to expect of all-black Greek organizations. The sorority's first public act was to march in the famous 1913 women's suffrage parade in Washington, D.C. Over the decades, DST's activism, commitment to improving black communities, and goal of uniting African American women across class lines, attracted such luminaries to its membership as Mary McLeod Bethune, the entertainer Lena Horne, dancer and choreographer Judith Jamison, Margaret Murray Washington (the wife of the famed educator, Booker T. Washington), and future U.S. representative Barbara Jordan. DST organized chapters in virtually every western city, many of the chapters forming on college campuses.

The important work of African American sororities in pushing for racial equality notwithstanding, black westerners, like their counterparts in other regions of the nation, relied principally on established civil rights organizations to break down racial barriers and seek a broader spectrum of employment opportunities. Black and white residents worked through established organizations like the NAACP and the NUL to challenge racial inequality in far western states such as California, Oregon, and Washington, and inter-mountain and midwestern states like Colorado and Kansas. But in concert with their counterparts throughout the nation, black westerners formed local chapters of national organizations and their own local institutions that encouraged direct action, confrontation, and mass protests, such as the Congress of Racial Equality (CORE).

Full equality, however, remained an elusive concept in the West, in sight but never entirely within the grasp of African Americans. Black westerners felt confident that the NAACP had served them effectively through World War II, and they continued to support the pioneering civil rights organization in the postwar era. But in many cities a new generation of leaders began to inspire a greater sense of urgency, with student leaders in particular demanding the immediate desegregation of public accommodations and schools. Racial segregation, despite the defeat of Nazism and fascism during World War II, remained a fact of life for the majority of African Americans in the United States. The southern states, as well as a few western states, such as Texas and Kansas, enforced state-sanctioned segregation through the courts. State and federal courts consistently upheld *Plessy* v. *Ferguson* (1896), which mandated separate-but-equal facilities for blacks and whites. For its part, the Lone Star State established segregated and grossly inferior public schools for black children. Kansas approached things differently, as its public schools were segregated at some grade levels but not at others; its elementary schools were strictly segregated by race. And unlike in Texas, in the Jayhawk State the quality of the education provided by the segregated schools was roughly equal in the all-black and all-white ones. During the postwar years, the majority of white southerners believed that segregation would continue to define and regulate race relations. The NAACP, however, had others ideas.

In 1951, the NAACP challenged segregated schools directly in the federal courts in a number of states, including Kansas. The Reverend Oliver L. Brown, a welder for the Santa Fe Railroad and assistant pastor at the St. John African Methodist Episcopal Church, an unlikely activist, served as the lead plaintiff. Reverend Brown's seven-year-old daughter Linda and the children of other black parents were prevented from attending the all-white Sumner Elementary School close to their homes because Kansas used *Plessy* v. *Ferguson* to justify its segregated system. So, rather than attending their neighborhood school, the black children attended an all-black school approximately a mile away and on the other side of a railroad switchyard, which, of course, made for a hazardous crossing.

The NAACP's decision to challenge *Plessy* stemmed in large measure from the success they had achieved in 1950 when the U.S.

Supreme Court ruled against segregation in three cases, ironically, all on the same day. In perhaps the most important of these decisions, the court ruled in *Sweatt* v. *Painter* (1950) that the University of Texas had to admit Heman Sweatt, an African American, to its law school, even though the university had set up an improvised all-black law school in the basement of the nearby state capitol. Thurgood Marshall, a brilliant African American lawyer who argued this case before the Supreme Court in behalf of the NAACP, maintained that the University of Texas' superior academic reputation and prestige in law meant that any segregated legal institution established in Texas would be substantially inferior. By unanimous decision, the Supreme Court agreed and ordered the University of Texas to integrate its law school. In *McLaurin* v. *Oklahoma* (1950) the Supreme Court ruled that the University of Oklahoma erred when it admitted George McLaurin as a graduate student but then required him to sit apart from white students in the classroom. The court ordered the University of Oklahoma to end this practice immediately. Finally, the court ruled in *Henderson* v. *United States* (1950) that segregated railway dining cars were unconstitutional. Each of these decisions, particularly *Sweatt* and *McLaurin*, encouraged the NAACP to challenge *Plessy* directly, and Marshall remarked that these decisions were "replete with road markings." The NAACP responded by filing lawsuits in Virginia, South Carolina, Louisiana, Kansas, Delaware, and Washington, D.C. Five of the cases reached the U.S. Supreme Court and were consolidated under *Brown* v. *Board of Education of Topeka*.

Oliver Brown proved to be the perfect plaintiff from the NAACP's perspective. A lifelong resident of Topeka, Brown, at thirty-two years of age in 1951, had not taken part in NAACP activities and was not regarded as either an activist or a militant. A World War II veteran, Brown worked as a welder for the Santa Fe Railroad and assistant pastor at the St. John African Methodist Episcopal Church. Although initially reluctant to get involved, Brown came to believe, as historian James T. Patterson writes, "That God approved of his engagement in the case." Because Topeka had integrated more of its public facilities than had the southern cities in which the other twelve plaintiffs resided, Oliver Brown probably feared little, if any, retaliation for his involvement in the case. A city of approximately 100,000 residents, Topeka segregated all twenty-two of its elementary schools, but not its only high school. Yet the high school, nonetheless, maintained racially separate basketball, swimming, wrestling, golf, and tennis teams. Even its pep teams and cheerleading squads were segregated. Topeka's public swimming pools were closed to African Americans except for one day of the year, and blacks were barred from six of the seven movie theaters in the city. Segregation also existed in the waiting rooms of the city's bus and train stations, although blacks were free to ride the city buses on an integrated basis. African Americans could also vote and run for political office in Topeka and throughout the state of Kansas, an impossibility in many southern states in the early 1950s. Thus the presence of segregation in Topeka notwithstanding, Oliver Brown never endured threats on his life and livelihood, as did plaintiffs who challenged integration in the South.

African American parents were initially discouraged in August 1951 when a federal district court ruled unanimously that the separate black and white schools in Topeka, Kansas, were substantially equal, thus falling within the scope of *Plessy*. Yet the Supreme Court, led by Chief Justice Earl Warren, overturned this ruling in May 1954. Speaking for a unanimous Supreme Court, Warren stated: "We conclude that in the field of public education the doctrine of separate but equal has no place. Separate educational facilities are inherently unequal." Although the *Brown* v. *Board of Education of Topeka* (1954) decision did not bring about immediate equality in the nation's schools, it forever struck down the legal basis and the underpinnings of segregation in Kansas and elsewhere. Thus a western state had emerged at the forefront of this legal revolution in education and civil rights.

The *Brown* decision also helps one see how segregation in the West both differed from and was similar to segregation in the South.

Every southern state contained a rigid pattern of segregation laws that regulated race relations in almost every conceivable aspect of life. These laws prohibited southern blacks from attending white schools, working certain jobs, supervising whites, and intermarrying with whites. They also barred them from public accommodations such as restaurants, public parks and beaches, and hotels. In the South, communities established separate hospitals, clinics, and even blood banks, making it almost inconceivable that black professionals, no matter how gifted or skilled in their profession, would supervise white employees. The South enforced this system of white supremacy both legally and extralegally, with incarceration, economic intimidation, and violence. The majority of black southerners knew their racial boundaries and crossed them at their peril. Although discrimination existed in many western communities, and segregation laws restricted African Americans in some areas, the widespread and pervasive pattern of segregation laws and practices as they had existed in the South since the 1890s never developed in the West. Rather than systematically codified in statutes or Jim Crow laws, discrimination was more sporadic and informal in the West. Black westerners also worked with progressive whites, as well as with Mexican Americans and Asians in some communities, in the fight for racial justice and full equality.

The national success of the NAACP in the *Brown* decision notwithstanding, the majority of NAACP branches in the western states and territories sought to improve conditions for African Americans on the local or regional level in other aspects of social, economic, and political life. Local activists organized NAACP branches during the post–World War II years in places as distant as Alaska and Hawaii, but, to be sure, the majority of NAACP branches in the West predated the war and many of them had led successful campaigns to protest de jure and de facto discrimination in their communities. In the wake of *Brown*, however, black and white activists began to demonstrate a new urgency to end racial inequality. African American leaders in the Great Plains were less inclined to form alliances with

Hispanics and Asians than their counterparts on the West Coast, mostly because so few members of the latter groups resided in the Plains, but also because the small Hispanic and Asian communities in this area were less stable and therefore less politically active.

Wichita proved a case in point. The largest city in the state of Kansas, Wichita, along with Lawrence and the state capital of Topeka, maintained some vestiges of formal segregation and second-class citizenship for African Americans. Much of this segregation was confined to public accommodations and public facilities, services that African Americans in Kansas used on a regular basis. In the city of Lawrence, for example, the home of the integrated University of Kansas, the state's flagship campus, some local restaurants, night clubs, and bars barred African American students. By 1958, the local Wichita NAACP Youth Council, led by Ron Walters, a Wichita State freshman, organized a four-week sit-in at the Dockum drugstore lunch counter.

Walters had been inspired by the NAACP's western regional director, Franklin Williams, who had visited Wichita in 1956 and spoke at a citywide NAACP conference. Williams informed Walters and other youth leaders about the sit-ins that CORE had organized in the 1940s and encouraged them to do their part to fight discrimination. When a young black female student stopped at Dockum's drugstore on her way home from work to order a drink, she was refused service. This event set the NAACP youth chapter in motion, which coordinated with the local chapter of the NAACP and its president, Chester I. Lewis, a talented African American lawyer and a leader who had challenged segregation in many establishments during his five-year residence in Wichita. Despite objections from the NAACP's national office that the organization did not approve of direct action, as it favored litigation in the courts as the preferred method to end segregation, about twelve members of the youth branch picketed Dockum's. Well dressed, orderly, and polite, the picketers sat quietly at the lunch counter day after day. Although white customers occasionally insulted the students with racial epitaphs, the protesters did not face the violence that met later groups of sit-in demonstrators in the 1960s. The two local white daily papers in Wichita, the *Wichita Beacon* and the *Wichita Eagle*, carried virtually no coverage of the sit-ins, a concession to the white business community to avoid placing the demonstrations in the spotlight. Wichita's black press, however, the *Enlightenment* and the *Midwest News Press*, did cover the sit-ins. Similarly, the A.P. and the U.P. wire services both reported the sit-ins nationally. The concerted pressure by student activists paid dividends when the vice president of Dockum's instructed all of his managers and clerks to serve all customers without regard to race, creed, or color.

The success in Wichita motivated other NAACP Youth Councils in the West to conduct similar campaigns. By August 1958, Clara Luper, an Oklahoma school teacher and the advisor of the Oklahoma City NAACP Youth Council, had heard this clarion call and organized a sit-in at the popular Katz drugstore. Within a matter of weeks, Luper and thirteen African American teenagers had integrated four downtown businesses. This successful protest notwithstanding, Jim Crow, formal segregation laws, and statutes that sanctioned separate and inferior treatment to African Americans did not die as quickly in Oklahoma as it did in Kansas. Another six years of protests, boycotts, and demonstrations transpired before the majority of Oklahoma City restaurants integrated.

In other cities in the West, such as Phoenix, Arizona, activism broke down discriminatory barriers. Phoenix had an especially active NAACP chapter. Led by Lincoln Ragsdale, a World War II veteran, and his wife, Eleanor, black residents of Phoenix pressed both public officials and the private sector to rid their city of Jim Crow. With the support of white politicians, black leaders integrated the Phoenix schools, despite overwhelming support by the white electorate for maintaining separate schools for black and white children. NAACP leaders in Phoenix also waged a protracted struggle for African Americans to rent and purchase housing in white, middle-class neighborhoods, and to gain employment in white-collar and professional jobs. Here, the Phoenix branch of the NAACP, under Ragsdale's leadership, allied with the Phoenix chapter of the NUL and the Greater Phoenix Civic Unity Council, both interracial organizations, to protest segregation. The prestige of the NAACP and the unwavering commitment of local leadership brought about these profound changes.

As the civil rights movement in Wichita and Phoenix suggest, in addition to local branches of the NAACP, other progressive organizations often took the lead in pressing for full equality in western cities. Securing access to public accommodations was relatively easy in the West compared to the South, where elected officials, local police, or angry white mobs often expressed their wrath toward African Americans. Gaining access to high-paying jobs in the white-collar and professional sectors proved a torturous process, for blacks had no local or statewide agency to investigate allegations of employment discrimination. In West Coast cities like San Francisco, Los Angeles, and San Diego, NAACP leaders made only marginal gains until they allied with local urban leagues and civic councils. In San Francisco, the Council for Civic Unity (CCU), a broad-based interracial organization that promoted racial equality, joined with numerous other organizations and individuals to eliminate discriminatory racial barriers in labor unions, the building trades, and the civil service. Under the leadership of Edward Howden, a white liberal and one of the most respected civil rights leaders in the Bay Area, the CCU achieved significant gains in several areas, most notably in employment and access to labor unions. By 1950, more than nine thousand black workers were members of seventy-six San Francisco locals, a significant gain in the space of a decade. As activists eradicated segregated locals and auxiliary unions during the late 1940s, black workers also succeeded in branching out into skilled and semiskilled positions in greater numbers. Likewise, black advancement in white-collar, civil service, and professional jobs advanced rapidly after 1950.

Urban leagues in the West also helped broaden employment opportunities for African American workers and improve the racial climate. Although they seldom possessed the degree of influence of the NAACP branches, urban leagues in cities like San Francisco, Los Angeles, San Diego, Seattle, Omaha, and Portland exhibited strong leadership and provided an array of community services. Western urban league executive directors like Seaton Manning in San Francisco and Floyd C. Covington in Los Angeles confronted deeply entrenched problems in their respective communities—segregated housing, low-performing schools for minority students, and an under-representation of African Americans in numerous employment categories. Percy Steele, Jr., who served as executive director of the San Diego Urban League from its founding in 1953 to 1963, challenged all forms of racial employment exclusion in San Diego. He personified the new black leadership in the West that came of age after World War II. Not content to operate solely within the African American community, Steele built bridges between interracial organizations and created opportunities for African Americans in employment, housing, and education.

Steele also insisted that African American leaders in San Diego work with the Mexican American community, a policy that set him apart from most urban league officials. In San Diego, a city where Mexican Americans outnumbered African Americans, Steele developed programs to assist Mexican Americans in the public schools, such as the creation of a vocational education program. Mexican American leaders also served on the San Diego Urban League board of directors. The most significant contribution of urban league officials like Steele was opening doors to a broader range of employment opportunities. In the majority of western cities, including San Diego, employment gains for African Americans came in slow increments. Employment progress came even slower to Mexican workers, their English-language skills, low levels of education, and the racial prejudice they faced putting them at even a greater disadvantage. Finally, urban league officials in the West compelled some local businesses to hire African Americans and Mexican Americans for white-collar and skilled positions for the first time and to expand the number of black and Mexican American workers in industrial jobs.

Western leaders also utilized more aggressive forms of protest to fight for racial equality. Direct action civil rights organizations like CORE organized local chapters in western cities and achieved varying degrees of success. Founded in 1942, CORE first came to public attention in 1947 when the interracial organization, which practiced nonviolence, conducted a Freedom Ride through the upper South to test the region's compliance with a recent Supreme Court decision, *Morgan* v. *Virginia*, that had outlawed discrimination in interstate travel. A group of sixteen CORE members, eight whites and eight African Americans, traveled by bus and train to fifteen cities in Kentucky, North Carolina, Tennessee, and Virginia seeking to publicize the decision in *Morgan* and encourage other blacks to enjoy their newly won rights. The 1947 Freedom Ride received virtually no attention by the media, and the riders who participated in the two-week experiment met with only several arrests. During the 1940s, CORE formed chapters in numerous cities, including Omaha and Lincoln, Nebraska, Lawrence and Wichita, Denver, and Los Angeles and San Francisco. Unlike the NAACP, which worked to gain equal civil rights through the courts, CORE activists sought racial progress through direct action protests such as picketing, boycotts, and sit-ins.

Western CORE chapters also challenged segregation head-on in public accommodations and employment, often with mixed or disappointing results. In 1948, thirty students at the University of Kansas for example, staged a four-hour sit-down strike at an all-white restaurant, to no avail. As noted above, in Wichita a decade later, students in Kansas would force businesses to desegregate. CORE chapters themselves would have greater success in Denver and Omaha when they boycotted and picketed local establishments to end discrimination. In the 1960s, the San Francisco CORE chapter waged a highly publicized campaign to end housing and employment discrimination by using direct action protest. It targeted public accommodations, local drive-ins, and other businesses that refused to hire African Americans except in the most menial positions. The largest protest organized by CORE, coordinated jointly by a group of high school and college students from Berkeley, involved San Francisco's Sheraton Palace Hotel. Considered one of the most storied and glamorous hotels in the city, the Sheraton Palace, which ironically had employed a sizable black workforce during the nineteenth century, now refused to hire African Americans. This stance triggered a massive protest in 1964, with more than 1,500 protesters joining picket lines and staging a sit-in. The demonstrators included Mario Salvo, a white activist who would later lead the Free Speech Movement at the Berkeley campus of the University of California. The demonstrations ultimately proved successful, for San Francisco mayor John F. Shelly negotiated a binding agreement with the Sheraton Palace to hire black workers, an agreement that other San Francisco hotels accepted in principle.

The direct action campaign waged by the San Francisco Freedom Movement, as these efforts became known, underscored the reality of employment discrimination in West Coast cities, particularly in strong union cities like San Francisco. Although black workers had gained access to the Boilermakers Union in 1945, they only slowly cracked racial barriers in other unions, where the history of racial exclusion went back to Gold Rush era efforts to keep out the Chinese. The trade unions in some West Coast cities had excluded or severely limited the number of African American workers in many service-industry jobs such as waiters, cooks, and bartenders, positions that blacks had dominated for more than two centuries in the South. Some western cities barred blacks from these jobs because white workers feared competition for them, but also due to the widespread concern that the white public would refuse to interact with African Americans in these positions. Many western cities, consequently, lagged behind even the Jim Crow South in offering service jobs to black workers.

The San Francisco Freedom Movement, though dominated by

two national organizations, CORE and the NAACP, represented the confluence of many groups and individuals. As such, it became a forerunner of the multiracial coalition politics that would later be commonplace in many other western cities. Thomas N. Burbridge, president of the San Francisco NAACP chapter and a pharmacological toxicologist, a medical professional whose specialty is to identify poisons and antidotes for poisons in drugs, played an instrumental role in organizing the demonstrations. But it was Tracy Simms, a black female student who attended Berkeley High School, and whom Burbridge described as "one of the most charming, charismatic personalities I have ever met," who served as the principal catalyst.

Prior to his election as the NAACP branch president, Burbridge, a New Orleans native, attended Dillard University and Talladega College, a historically black college located in Talladega, Alabama. A brilliant student, Burbridge received a Rosenwald Fellowship to study chemistry at the University of Minnesota, after which he served in the U.S. Navy before attending medical school.

Simms was a member of the Du Bois Club, a youth group loosely (not officially) associated with the Communist Party. Du Bois Club members worked with African American youth throughout the Bay Cities, and they organized some of the earliest picket lines in San Francisco. The club targeted the popular eatery Mel's drive-in restaurant in San Francisco, for example, when black youth informed Du Bois Club members that blacks could eat at Mel's but not work there. Simm's presence in California was significant for another important reason. Heretofore, students had played only a minor role in California's civil rights protests, unlike their student counterparts in Wichita and Oklahoma City. But unlike the student-led demonstrations in Wichita and Oklahoma City, in California, numerous demonstrators were arrested. Simms served a sentence of sixty days, while Burbridge was sentenced to nine months. He was released after California governor Pat Brown reduced his sentence to thirty days.

The organizers of direct-action campaigns in California now joined the more conservative, though still effective, lawyers and leaders of the NAACP, and these campaigns, while not ending employment discrimination, accelerated the pace of reform. Finally, the direct- action campaigns orchestrated by CORE and the NAACP were multiracial, with white college students composing the overwhelming majority of picketers.

Encouraged by the historic *Brown* decision of 1954, black and white activists across the West protested de facto segregation in public schools more vigorously in the 1960s. In many western cities during this time, a map of school integration would have resembled a checkerboard pattern: in some places, a smattering of black, white, Mexican, Chinese, Japanese, and Filipino students sat in the same classroom; more often, western public schools reflected the housing patterns of western cities, with students attending local schools in their neighborhoods, thereby dominated heavily by members of one or two ethnic groups or racial minorities. So in the large West Coast cities–San Francisco, Los Angeles, Seattle, Oakland–African Americans made up a disproportionate number of pupils in their neighborhood schools. While segregation was not officially the law of the land, housing covenants and other restrictions led to de facto segregation. In San Francisco, where African Americans composed 25 percent of the school-aged population, the Benjamin Franklin Junior High School, located in the Western Addition, was 95 percent African American. The Raphael Weill Elementary School, also in the Western Addition, contained a black student population of 80 percent, while Asians composed 12 percent. Not only were these two schools heavily occupied by one or two races, the faculty contained virtually no black teachers or administrators, and black students performed poorly in their academic subjects compared to their white peers. Lois Barnes, the education chair of the San Francisco NAACP, pressed the San Francisco Unified School District to hire more black teachers and adopt an aggressive program to integrate the public schools. She did not succeed on either score.

The disproportionate number of African American students in a select group of public schools was hardly unique to San Francisco, as cities throughout the West reported that their student bodies had become even more segregated following *Brown*. In some instances, white parents had removed their children from mixed schools in the West—as did some whites in other regions of the nation—because they feared racial mixing of any type and also believed that the quality of these schools would deteriorate with the enrollment of black children. As early as the first day of school in 1947, five hundred white students walked out of the all-white Fremont High School in Los Angeles because a small group of black parents had enrolled six of their children. Presaging the ugly behavior of white students at Central High School in Little Rock, Arkansas, following court-ordered integration of the school in 1957, white students at Fremont High hanged an African American figure in effigy and carried racist placards. Clearly, racial integration of the public schools in the West could be a highly sensitive matter. This behavior underscored a harsh racial reality in the West, and the situation at Fremont High reveals that some western cities bitterly resisted integrated public schools. Nevertheless, black children were still far more likely to sit in an integrated classroom in the West than in the Jim Crow South. And by the 1960s, western states had eliminated many racial practices designed to keep African Americans "separate-but-equal."

Sports and Entertainment

During the postwar years, black westerners made headlines in sports, music, and the arts. They were especially prominent in collegiate and professional sports. Unlike public universities in the South, which discriminated against black students by state law, public and private colleges in the West had permitted a small number of black collegiate athletes to participate in their respective sports and attend the private and public colleges. As early as 1891, George Albert Flippin played football for the University of Nebraska; opposing coaches regarded Flippin as one of the most dominant football players in the nation. A superb athlete, Flippin also excelled in baseball, track and field, and trap shooting. He later became a successful physician and surgeon in Stromsburg, a small, rural, predominately Swedish community, and was inducted into the University of Nebraska Football Hall of Fame in 1974. The fact that the University of Nebraska had integrated its football team as early as 1891 suggests that a more benign pattern of race relations had evolved in the Great Plains states than in the Southwest, the Deep South, or the border states such as Kentucky and Tennessee. No southern state permitted black athletes to compete on football teams at the major state-supported universities until the mid-1950s, and many, such as Texas A&M University and the University of Texas, excluded blacks until the 1960s.

Western cities offered opportunities for African Americans to compete on integrated teams and to display their athletic prowess. Jackie Robinson, whose family had migrated in 1919 from Cairo, Georgia, to Pasadena, California, when Jackie was a young child, excelled in four sports at Pasadena City College and later at the University of California, Los Angeles (UCLA). In 1947 he became the first African American to play major league baseball, after having served, as mentioned, in the military during the war. Basketball legends Wilt Chamberlain and Bill Russell each played collegiate basketball at western schools, the University of Kansas and the University of San Francisco respectably. They dominated opposing players and their respective conferences, in the process redefining how the game of collegiate basketball was played. Opposing coaches tried to devise new defenses in an effort to stop Chamberlain and Russell, but met little success. Chamberlain's arrival in Lawrence also challenged segregation in the town and on the campus, which had been slow to embrace integration. Chamberlain's celebrity also helped to integrate some local restaurants and night clubs, establishments that had heretofore been off limits to African American students. Chamberlain boasted in his later years, "I single-handedly integrated Kansas," a claim that is unsupported by the historical record, for Lawrence remained segregated in many areas. Nonetheless, his celebrity certainly played a role in a process.

Russell's impact on collegiate basketball was even more dramatic than Chamberlain's. A native of Monroe, Louisiana, Russell's family had moved during the war to Oakland, California, where Russell eventually attended McClymonds High School. The gangly, awkward athlete had none of the attributes of a future superstar as a young boy, but Russell blossomed at the University of San Francisco (USF) under the leadership of coach Phil Woolpert. Like Chamberlain, Russell had to adjust to his relative isolation as a black student on campus, in Russell's case a small, private, Jesuit one. He also had to adapt to the staid playing style of his teammates. Coach Woolpert's stern guidance and patience with Russell paid off, as the USF Dons won fifty-six consecutive games, a record that stood until 1974 when UCLA broke it. The Dons also won the NCAA collegiate basketball championship in 1955 and 1956, and Russell won a gold medal as a member of the victorious U.S. Olympic basketball team that competed in Melbourne, Australia, in 1956.

The USF Dons were unusual in another respect. They were one of the earliest teams at a predominantly white college or university to permit more than two black players to take the court against opposing players at the same time. An unspoken, though well-understood quota existed in college basketball, where fans, coaches, and alumni expected white players to dominate numerically the rosters of collegiate basketball programs. In the majority of cases, college coaches adhered to this tradition, as they feared the wrath of athletic directors and fans alike. Coach Woolpert bucked this rule, starting Russell, K. C. Jones, and Hal Perry, three African Americans. It was an unprecedented lineup, this on a team roster that included a total of five black players. The decision paid huge dividends, as USF emerged as one of the greatest basketball programs in the nation. Later Jones and Russell both played on the same Boston Celtics team, the franchise winning an astonishing eleven NBA championships during their years.

Only a decade later, coach Don Haskins shocked the college basketball world when his Texas Western starting lineup included five

African American players and won the 1966 NCAA championship game against the powerful University of Kentucky basketball team led by Adolph Rupp, one of the greatest coaches in the history of college basketball, whose teams had won four national championships. Rupp and Kentucky administrators had steadfastly refused to recruit African Americans, and Rupp's 1966 team included only white players. That year, Haskins and his Texas Western squad defeated the heavily favored Kentucky Wildcats by the score of 72 to 65 in one of the greatest upsets in the history of college basketball. Like USF, Texas Western's victory had a profound impact on college basketball. Now, even predominantly white universities in the South began to recruit African American athletes in earnest in order to compete with schools with talented black players. As Phil Woolpert had demonstrated at USF, an integrated athletic program could not only compete but also win championships. Although the black athletes at Texas Western did not view themselves as activists or reformers, David Lattin, Bobby Joe Hill, Willie Worsley, Orsten Artis, Nevil Shed, Willie Cager, and Harry Flournoy changed both the face and the style of college basketball with their historic victory. The Texas Western Miners' star center, Lattin, probably spoke for the other black players when he stated, "we were just kids playing basketball, having fun. It was not that big a deal to us. We were just out there trying to win."

Black westerners also dominated the skilled positions in collegiate football during the 1960s and 1970s, but none more so than those on the University of Southern California (USC) Trojans. USC recruited a steady stream of gifted African Americans to play skilled positions such as linebacker, safety, corner back, wide receiver, and running back. The Trojans were defined first and foremost by the running-back position, the heart of their potent run-oriented offense. Mike Garrett, a star half back, set fourteen NCAA and USC records and won the Heisman Trophy in 1965, the first Trojan ever to receive that award and only the second player on the entire West Coast to be so honored. Other talented players followed in Garrett's footsteps, including O. J. Simpson, Clarence Davis, Anthony Davis, Sam Cunningham, and Marcus Allen. Simpson and Allen both won Heisman Trophies, in 1968 and 1981, while Davis finished second in the Heisman voting in 1974. Simpson and Allen also went on to have outstanding professional careers, earning induction in the National Football Hall of Fame. The dominance of African American football players in some instances accelerated the pace of integration at southern colleges. For example, shortly after USC fullback Sam Cunningham decimated the University of Alabama's defense with his running and blocking in 1970, Alabama's legendary coach Paul "Bear" Bryant decided to recruit African American players for his roster.

Black westerners dominated collegiate track and field during the 1960s, with athletes from California and Texas leading the way. Rafer Johnson left the brutal poverty of a Texas ghetto to attend UCLA, an institution with an outstanding academic reputation and whose alumni included Jackie Robinson and Ralph Bunche. An outstanding multisport athlete, Johnson excelled in the decathlon, an event in which he won a gold medal in the 1960 Olympic Games, establishing a new Olympic record. By the late 1960s, San Jose State College became the focal point of track and field, particularly the sprints. The stars of this program were Tommy Smith, Lee Evans, and John Carlos, who dominated the 200- and 400-meter sprints at the 1968 Olympics in Mexico City, also setting new records in the process. Smith won the 200 meters, while Carlos earned a bronze medal in the event. Lee Evans earned a gold medal in the 400 meters, with an Olympic record time of 43.86. Evans became the first runner ever to break 44 seconds in this event, a record that stood for twenty years.

Many black athletes throughout the West were deeply concerned about the widespread poverty and racial inequality that gripped the nation in the midst of the 1950s-1960s civil rights movement, and Smith and Carlos agreed to make a symbolic gesture to show their solidarity at the 1968 Olympic Games. As they stood on the Olympic podium during the playing of the national anthem of the United

States following their first- and third-place finishes in the 200 meters, both young men slipped on a black glove, bowed their heads, and raised their hands with a clenched fist, representing the Black Power salute (see below). For the first time in the history of the Olympic Games, African American athletes affirmed before an international audience that even their lives as elite athletes were intimately connected to the ongoing struggle for equal rights, equal opportunity, and racial equality.

Professional sports teams were much slower in moving west than were collegiate ones, for the centers of the nation's population remained in the eastern and midwestern states. But, as western states began to grow in population and power, this, too, began to change. In a sign of the times, in 1958 the New York Giants baseball team went west, relocating their franchise to San Francisco. By 1962, the San Francisco Giants won the National League pennant, and voters chose their star player, Willie Mays, as the league's most valuable player. A native of Birmingham, Alabama, Mays had played briefly in the segregated Negro Leagues before signing with the New York Giants as a rookie in 1951. Few players of any race had ever taken professional baseball by storm so early in their careers, but Mays possessed a phenomenal talent. With speed, power, and the ability to hit for a high batting average, he emerged as one the greatest center fielders in the history of professional baseball. Baseball aficionados still regard his over-the-shoulder catch in the 1954 World Series against the Cleveland Indians as one of the greatest plays by an outfielder in the history of the game. When Mays concluded his professional career in 1973, he had hit 660 home runs, third all time behind Hank Aaron and Babe Ruth, made 7,095 putouts, ranking first all-time among outfielders, stolen 338 bases, and compiled a lifetime batting average of .302. A panel of baseball experts at *The Sporting News* ranked Mays the second greatest baseball player of all time, behind only Babe Ruth. In his glory days with the Giants, Mays combined with two Hall of Fame first basemen, Willie McCovey, a tall, powerful slugger, and Orlando Cepeda, a native of Puerto Rico and an equally strong hitter, to form one of the most feared lineups in professional baseball.

Like the New York Giants, the Brooklyn Dodgers also left New York for the West Coast, relocating their storied franchise to southern California in 1958. The Dodgers had signed the great Jackie Robinson in 1947 to break the color line in the major leagues, but their team also included Roy Campanella, a gifted catcher of mixed African American and Italian parentage. Campanella, who possessed a quiet demeanor in contrast to the fiery Robinson, excelled as both a fielder and a hitter and won the coveted National League Most Valuable Player award three times. The Los Angeles Dodgers, in contrast to the old Brooklyn franchise, built their teams around pitching and speed, with Maury Wills, an African American shortstop, personifying their new look. Regarded as one of the greatest base stealers of his era, Wills led the National League in stolen bases six times and was the first ballplayer ever to steal more than one hundred bases in a single season. In 1962, baseball writers voted Wills the league's Most Valuable Player.

Even as Americans increasingly turned their eyes to western athletes, the West also became fertile ground for black entertainers. Although widely known as a photographer, the Kansas-born Gordon Parks broke new ground when he directed *The Learning Tree* (1969), the first feature film directed by an African American in Hollywood. Based loosely on Parks' early life in Kansas, the film depicts the struggles of a tight-knit black farm family to scratch out a living on the Great Plains. Parks' popularity soared when he directed the film *Shaft* (1971), which followed the exploits of John Shaft, a savvy and street-smart black private detective in New York. Although criticized in some circles as playing to demeaning stereotypes of African Americans, the film drew a wide audience and was accompanied by a similarly popular film score written and performed by the gifted soul-singer Isaac Hayes. In 1972, the "Theme from Shaft" received an Academy Award for the best original song, earning Hayes the distinction of being the first African American to win an Academy Award in a nonacting category.

Black musicians likewise earned wide acclaim in the postwar West, with Los Angeles' Central Avenue and San Francisco's Fillmore District serving as particularly vibrant centers of creativity. West Coast jazz, which was performed by artists of all races, gained national attention and competed with its East Coast counterpart. Artists such as Dexter Gordon, Lionel Hampton, Charles Mingus, and Chet Baker played regularly at Central Avenue night clubs and ballrooms. Nat King Cole, one of the most popular black entertainers in the nation, performed on a regular basis in Los Angeles, and he even hosted a variety show on NBC for a brief time in 1956, the first African American ever to host a variety show on a major network. Cole's skill as a pianist and smooth, velvety voice attracted a national following with fans of jazz, show tunes, and even Christmas music. His popular version of "The Christmas Song," remains arguably one of the most popular and recognizable Christmas songs ever recorded. San Francisco's Fillmore District, the city's largest African American community during the 1950s and 1960s, also contained a renowned jazz and blues scene. Unfortunately, even as black westerners made impressive gains in sports and the arts and entertainment, their communities would soon become embroiled in violent responses to deep-seated frustrations.

Urban Violence

The last push of the national civil rights movement, both its achievements and limitations, had a profound effect on African Americans in western cities, who, like their southern and northern counterparts, demonstrated their unwillingness to continue to accept second-class citizenship. In 1964 Congress passed the most comprehensive civil rights law in the nation's history, outlawing a wide range of discriminatory practices. A federal law passed the following year granting all Americans the right to vote without regard to race or ethnicity. Then, in the wake of the assassination of Dr. Martin Luther King, Jr., in 1968, Congress passed the Fair Housing Act. This act guaranteed all Americans the right to rent, lease, or purchase homes on a nonracial basis. Yet black westerners, despite the passage of these momentous federal laws, lost ground in some areas during the 1960s, and by 1970 they still had not attained equality.

African Americans in western cities, many of whom found themselves the victims of indiscriminate stops and random searches by police, as well as unprovoked violence at the hands of law enforcement officers, found police brutality an especially odious and frustrating problem. They seemed perplexed that police brutality could occur so often and so openly and that they had so little recourse when they complained publicly. City officials and police commissions appeared indifferent to any complaint filed against a fellow officer, and western cities had hired only a token number of African Americans for urban police forces prior to the 1960s. Charges of police misconduct surfaced in every western state and touched African Americans of all social classes.

The black residents of Watts, a neighborhood in South Central Los Angeles, had long had an especially contentious relationship with the police, and frustration with the situation and wider socioeconomic problems related to housing segregation and unemployment led to the eruption of six days of rioting that shook the city, state, and nation. On August 11, 1965, Lee Minikus, a white California Highway Patrolman (CHP) stopped a twenty-one-year-old black male named Marquette Frye for driving recklessly at Avalon Avenue and 122nd Street near Frye's home. His younger brother, Ronald, was a passenger in Frye's vehicle. Like many African American males in California, Frye was unemployed, had a juvenile record, and had not completed high school. Born in Lima, Oklahoma, Frye grew up in Hanna, Wyoming, a small integrated community about an hour north of Laramie, home of the University of Wyoming. Frye, by his own admission, had been drinking that evening, and officer Minikus decided to issue a sobriety test, which Frye failed. This seemingly routine arrest escalated when a crowd gathered; soon Frye's mother, Rena, was also on the scene. The sight of his mother among the crowd prompted Marquette to become loud and uncooperative. As the crowd grew larger and tempers flared, the CHP officers called for backup, and when both Los Angeles police and more CHP officers arrived, Frye resisted arrest. Rena Frye attempted to intervene on behalf of her son by jumping on the back of the arresting officer, which only further agitated the crowd. When word spread that a police officer had struck Rena Frye or handled her roughly, the crowd, which now numbered more than one hundred people, became louder and a ruckus started. The crowd surged toward the fleeing patrol cars that carried Marquette and Rena Frye, throwing rocks, bottles, and whatever else was within reach. By the following morning, this altercation had spread to a full-blown riot that lasted for six days, as angry blacks burned and looted retail stores, assaulted passing motorists, and fought firefighters, National Guard troops, and the L.A. police.

The violence spread quickly throughout Watts and to other areas of Los Angeles. Indeed, the riot zone encompassed about forty-six square miles, spreading throughout South Central Los Angeles, an area about the size of San Francisco. Rioters, who were mainly young black males, targeted white businesses and retail stores in their community. As Bayard Rustin, a prominent CORE leader noted, black rioters singled out white-owned stores which, in their estimation, had exploited them by charging exorbitant prices for their goods. In the final tally, arsonists destroyed more than 261 buildings and looted hundreds of others. Rustin's astute observation was also borne out by the number of fatalities, for not a single white person died at the hands of the rioters. Instead, rioters directed their anger and frustration at the police, who they resented because of decades of mistreatment and unrestrained brutality toward inner-city residents. In one of the most egregious examples, the LAPD shot a group of unarmed black Muslims in April 1962 during a confrontation outside of one of their mosques, killing one person, wounding five others, and leaving another one paralyzed.

Before it ended, the riot claimed the lives of thirty-four people, twenty-nine African Americans and three Latinos. It left more than a 1,000 people injured, resulted in 4,000 arrests, and caused some $200 million in property damage. Born of the hopelessness and frustration in which many young urban blacks mired in poverty lived, the riot began just five days after the passage of the historic 1965 Voting Rights Act. It appeared on the surface that the national civil rights movement, which had brought such significant legal progress to African Americans as a race, had yet to improve their lives appreciably. Many of the individuals who took part in the riot lived in substandard housing, attended all-black schools, and worked menial jobs, if they worked at all. Indeed, by the mid-1960s, a sizable number of African Americans living in Watts received some form of public assistance, a stark change from previous generations. Their collective plight did indeed reveal some of the stark limitations of the civil rights movement, which had insisted on winning legal equality for African Americans but had not attempted to transform the dismal economic plight that blacks faced relative to most whites. The increasing ghettoization of African Americans in Watts after 1960 and their physical separation from whites in housing and neighborhood schools reinforced the isolation of blacks from the white middle class. Sadly, the quality of life for many African Americans in communities like Watts had only declined since the World War II years, when job opportunities were plentiful and a sense of optimism permeated the community. For the majority of African Americans, there was no escape from this conundrum, and their prospects to rise from poverty and despair grew dimmer as the 1960s came to a close.

So, one might well ask, what factors account for the growing gap between the haves and the have-nots in communities like Watts? There were several interrelated reasons for growing disparities between blacks and whites and even between the black middle class and the black working class. Many African Americans, despite their earlier optimism, had not kept pace with white levels of employment. Black unemployment rates consistently remained twice as high as white rates in the region. African Americans, particularly young black men, possessed the lowest levels of formal education, which slowed their advancement into better-paying and more secure jobs. Because these individuals represented the most recent hires in an industry, they lost their jobs quicker than whites during economic downturns. African Americans also possessed far fewer assets such as homes or savings accounts, things that might sustain them during periods of economic hardship. Consequently, the poverty rate rose for African Americans in Los Angeles and many other American cities during the 1960s, this at the very time that opportunities for the black middle class were seemingly expanding greatly.

The residents of Watts had also felt powerless because the city of Los Angeles had hired few black policemen to patrol their neighborhood. And black Angelenos had even fewer black elected officials to protect their interests. In some cities black westerners came to fear all white policemen, and with good cause. African Americans were too often, along with Latinos, the object of a policeman's billy club or a fatal shooting that local authorities would quickly deem a justifiable homicide. In the two and a half years leading up to the 1965 Watts riot, the Los Angeles police force shot and killed sixty-five African Americans. Twenty-seven of these individuals were shot in the back, twenty-five were unarmed, and twenty-three were suspected of theft or other nonviolent crimes. The absence of citizen review commissions compounded the problem of police brutality, giving local residents the all too accurate impression that the police lacked accountability for their actions and that local elected officials did not care. Some black residents thus perceived white policemen as an occupation army rather than as public servants who were sworn to maintain law and order. These same factors, therefore, resulted in race riots in West Coast cities like Oakland and San Francisco (1966), and in other parts of the nation, where the loss of life, though less severe than that in Los Angeles, revealed a more serious racial problem in the West than most Americans knew existed and many white westerners were unwilling to admit.

Black Power

The violence in western cities during the 1960s led to the realization that racial disparities were as stark and real in Oakland and Los Angeles as they were in Birmingham, Alabama, Oxford, Mississippi, or Detroit, Michigan. Many black westerners pointed to their slum housing, menial jobs, the high rate of youth unemployment, de facto segregated schools, the absence of political representation, and the widespread pattern of police brutality as evidence that their conditions were not markedly different from those facing African Americans in the Deep South. In their opinion, it boiled down to a matter of degree. In the meantime, legal desegregation and improved voting rights had done little to address these problems. Frustration gave rise to increasing calls for Black Power, community empowerment, and the election of more black officials. Now, established black civil rights leaders and young black militants alike attempted to seize greater control over their lives.

In the West, expressions of Black Power took many forms, from adopting the militant rhetoric and language of Marxist and African revolutionaries, to wearing Afro hairstyles and African daishikis (African-style clothing for men and women), to organizing local communities to work toward improving schools, job opportunities, the rate of voter registration, and document cases of police brutality. Dozens of new organizations and leaders emerged, including some leaders collectively dubbed the Young Turks. These individuals, many of whom came of age during the 1950s and early 1960s, surfaced within established civil rights organizations like the NAACP. In Wichita, Kansas, Chester I. Lewis, the local branch president, boldly challenged the established leadership within the Wichita NAACP branch to become more assertive in pressing for racial equality by adopting direct action tactics. The Young Turks also pushed for change in the national NAACP, insisting that younger people, rather than the old guard, be elected to sit on the national board. Lewis' hope was that these individuals could better represent the grassroots of the NAACP, a group whose voice was often missing at the national conventions. These individuals succeeded in 1964 when the NAACP's national nominating committee selected six people for six seats to be elected by the branches. Yet no organization in the West that epitomized the emerging militancy had a more profound impact than the Black Panther Party for Self Defense.

Huey P. Newton and Bobby Seale established the Black Panther Party in 1966 in Oakland, California, a year after the Watts riot and the assassination of Malcolm X, the former spokesman for the Nation of Islam and the most articulate advocate of Black Power. The Black Panther Party preached revolutionary nationalism and community empowerment. Newton and Seale were migrants from the South and products of the mean streets of West Oakland, whose families having brought them to California after World War II in what turned out to be a fruitless search for a better life. They founded the new organization to carry on the work of Malcolm X. In many respects, their lives mirrored the despair, anger, and disillusionment of many other young black men who had come West after 1945.

The majority of black westerners did not live in abject poverty during the post-World War II era, but a growing number of them found little opportunity and envisioned a dismal future. Growing up in the ghettos and the public housing projects of Berkeley and West Oakland, neither Seale nor Newton felt that he had been educated to compete in modern society, except in menial jobs. Poor schools, high unemployment (or employment only in lousy jobs), uninspired teachers, and occasional run-ins with the Oakland police encouraged both men to reject the gradualism of traditional civil rights organizations and embrace instead the militant rhetoric of Malcolm X and Marxism. Newton, Seale, and a small but dedicated group of followers called for armed self-defense of black communities, an immediate end to all forms of racial discrimination, and black community empowerment. Prowling the streets of West Oakland, Newton, a charismatic leader, recruited an equally disaffected and dissatisfied group of African Americans. One such recruit was

Eldridge Cleaver, a writer for the left-wing *Ramparts* magazine who himself had served time in a California prison for rape. Cleaver's writings, some of them in national publications, helped to catapult the Black Panther Party into the regional and national limelight. Cleaver's book, *Soul on Ice* (1967), a collection of provocative essays, attracted a large readership.

The Black Panthers grew slowly between 1966 and 1970, but they earned notoriety beyond their numbers for their theatric militancy. Members established chapters in cities as far away as New York and Chicago, as well as in some foreign countries, and the Black Panthers helped to inspire the similarly radical American Indian Movement. While the organization never attracted the mass appeal of more mainstream civil rights organizations like the NAACP or Dr. King's Southern Christian Leadership Conference, the Black Panthers gained nationwide attention. In May of 1966 they staged a protest in Sacramento, California, at the state capitol, to challenge a bill that would have prohibited the possession of firearms in public places. Dressed in black leather jackets, turtleneck sweaters, and matching black berets, the Panthers struck a menacing pose in the minds of white Americans, as photographers captured images of the highly stylized and clearly armed Panthers entering the state assembly chamber. The Black Panther Party's membership reached approximately twelve hundred in 1968. Thousands of young African American males in the inner city ghettos openly identified with the bravado of the organization and supported many of its programs. Black Panthers patrolled neighborhoods, armed, to prevent police brutality, and they provided social services. They also worked to educate African Americans about their rights and inspire pride in their African heritage. Their militant and charismatic style and the breadth of their programs gave them widespread influence.

By the early 1970s, however, the Black Panthers were merely a shell of the organization during its heyday. Repeated clashes between the Panthers and local police forces in western cities and across the nation crippled the party's leadership and led to the deaths or long incarcerations of many of their members. In the most notable instance, Huey P. Newton, the organization's founder, was tried for murder in the death of an Oakland police officer following Newton's arrest for a routine traffic violation. Newton's trial, which resulted in a hung jury and the dismissal of criminal charges, attracted thousands of supporters of all races and nationalities in Oakland and across the nation. But this trial was merely the beginning of Newton's and the militant organization's troubles. The Federal Bureau of Investigation (FBI) under its director, J. Edgar Hoover, launched an extensive counterintelligence program dubbed COINTELPRO, the purpose of which was to disrupt and crush radical organizations such as the Black Panthers or any other civil rights organization that Hoover believed threatened the peace and security of the nation. COINTELPRO proved remarkably successful in squelching groups like the Panthers, though it was investigated by Congress in 1975 for violating the civil rights of radical groups ranging from the Black Panthers to Students for a Democratic Society and the Weather Underground.

Despite their relatively brief history, the Black Panthers contributed to the emerging civil rights struggle in several important ways. The organization supported its vision of local empowerment by establishing dozens of community-oriented programs in inner-city ghettos. Indeed, many of these initiatives, such as free medical screening, voter registration, free breakfast programs for children, and food banks to distribute food to needy families have become fixtures today in numerous urban locales that operate through churches and private charities. African American women played a critical role in the organization, although they were restricted from occupying many leadership positions and often had to put up with the sexist attitudes and behaviors of male leaders. One exception was Elaine Brown, who led the organization briefly after legal troubles forced Huey Newton into exile in Cuba.

The Black Panthers' community programs, run largely by African American women, were the most identifiable symbols of the organization in many local communities. In the same manner that they had led the outreach and missionary programs in African American churches, women's clubs, and sororities in previous generations, black women spearheaded the dozens of community programs that the Black Panthers established. Similarly, the organization's newspaper, *The Black Panther*, contained news on both national and international events that progressive readers of any race were unlikely to find in their daily newspapers. The Black Panthers also promoted voter registration in the black community and encouraged African Americans and progressive whites to elect political leaders who openly campaigned to improve services in the black community. Although Bobby Seale ran an unsuccessful campaign for political office in 1973, the Panthers' support of Lionel Wilson in 1977 led to the election of Oakland's first African American mayor. Finally, by calling attention to police brutality in the African American community in the West and across the nation, the Panthers sparked a discussion to hire more minority police officers and establish citizen review boards.

Conclusion

As the 1960s came to a close, black westerners, like the majority of their northern and southern counterparts, were probably less concerned with race than with supporting their families, finding affordable and decent housing, and sending their children to high-performing schools. Indeed, African Americans in all regions of the West could claim significant progress in many areas. While the West had never been and not yet become the Eldorado that many African Americans had hoped it might be, it had come a considerable distance from the widespread and systematic discrimination and blatant racism of the nineteenth and early twentieth centuries. The black middle class had grown significantly since World War II and many African Americans found employment and careers in white-collar and professional jobs.

Nonetheless, the race riots in western cities, the growth of urban ghettos, widespread unemployment, and a growing pattern of de facto segregation in public schools also revealed that black westerners had fallen behind white westerners in many areas. Indeed, the struggle over civil rights, and resistance to such change had sparked violence on occasion in the West and in other parts of the country. Most black westerners doubtlessly agreed that a considerable amount of work remained to be done.

Suggested Readings

Brown, Elaine. *A Taste of Power: A Black Woman's Story*. New York: Anchor Books, 1992.

Collier-Thomas, Bettye. *Jesus, Jobs, and Justice: African American Women and Religion*. New York: Random House Books, 2010.

Demas, Lane. *Integrating the Gridiron: Black Civil Rights and American College Football*. Newark: Rutgers University Press, 2010.

Eick, Gretchen. *Dissent in Wichita*. Urbana: University of Illinois Press, 2001.

Fitzpatrick, Frank. *And the Walls Came Tumbling Down: Kentucky, Texas Western, and the Game that Changed American Sports*. New York: Simon and Schuster, 1999.

Giddings, Paula. *In Search of Sisterhood: Delta Sigma Theta and the Challenge of the Black Sorority Movement*. New York: HarperCollins, 1988.

Goldberg, Robert A. "Racial Change on the Southern Periphery: The Case of San Antonio, Texas, 1960–1965." *Journal of Southern History* 49 (1983): 349–379.

Goudsouzian, Aram. *King of the Court: Bill Russell and the Basketball Revolution*. Berkeley: University of California Press, 2010.

Hirsch, James S. *Willie Mays: The Life, The Legend*. New York: Scribner, 2010.

Horne, Gerald. *Fire This Time: The Watts Uprising and the 1960s*. Charlottesville: University of Virginia, 1995.

Joseph, Peniel E. *Waiting 'Til the Midnight Hour: A Narrative History of Black Power*. New York: Macmillan, 2007.

Martin, Charles H. *Benching Jim Crow: The Rise and Fall of the Color Line in Southern College Sports, 1890–1980*. Urbana: University of Illinois Press, 2010.

Meier, August and Elliott Rudwick. *CORE: A Study in the Civil Rights Movement, 1942–1968*. New York: Oxford University Press, 1973.

Melcher, Mary. "Blacks and Whites Together: Interracial Leadership in the Phoenix Civil Rights Movement." *Journal of Arizona History* 32 (Summer 1991): 195–216.

Patterson, James T. *Brown v. Board of Education: A Civil Rights Milestone and Its Troubled Legacy*. New York: Oxford University Press, 2001.

Rampersad, Arnold. *Jackie Robinson, A Biography*. New York: Random House, 1998.

Ross, B. Joyce. "Mary McLeod Bethune and the National Youth Administration: A Case Study of Power Relationships in the Black Cabinet of Franklin D. Roosevelt."

John Hope Franklin and August Meier, eds. *Black Leaders of the Twentieth Century.* Urbana: University of Illinois Press, 1982.

Tygiel, Jules. *Baseball's Great Experiment: Jackie Robinson and His Legacy, 25th Anniversary ed.* New York: Oxford University Press, 2008.

Van Deburg, William L. *New Day in Babylon: The Black Power Movement and American Culture, 1965–1975.* Chicago: University of Chicago Press, 1992.

White, Deborah Gray. *Too Heavy a Load: Black Women in Defense of Themselves, 1894–1994.* New York: W. W. Norton, 1999.

Sarah Hastings, a World War II migrant from Kansas City, Missouri. *Courtesy Broussard Family Collection*

Below: Welder-trainee Josie Lucille Owens working at the Kaiser Shipyards in Richmond, California. *National Archives 208-NP-1KKK(6)*

Women war workers at the shipyards. *Library of Congress, LC-USW33-028624-C*

Joseph James, San Francisco Bay Area shipyard. *Courtesy: Moorland-Spingarn Research Center, Howard University*

Doris "Dorie" Miller receiving the Navy Cross from Admiral Chester W. Nimitz aboard a U.S. Navy warship in Pearl Harbor, T.H., May 27, 1942. *Official U.S. Navy Photograph, Library of Congress, LC-USZ62-131712*

U.S. Army WAC Major Charity E. Adams and Captain Abbie N. Campbell inspect members of the 6888th Central Postal Directory Battalion, England, February 15, 1945. *National Archives 111-SC-20079*

Lincoln Ragsdale, Sr. (middle) with fellow Tuskegee Airmen. *Courtesy Matthew C. Whitaker*

Widening the roadway of the Alcan Highway, 1942. *Library of Congress, LC-USW33-000938-ZC*

Jackie Robinson, in miltary uniform, signs a contract with the farm team for the Brooklyn Dodgers, becoming the first African American to sign with a white professional baseball team, circa 1943. © *Bettman/CORBIS (BE044191)*

Brown v. *Board of Education.* The children involved in the landmark lawsuit which challenged segregation in public schools. Topeka, Kansas, 1953. From front, Vicki Henderson, Donald Henderson, Linda Brown, James Emanuel, Nancy Todd, and Katherine Carper. *Photo by Carl Iwasaki/Time Life Pictures/Getty Images, 50680730*

Clara Luper, late 1950s, Oklahoma. *Oklahoma Historical Society*

Willie Mays with his arm around the shoulders of Roy Campanella. *World Telegram & Sun photo by William C. Greene. Library of Congress LC-USZ62-112029*

1966 NCAA Champions, the Texas Western College Miners, after defeating the top-ranked Kentucky Wildcats in a game of historic and social significance. *University of Texas at El Paso*

Barbara Jordan, following her speech given during the comissioning ceremony for the U.S.S. *Miller*, the first U.S. Navy ship named after an African American, Doris "Dorie" Miller. UT Institute of Texan Cultures at San Antonio 073-1031. *Loaned by U.S. Department of the Navy. UTSA Libraries, Special Collections (073-1031)*

Tom Bradley
(right) and Nate
Holden, ca. 1972
© *Nate Holden,*
www.NateHolden.
com

Watts Riots. Three buildings burn on Avalon Blvd. and a surplus store burns at right as a looting, burning mob ruled the Watts section of Los Angeles. *Library of Congress, LC-USZ62-113642*

Robert B. Flippin, parole officer at the California State Prison at San Quentin, talking with an inmate. *Courtesy: Moorland-Spingarn Research Center, Howard University*

"Cadillac, Get Off My Back. Freedom Now!" Tracy Simms at the San Francisco Cadillac Demonstrations. *Photo courtesy Shirley Streshinsky*

Black Panther Party members participate in a drill during the funeral service for Black Panther Bobby James Hutton, age 17, who was killed by police officers during a gun battle in Oakland, California, April 15, 1968. Hutton's death was called a "political assassination" by a speaker at the funeral. © *Bettman/CORBIS (BE020828)*

Taken in Los Angeles on April 30, 1992 near the intersection of Kenmore Avenue and Beverly Boulevard. Later that day a dusk-to-dawn curfew was imposed in areas throughout the city. *Polaroid photo by Dana Graves.*

CHAPTER 6

The Modern Era: The Search for Equity

With the election of Richard Nixon as president in 1968, and his reelection in 1972, the executive branch's focus shifted to law and order and ending the divisive war in Vietnam, rather than achieving full equality and equity for African Americans. Indeed, following the passage of the 1968 Fair Housing Act, the last major civil rights law enacted by Congress, public opinion polls revealed that the majority of white Americans felt that the government had done enough to end segregation and racial inequality in America. Some polls revealed that a majority of Americans had felt this way as early as 1965, just ten years after the start of the famous bus boycott in Montgomery, Alabama, that had been inspired by Rosa Parks' defiant act of refusing to surrender her seat to a white person on public transportation. These polls indicated that a significant portion of white Americans, in every region of the nation, did not believe that granting full citizenship rights to African Americans should have been a national priority. Yet black westerners appeared as relieved as any right-wing conservative in the nation that the tumultuous and fractious decade of 1960s had come to a conclusion. Rather than taking to the streets and staging large-scale protests, as African Americans and their supporters had done during the 1950s and 1960s, in the 1970s and 1980s black westerners turned increasingly to Congress and the courts to open doors in unions, white-collar, managerial, and professional jobs, and gain access to colleges and professional schools. As they had done so often since the early decades of the twentieth century, African Americans turned to the NAACP to wage many of their battles. But for the first time in the nation's history, black westerners also had the backing of effective civil rights legislation and the weight of the federal courts in their fight against racial inequality.

Political Success

Black voters across the nation took the right to vote quite seriously, and they believed that sharing political power with other racial and ethnic groups would accelerate the process of gaining full access to good jobs, better housing, and integrated schools. The quest for political power in the West after 1970 was part of a national campaign by African Americans to exert pressure on entrenched white power through the ballot box. Following the passage of the Voting Rights Act in 1965, the number of African American officeholders increased dramatically throughout the nation. About 500 black elected officials served in 1964, of which approximately twenty-five resided in the South. That large a number of black elected officials had not been evident in the South since the era of Reconstruction. By 1980, the number of black officeholders throughout the nation had soared to nearly 4,000. By 1990, more than 8,000 black elected officials served a broad-based constituency of all races, a staggering increase in the space of twenty-five years. The majority of these elected officials (approximately 60 percent) resided in the South, where African American voters composed a sizable voting bloc, and even majorities in some locales. By 1994, the thirty-seven black congresspersons in the House of Representatives composed 8.5 percent of that body.

Despite their relatively small numbers in most western states, African Americans discovered that white and Hispanic voters often supported their quest for political office. California served as a bellwether, once again. Tom Bradley, a former policeman in Los Angeles, serves as a case in point. A native of Calvert, Texas, and the grandson of former slaves, Bradley graduated from UCLA. When he discovered that opportunities in law enforcement were available to African Americans, he joined the Los Angeles Police Department (LAPD) and moved quickly through the ranks. When the LAPD promoted him to lieutenant, Bradley attained the highest rank of any African American on the force. But he also was determined to pursue a career in politics, so he earned a law degree at Southwestern University in Los Angeles and served on the Los Angeles City Council from 1963 to 1972, building a political base that included many progressive white voters as well as middle-class African Americans.

By 1969, Bradley had decided to challenge incumbent mayor Sam Yorty. Because many polls showed Bradley in the lead, Yorty falsely portrayed Bradley as a supporter of the Black Panthers and someone to be feared. Although Bradley lost the 1969 mayoralty race, he challenged Yorty again in 1973. This time he won a close election to become the first African American mayor of L.A. since Francisco Reyes, a mulatto from central Mexico, was the *alcalde* of the pueblo of Los Angeles in the 1780s. Mayor Bradley served a total of five terms in office, increased civilian control over the LAPD, and started building a mass-transit system that would connect the sprawling greater Los Angeles region. He also dramatically improved the city's race relations by bringing a broader number of racial and ethnic groups into city government and serving on city commissions. Bradley's twenty years as mayor of Los Angeles, the largest city in the West and the second largest in the nation, revealed that African American politicians could govern effectively, provided that they build coalitions and cater to middle-class voters of all races. His tenure as mayor of L.A. also illustrated the importance that African American voters placed on their vote to elect candidates to office who supported their interests.

African American mayors in other western cities followed in Bradley's footsteps. The Black Panther Party organized a grassroots campaign in Oakland, California, which led to the election of Lionel Wilson as that city's first black mayor in 1977. Wilson's election owed as much, however, to a longstanding black political organization, the East Bay Democratic Club. The club was based in Oakland and Berkeley and had been established in the 1940s by D. G. Gibson, William Byron Rumford, and other black leaders in Oakland. Like that of Tom Bradley in Los Angeles, Gibson's strategy involved building successful coalitions to elect African Americans to political office. The East Bay Democratic Club under Gibson's leadership had helped elect Rumford to the California State Assembly in 1948.

African American women also benefitted from the surge in black voting during the 1960s and 1970s, one fueled in part by increased voter registration among African Americans and the successful assault on voting restrictions against blacks led by the NAACP. Barbara Jordan rose from the grim poverty and despair of Houston's Fifth Ward to win a seat in the Texas State Senate in 1967, the first black Texan elected to that body since 1883, when the violent imposition of Jim Crow had ended the success of black politicians in the South during the post–Civil War era of Reconstruction. Almost a century later, in 1972, the Texas Senate elected Jordan president pro tempore of the Texas Senate. A skilled and adroit legislator, she ran successfully in 1973 for the U.S. House of Representatives from the Eighteenth Texas District, becoming the first woman from a southern state to serve in the United States Congress. Jordan led a distinguished career in that body, and the esteem held for her in the Democratic Party was a pivotal factor in her selection to deliver the keynote address at the 1976 Democratic National Convention, the first woman of any race to do so. Congresswoman Jordan is perhaps best remembered, however, for her role as a member of the House Judiciary Committee during the 1974 Watergate hearings, which investigated the illegal conduct of President Richard M. Nixon and his White House associates. A compelling orator, Jordan presented what was arguably the most brilliant speech at that proceeding. Facing television cameras and speaking before the entire nation, she asserted boldly, "my faith in the Constitution is whole, it is complete, it is total. I am not going to sit here and be an idle spectator to the diminution, the subversion, the destruction of the Constitution."

The political rise of Willie L. Brown, Jr., was nearly as spectacular. This black migrant from the small East Texas town of Mineola came to San Francisco in the early 1950s and earned a law degree at the University of California's Hastings School of Law, where his class elected him president. In the early 1960s, Brown settled into the Western Addition, a heavily populated African American neighborhood of San Francisco, and launched his political career. Though Brown lost his initial bid for elective office in 1962, he won election to the California State Assembly in 1964. His leadership and political savvy ultimately earned him the powerful position of Speaker of the Assembly. In 1996, in a close contest, voters elected Brown mayor of San Francisco, and he easily won reelection for a second term. Brown's success revealed that African Americans had made tremendous progress politically, in gaining a seat at the table and access to power after 1964. But Brown's political victories and access to power also spoke to the enormous changes that had transpired racially and politically in the West and the nation since the end of World War II. Who would have predicted in 1940 or even 1950, given the enormous racial barriers that black westerners had faced, that African American migrants from the South could be elected mayor of two of the most important cities in the nation—San Francisco and L.A.?

Conservative southwestern cities such as Dallas, Houston, and San Antonio also changed politically, as both African Americans and Hispanics voted in larger numbers and won political office. Following the passage of the 1965 Voting Rights Act, which Congress extended in 1970, 1975, and 1982, African American voting turnout increased significantly. The percentage of African Americans who registered to vote in Texas, for example, grew from 35 percent in 1960 to 65 percent in 1976. The federal government also placed Texas and a number of southern states under close federal supervision, because the states historically had prevented blacks and Hispanics from voting through clever ruses such as poll taxes, literacy tests, all-white primaries, and shortened registration periods. African Americans, Hispanics and progressive white voters also challenged the legality of at-large districts, which diluted minority voting strength. At-large elections hurt minority candidates in general because the strength of their voting bloc lay in predominantly minority communities. These changes bore fruit in many large Texas cities, for forty-one African Americans held local office in Texas in 1970. Indeed, the number of blacks who held office in Texas soared to 158 by 1977. Dallas, a city that had been dominated by conservative white business elites into the 1970s, elected Ron Kirk, its first African American mayor, to office in 1994. A native of Austin and a graduate of the University of Texas Law School, Kirk had the strong support of Dallas' business community as well as the overwhelming support of African American voters. A political moderate, Kirk received 62 percent of the total vote. His strong leadership, coalition building, and desire for consensus resulted in his reelection as mayor in 1999, when he received an impressive 74 percent of the vote. Nor did Kirk's political career end when he stepped down as mayor of Dallas. In 2009, the U.S. Senate confirmed him as the first African American to hold the position of United States Trade Representative.

Denver, an inter-mountain city, also strongly supported black politicians such as Wellington Webb, a former city auditor, who served as mayor from 1991 to 2003. Like Willie L. Brown, Jr., and Ron Kirk, Webb successfully courted business interests and promoted downtown economic development in the Mile High City. He also governed during an era of rapid economic expansion. Webb received strong support from Denver's Hispanic community, an important political constituency that made up 20 percent of the population. His three terms in office proved remarkably successful. Under his watch the city of Denver built Coors Field, the home of the Colorado Rockies, a new international airport, and a new convention center.

Norman Rice served with similar success for two-terms (1989–97) as mayor of Seattle, a city with a relatively small black community.

Rice's moderate policies won him the support of Seattle's business class as well as that of the white and Asian middle class. The success of westerners like Tom Bradley, Lionel Wilson, Ron Kirk, Willie L. Brown, Jr., Wellington Webb, and Norman Rice displayed the political savvy and maturity of a new group of black politicians who had come of age during the 1960s and 1970s. Their success also suggested that many white, Asian, and Hispanic voters in the West saw African Americans as eminently qualified to lead them and represent their cities.

African American women had far less success winning political office in the West, but they, too, began to receive important political appointments. Hundreds of them served on school boards, city councils, and in local and statewide offices. Some were elected to local courts, and a small number, such as Barbara Jordan, Yvonne Burke, and Maxine Waters, served in state legislatures or in Congress.

Socioeconomic Challenges

Black political power in the West did not always translate into progress for African American. In Oakland, for example, white voters increasingly fled to suburban communities, taking their tax dollars and leaving the central city populated largely by impoverished people—African Americans, other minority groups, and whites. This pattern was not unique to the West, it should be noted, as middle-class whites and blacks left inner cities in hundreds of communities throughout the nation. The situation in Oakland was exacerbated, however, by the passage of Proposition 13 by California's voters in 1978, a tax revolt that severely limited the amount of property tax that any locality within the state could levy on homeowners. Because of a declining tax base, despite his best intentions Mayor Wilson lacked the resources to enact any of the bold initiatives to assist African Americans and other economically marginal groups that he had promised in his campaign. Oakland, like post–World War II Detroit and numerous cities by the 1970s, became an urban symbol for high crime, drug wars, decaying ghettos, low-performing schools, and thousands of impoverished residents with broken spirits and little hope.

Nor did African Americans fare particularly well during Willie L. Brown's two terms as mayor of San Francisco (1996–2004). Unlike Wilson, who faced massive white flight and a declining tax base, Brown governed during an era of prosperity in San Francisco, one in which white-collar, professional, and high-tech jobs were in great demand and real estate prices soared, in some years increasing as much as 20 to 25 percent. But Brown's policies as mayor did little to help low-income residents of any race. Spending money to create affordable housing proved unpopular and contrary to the interests of big business and real estate developers in the city, and Brown depended heavily upon this important constituency for fund-raising and to support other major programs as mayor. As a consequence, low-income residents of every race faced a serious housing crisis during his administration.

These policies left African Americans and other minority group residents, mainly Asians and Latinos, to compete for housing in the same manner as any San Franciscan in a competitive housing market marked by skyrocketing rents and home prices. Many African Americans, even those whose families had resided in San Francisco for generations, found the city's housing too expensive by the 1980s and moved to East Bay cities such as Oakland, Berkeley, Richmond, and Vallejo. Some relocated as far away as Sacramento, a distance of approximately ninety miles. Still others moved to adjacent western states or returned to the South or to Sunbelt states, where jobs were plentiful and housing less expensive.

These factors led to the dramatic decline of African Americans in one West Coast city. For the first time since the turn of the twentieth century, the number of African Americans who resided in San Francisco declined in the federal census, and the out-migration proved even more dramatic than anyone could have imagined. The San Francisco *Chronicle* reported that the city's black population dropped faster than that of any large U.S. city in the nation between

1970 and 2005. In 1970, 96,078 African Americans lived in San Francisco, 13.4 percent of the total population and an increase of 29.1 percent from the previous decade. By 1990, the city's black population had fallen to 79,039 or 10.9 percent of the city's total population. And by 2005, the African American population in San Francisco had declined to 6.5 percent of the city's total residents, less than one-half the percentage reported in 1970. Declining economic opportunities, inferior schools, and a tight and expensive housing market prompted many African Americans to reconsider living in the Golden Gate City, and a surprisingly large number of them voted with their feet. Whatever magic that San Francisco had formerly possessed to attract African Americans to its Golden Gates was now clearly a thing of the past. Many black westerners no longer perceived San Francisco as a locale where they could advance.

And troubling vestiges of segregation and de facto inequality persisted in the West after 1970. Housing and employment patterns in the region remained stubbornly resistant to change, two painful reminders that the West was no oasis of equality but reflected racial patterns one could find in cities throughout the nation. White homeowners welcomed African Americans to their neighborhoods reluctantly, if at all. Even after the U.S. Supreme Court ruled in 1948 that racially restrictive covenants were unenforceable, white property owners, real estate agencies, and neighborhood improvement associations used a variety of ruses to avoid selling, renting, or leasing property to African Americans in certain neighborhoods. Such discrimination cut across all economic classes in the African American community. A black Harvard-trained physician was just as likely to be denied access to purchasing a home in a predominantly white neighborhood as was a skilled tradesman or a longshoreman. Remember how the baseball great Willie Mays found that his exploits on the baseball diamond bore little relationship to where he could purchase property in San Francisco, when a white homeowner refused to sell his home to Mays because of his race? Only after this episode made national headlines and became an embarrassment to the city, and after the mayor of San Francisco intervened in Mays' behalf, did the reluctant white homeowner relent. The overwhelming majority of black westerners, however, did not possess the political clout or the influence of Mays, a future Hall of Fame ballplayer. Even Willie L. Brown, Jr., the most powerful black legislator in the state of California, had a similar experience in the early 1980s, when a realtor in the exclusive Cathedral Hills neighborhood of San Francisco initially denied him an opportunity to rent an apartment. Widespread publicity regarding this incident and the threat of an expensive lawsuit also forced the hand of this realtor.

Black westerners also had far greater difficulty escaping the central cities for suburbs than did white homeowners, who moved increasingly to suburban communities in the West after 1970, mirroring a pattern of white flight that existed across the nation. As historian Robert Self demonstrated in his excellent study of Oakland, African Americans faced considerably more difficulty obtaining loans to move to suburban housing in the greater Bay Area. Much as it had with the G.I. Bill program in the post–World War II era, the federal government also discriminated openly against blacks and other racial minorities in providing access to federally-backed mortgages to minorities who wished to move to predominantly white neighborhoods. With fewer options at their disposal, black westerners crowded into the city centers of Los Angeles, Oakland, Kansas City, Portland, Seattle, and Denver in larger numbers, just as they had during the boom of World War II. As industrial jobs slowly disappeared, and as white homeowners moved to suburban communities—removing a significant percentage of the property tax base—many of these cities became mired in poverty. With less tax dollars at their disposal, city officials performed fewer services, and the quality of many working-class neighborhoods declined. White flight also affected the racial composition of inner-city schools in the West, which became dominated by African American, Latino, and Asian students, many of whom performed well below the academic level of white middle-class students. Residential segregation also reinforced the racial patterns in many schools.

Although Oakland was one of the nation's most egregious examples, the number and size of black ghettos in the West multiplied significantly after 1960. The South Central District of Los Angeles, where the majority of blacks in the city resided, became a ripe recruiting ground for gangs such as the Bloods and the Crips, each of whom staked out city blocks, public housing projects, and entire neighborhoods in an effort to control the drug trade and strike fear and terror into local residents. Poorly educated, often high school dropouts, products of broken homes and single mothers raised in poverty, and facing high rates of unemployment, these young men and women embodied the hopeless despair of many urban ghettos. The legal and political gains of the civil rights movement had not improved their lives appreciably or provided them the kind of socio-economic opportunities that would let them compete in a highly competitive society.

Adding insult to injury, urban redevelopment projects in the 1960s and 1970s contributed to the fragmentation of many western black neighborhoods and the dispersal of black businesses and the black middle class. Whether by design or unintentionally, redevelopment usually tore through the heart of existing black western neighborhoods, severely disrupting residents and crippling many black-owned businesses. In San Francisco's Fillmore District, one of two large black communities in the city, the San Francisco Development Commission voted to condemn hundreds of homes and apartments occupied at the time by African American and Japanese residents. Many of these properties stood in the path of a proposed expressway, whose purpose was to ease the commute of white workers who resided on the outskirts of the city to downtown, where they worked. Roy Wilkins, the NAACP's national executive secretary, struck a responsive chord with many African Americans in the West and across the nation when he referred to redevelopment as "Negro removal," hinting back to governmental Indian removal policies in the West.

Redevelopment projects did far more than merely remove or relocate people, however; they arbitrarily forced businesses to move and destroyed communities that had taken people many years to build. For decades, residents had visited a local barber shop or beauty parlor, shopped at a local grocer or fish market, frequented a neighborhood pool hall, shoe shine parlor, or theater, Outsiders now informed residents that their community, homes, and local institutions would be condemned because they stood in the way of *progress* or *urban renewal*. Before 1970, black neighborhoods like San Francisco's Fillmore District, Los Angeles's Central Avenue, Houston's Fifth Ward, or Seattle's Central District contained thriving and bustling businesses that catered to their ethnic diversity and residential concentration. These institutions—symbols of community pride and stability—had provided mentors and role models for African American children, who saw black doctors, pharmacists, lawyers, editors, and other professionals on a daily basis in their neighborhoods. They were part of the social fabric of the African American community, and redevelopment tore this social fabric asunder when it forced these individuals and their businesses to move to other, more-integrated neighborhoods. The absence of the black middle class revealed in stark terms the widening class gap that now existed in the African American community nationwide, where two-thirds of all black children were born to unwed mothers by 1991, 40 percent of all African American girls had become pregnant by the age of eighteen, and the majority of black female-headed families were poor. The black middle class had taken advantage of civil rights legislation and political success, but many African Americans in western cities and throughout the nation benefitted comparatively little. Redevelopment projects that gutted African American neighborhoods further showed the impotence of black leaders, black politicians, and civil rights organization like the NAACP and CORE. Each individual and organization stood powerlessness to halt this process.

Despite the difficulties many African Americans faced in escaping inner cities, suburban communities did attract numerous black westerners after 1970. Over 80 percent of the nation's population growth took place in suburbs between 1950 and 1970; by 1990, more than half of all Americans resided in suburbs. Blacks also followed this wave out of the central cities—and in impressive numbers. By the end of the 1960s, about 250,000 blacks per year moved to the suburbs, approximately ten times the number who had moved at the start of the decade. African Americans in the West cited the same reasons as middle-class whites, Latinos, or Asians when they left the central cities. Suburbs offered spacious and affordable housing, superior schools, access to shopping malls and industrial parks, and a safer environment. The relocation of jobs from the central cities to the urban fringes proved an especially powerful motivator for all westerners, as more than three-fourths of all new manufacturing and retail jobs between 1950 and 1970 were based in suburbs. The enormous changes in state and federal law brought on by the Civil Rights Act of 1964 and the Fair Housing Act of 1968 also encouraged African American movement to western suburbs. No longer did the Federal Housing Administration (FHA) refuse to guarantee mortgages when blacks or members of other minority groups considered undesirable to whites wished to move into white neighborhoods. In 1966 the California Supreme Court overturned Proposition 14, a widely popular referendum that had prohibited the state from denying any property owner the right to sell, rent, or lease their property at their discretion. The Civil Rights Act of 1968's fair housing provision, Title VIII, also prohibited most forms of discrimination based on race, national origin, and religion. This federal law, which was passed in the wake of Dr. Martin Luther King's assassination in 1968, attempted to remove the remaining legal loopholes that prevented African Americans and other racial minorities from occupying housing in predominantly white neighborhoods. Collectively, these laws, combined with changing public attitudes toward nonwhites, supported African Americans who sought housing in western suburban communities.

Although employment opportunities varied widely from one suburban community to the next, African American residents who resided in suburbs generally had higher incomes, lower unemployment rates, and experienced less poverty than black residents of inner cities. Those who resided in the numerous suburban communities surrounding Los Angeles fared especially well, although considerable disparities existed in their incomes. An African American business-man who moved from Texas to Orange County, California, in 1969, for example, referred to his move as "the best thing that could have happened to me, especially coming from Texas. The opportunity here is great." Similarly, by the 1980s, the Los Angeles suburb of Ingle-wood reputably had the highest income and lowest poverty level of any predominately black city in the nation. By 1990, 61 percent of the black labor force in California held white-collar jobs, a figure that mirrored the state's general population, and a sizable percent-age of these African American workers lived in suburbs. In contrast, no central city in California in 1990 had two-thirds of its African American workforce in white-collar jobs. Moreover, the dramatic growth in white-collar employment among blacks by 1990 contrasts sharply with the meager gains that African American migrants as well as native black Californians had achieved during World War II and the decade of the 1950s.

The success of middle-class African Americans living in sub-urbs contrasts sharply with the fortunes of those, along with other groups, who remained trapped in inner cities with declining levels of employment, tax bases, and government services. As a result, a growing class divide marked the black population in the West and around the nation, one exacerbated by the increasing spatial separa-tion of middle- and lower-class African Americans. As in the 1960s in Watts, the deep frustration of inner-city people would erupt in rioting in Los Angeles in 1992, by both black and Latino residents (see below).

Education

The quest of African Americans in the West for equity and full citi-zenship included gaining access to better elementary and secondary schools for their children—giving them an education that would enable them to compete effectively in a global, information-age society—as well as access to colleges, universities, and professional programs. Indeed, much progress had been achieved in these areas by the 1970s, as public and private colleges and universities, as well as professional schools, slowly began to open their doors to African American students. Prestigious state universities like UCLA, Berkeley (also part of the University of California system) the University of Colorado, the University of Arizona, the University of Oregon, the University of Kansas, and the University of Washington, where a small cohort of African American students had matriculated prior to World War II, enrolled black students in record numbers during the 1960s and 1970s. Even schools like the University of Texas at Austin and Texas A&M University, which had formerly prohibited African American students strictly because of their race since their founding in the 1870s, enrolled a modest number of black students by the early 1960s. These individuals, many of whom were first-generation college students and the sons and daughters of black southern migrants who had come West during World War II, fulfilled the dreams of their parents when they pursued college degrees.

Unfortunately, many of these students found themselves socially isolated on predominately white college campuses. Black students also found out that white students refused to room with them, in some instances, while others viewed them as exotic curiosities. Their experiences were similar, perhaps, to that of Malcolm X, who referred to himself as the "mascot" in his classes when he attended school in Michigan as a young boy. Other white students expected their black classmates to serve as authorities on every aspect of black history and culture. In order to assist African American college students, student leaders and university officials formed a variety of organizations and social support networks to help them adjust. Black Student Unions or associations became common on college campuses in the West and throughout the nation, and more militant students used these organizations to encourage African Americans to push for a variety of demands. At San Francisco State College in 1969, African American, Asian, Latino, and Native American students formed the Third

World Liberation Front, and pressed for the creation of a Black Studies Program. The students, who were joined by a small number of supportive faculty and community leaders, succeeded after more than a year of confrontations between S. I. Hayakawa, the college's acting president, and the multiethnic coalition. Instead of bending to the demands of student and faculty demonstrators, Hayakawa called in the local police, who arrested demonstrators. The five-month student-led strike is widely regarded as the longest campus strike in U.S. history (November 6, 1969 to March 20, 1969). African American students at other western colleges and universities staged milder forms of civil disobedience when they demanded that administrators increase black enrollment, hire black faculty members and administrators, and diversify the curriculum by creating black or ethnic studies programs. Occasionally these protests bore fruit, as when Stanford University hired the renowned scholar St. Clair Drake to chair its inaugural African American Studies program in the wake of a black student protest in 1969. The Program in African and African American Studies at Stanford University was the first such one established at a private institution of higher learning in the United States.

By the late 1970s, one could see the effects of the white backlash against civil rights on college campuses. Many conservative groups and some Jewish organizations demanded an end to affirmative action programs, which they interpreted as racial preferences, wholly ignoring the longstanding and entrenched policies on many college campuses of granting special admission preference to the children of trustees, alumni, generous donors, and athletes, which in effect privileged whites. White students, who for the first time had to compete with nonwhites for coveted positions at many colleges and professional schools, felt aggrieved, and they pressed their case in courts. In the most celebrated such case of the decade, Alan Bakke, a white student, applied to the University of California at Davis Medical School, which then denied him admission. When Bakke learned that the university had admitted minority students with lower scores, he sued the University of California on the grounds that his civil rights had been violated as a victim of reverse discrimination. This important legal case drew national attention, and many civil rights organizations believed that the future of affirmative action itself lay at stake. A divided United States Supreme Court in 1978 rendered a verdict that favored Bakke, but struck down neither the principle nor the legality of affirmative action. By a vote of 5 to 4, the court ruled that the medical school admissions program that the University of California at Davis had established was illegal because it arbitrarily set aside sixteen of the one hundred available slots for minority students. This program amounted to a quota system, the court ruled, and on this specific ground was illegal. Moreover, as Justice Lewis F. Powell wrote, the medical school admissions program insulated minority students from comparison with all other students. For this reason, the court ordered the University of California to admit Alan Bakke to its medical school.

Yet the Supreme Court had, in the same stroke, also upheld the legality of affirmative action programs, if by a narrow margin. In a series of separate opinions, the justices weighed in on one of the most controversial issues to come before the court in years. They ruled that the long history of slavery, segregation, and de facto discrimination against African Americans justified affirmative action programs in some instances; but the court was also clear that strict racial quotas were unconstitutional. The five justices who voted to uphold the principle of affirmative action also agreed that having a diversified student body or workforce was a healthy condition for a public university and for American society as a whole. Justice Powell, the swing vote in this case, argued that there was a "compelling state interest" in racial diversity. The nine Supreme Court justices were just as sensitive, however, to the complaint of white students that affirmative action programs gave blacks and other nonwhite minorities an unfair advantage, an argument that a majority of justices rejected in light of the second-class status that African Americans in the West and the nation had endured for more than two centuries.

The United States Supreme Court affirmed the legality of *Bakke* in 2003 when it ruled by a 5 to 4 vote in the case *Grutter* v. *Bollinger*. This time the court weighed whether race could still be used as one of many considerations in the admissions process of the University of Michigan Law School. Writing for the court majority, Justice Sandra Day O'Connor stated emphatically the value of diversity, saying: "In order to cultivate a set of leaders with legitimacy in the eyes of the citizenry, it is necessary that the path to leadership be visibly open to talented and qualified individuals of every race and ethnicity." O'Connor and four other justices ruled that the University of Michigan Law School had used race as just one of many variables in deciding admission to its prestigious law school. This narrowly tailored use of race in admissions was therefore consistent with *Bakke* and did not violate the Equal Protection Clause of the Constitution. The court's narrow vote, 5 to 4, revealed that questions regarding affirmative action, access, and equity were just as divisive in the twenty-first century as they had been thirty-five years earlier.

On the same day that the Supreme Court ruled in *Grutter* v. *Bollinger*, it voted 6 to 3 to invalidate the University of Michigan's affirmative action program for admission to its undergraduate college in the case *Bollinger* v. *Gratz*. In contrast to the law school, where race counted as one of numerous factors that the admissions committee considered, and did not unfairly insulate minority students from other applicants, the undergraduate school used a point system based in part on race. The court's majority concluded that this program violated the Constitution's guarantee of equal protection.

The *Bollinger* v. *Gratz* case revealed that the courts would be far less receptive in some instances to claims by African Americans and other racial minorities that the playing field was unequal or that they faced special disadvantages because of their race. If black westerners hoped to improve their status, admissions' committees expected them, like white students, to work hard and use their own initiative. It remained true that colleges, universities, professional schools, and employers could utilize affirmative action programs in order to diversify their student body or workforce, but the courts had reduced significantly the range and scope of these programs. Small wonder that the enrollment of African American students at many western colleges and universities remained static throughout the 1990s. At Texas A&M University and the University of Texas at Austin, the flagship public universities in Texas, the number of black undergraduate students barely increased at all between 1992 and 2000. First-generation African American college students, in particular, had relied heavily on affirmative action programs to attend college. It remained unclear, as result of these court decisions, how African American enrollment patterns would evolve in the future.

Social Marginalization

African American westerners also continued to rely on local, state, and national protest organizations to challenge racial inequities or disparities in their treatment relative to whites. Interracial cooperation and coalitions with a variety of racial groups emerged as an important strategy to bring about full equality and equity as the twentieth century came to a close. African American leaders noted, for example, that Hispanic children were as likely to drop out of high school as were African American children, and leaders from each group worked to improve the graduate rates of their students. Yet even when black westerners allied with other groups in the West, they lagged behind whites in such critical areas as access to health care, affordable child care facilities, job training, and promotions. White women had long complained about a so-called glass ceiling that prevented them from moving up the employment ladder and securing better-paying jobs on parity with their male counterparts. Black westerners had even more reason to complain, for their access to managerial and supervisory jobs lagged behind every other group in the West. African American family median income in 2006 was $31,969 compared to $37,781 for Hispanics and $50,673 for whites. These figures suggest that African Americans, who had made significant strides in closing the disparity between their median income and that of white workers during the 1950s and 1960s, had lost considerable ground by the turn of the twenty-first century. The surge in Hispanic family median income also suggests that Hispanics had become serious competitors with African Americans for many jobs.

Equally disturbing, the jails and prisons in the West overflowed with African Americans, particularly young black males, who had become entangled in the avalanche of illegal drugs, especially heroin and cocaine, which flooded into minority communities and the nation during the 1970s and 1980s. The African American prison population alone exceeded the total of all individuals incarcerated in many industrialized nations in the final decades of the twentieth century. While the rate of incarceration in the United States had remained relatively constant between 1945 and 1970, it soared to unimaginable levels in the next three decades. By 1996, the state and federal prison population reached 1.2 million, a six-fold increase since 1970; and by the turn of the twenty-first century, the total prison population of the United States had passed 2 million.

That African Americans made up the majority of this sizable increase in the nation's prison population after 1970 cast a dark cloud on the future of many African American families, access to numerous opportunities, and contemporary race relations. African Americans comprised half of all prisoners in the United States in 1998, despite the fact that they composed only 13 percent of the nation's population. In California, the most populous state in the West and the nation, four times as many blacks served time in prisons as were enrolled in the state's colleges and universities. In Texas, where African Americans composed 12 percent of the population in 2009, blacks not only swelled the prison population but also represented nearly 39 percent of all inmates on death row. The war on drugs launched by Presidents George H. W. Bush and Bill Clinton exacted especially harsh penalties on individuals who used or sold crack cocaine, the preferred drug in numerous African American inner-city communities. Not surprisingly, by 2000, one-quarter of all prison inmates served prison sentences for nonviolent drug offenses. The disparity in sentencing offenders for crack cocaine compared to powder cocaine, a drug used predominately by whites, was especially glaring. A 1986 law passed by Congress sentenced a person convicted of crack cocaine possession to the same mandatory prison term as someone with 100 times the same amount of powder cocaine. More than 80 percent of the inmates serving time in U.S. prisons for distributing or possessing crack cocaine in 2009 were African American. In 2010, Congress acknowledged the unfairness of the law and voted to significantly reduce the disparity in crack and powder cocaine sentencing.

The War on Drugs, overseen by the U.S. Department of Justice, targeted large urban centers as well as rural communities throughout the West and the nation. Overzealous law enforcement and motivation to secure federal grants from the Department of Justice to assist impoverished communities occasionally caused local police forces to raid black neighborhoods and falsely accuse law-abiding citizens of drug trafficking. One such raid on a black neighborhood in Hearne, Texas, in 2000, for example, led to the arrest and incarceration of twenty-six African American residents on the sole testimony of a paid informant. The events in this case were dramatized in the 2008 feature film *American Violet*. Only after the American Civil Liberties Union waged a vigorous defense in behalf of these individuals and the testimony of the sole confidential informant was discredited, did the courts release and exonerate victims of this miscarriage of justice.

The most spectacular case of racial targeting in the war on drugs, however, involved the small rural community of Tulia, Texas, a West Texas farming community of five thousand residents. In 1999, the police arrested and charged forty-six African Americans, who comprised 13 percent of the town's total black population, with selling cocaine to a white confidential informant. The majority of these people had never been arrested for any offense, nor did they have a history of drug trafficking. Yet on the uncorroborated word of a single white informant, who had been hired by the town's sheriff the previous year to expose drug dealers in Tulia, forty-six men and women had their lives turned upside down. One of them, Joe Moore, a local sixty-year-old hog farmer who had lived much of his life in a one-room shack, received a sentence of ninety years. Freddie Brookins, Jr., a former high school star athlete with no criminal record, was sentenced to twenty years in prison. Additionally, the majority of white residents in Tulia agreed that the forty-six defendants were guilty as charged despite the fact that the arrests had uncovered no cocaine, drug paraphernalia, or any creditable evidence of drug dealing. It became clear, however, to a state judge who was assigned to hear appeals from some of those convicted in Tulia that the testimony of Tom Coleman, the lone confidential informant in this case, was "absolutely riddled with perjury." Coleman was a white former police officer who had been arrested previously on charges of stealing from a county in which he had worked. The presiding judge called him "the most devious, non-responsive law enforcement witness this court has witnessed in 25 years on the bench in Texas." It became clear that Coleman had fabricated much, if not all, of the evidence when victims produced irrefutable evidence that they had been working or in other locales when Coleman reported that he had purchased drugs from them. One victim, an African American woman, was at an Oklahoma City bank at the time of her alleged drug sale, and she produced her signature on a withdrawal slip to refute Coleman's testimony. In time, the NAACP's Legal Defense Fund, the legal arm of the pioneering civil rights organization, led the successful effort to free the Tulia defendants.

The events in both Hearne and Tulia reveal that despite considerable progress in race relations throughout the West, black westerners could still have their lives uprooted by the government, in this case to fight the so-called war on drugs, without the evidence necessary to convict middle-class white Americans. That the war on drugs in some western communities has been racially motivated, and that it even involved specific racial targeting, as in Hearne and Tulia, is indisputable. All of the victims arrested and indicted in these two communities for drug trafficking were African American, and in their haste to capitalize on the financial incentives to participate in the war on drugs, local officials deemed the lives of African Americans, the most vulnerable members of the community, expendable. Furthermore, the exorbitant lengths of the sentences meted out to the black defendants in Tulia harkened back to the famous Scottsboro Boys trial of the 1930s, in which juries were willing to convict African Americans for extraordinary long prison sentences. Finally, only one African American served on a jury in the Tulia case, a revealing statement in-and-of-itself. In the eight separate trials held in that community, blacks were convicted by all-white juries, a throwback to a dark era in the American West.

African Americans in the West also had less access to health care than did whites, a discrepancy that manifested itself in a variety of ways. Black westerners, for example, had the shortest life span of any racial or ethnic group, and black males had the shortest life span of all. The Centers for Disease Control reported that black males in 2007 had a life expectancy of 70 years compared to 75.9 years for white males. Black females fared somewhat better, as they averaged 76.8 years compared to 80.8 years for white females. Black children contracted more childhood diseases than white children and were more likely to suffer from asthma, poor nutrition, and an array of learning disabilities. Poor diets, the lack of prenatal care, indifference, neglect, poverty, and environmental conditions all contributed to these problems. Black expectant mothers who lived on the margins of society economically were far less likely than white middle-class mothers to receive adequate prenatal care or to provide proper nutrition for their infants. Similarly, modest incomes almost guaranteed that black children in the inner cities had higher obesity rates than whites, although Hispanics were not far behind.

African Americans in the West, and throughout the nation, have also been disproportionately affected by the HIV-AIDS epidemic, which has had a devastating impact on many African American communities. African American leaders were slow to grasp the severity of HIV-AIDS, and believed incorrectly that the disease unfairly stigmatized African Americans. The HIV-AIDS crisis constituted an epidemic in some African American communities. The Black AIDS Institute, an independent advocacy group, reported that nearly 600,000 African Americans lived with HIV, and up to 30,000 African Americans become infected every year. The United Nations reported in 2009 that fewer persons worldwide are dying of AIDS, yet the number of AIDS deaths in the African American community continues to rise, despite the wealth of the American nation—surely a marker of ongoing racial-economic inequality among African Americans. Young black females in particular have borne the brunt of this disease. In 2004, AIDS was the leading cause of death for black women between the ages of 24 and 35. In that year, black females were 13 times more likely to die of the disease than white females. The large number of African Americans who contracted HIV-AIDS prompted a number of established civil rights and service organizations such as the NAACP and Delta Sigma Theta Sorority to include AIDS education as part of their community outreach programs.

The large percentage of impoverished black female-headed families in the West served as another indicator that African Americans had lost ground. In 1965, about one in four black families nationally was female headed. By 2000, nearly seven in ten was headed by a woman, and the majority fell at or below the poverty line. By 2006, the *New York Times* reported less than one-in-ten black children under the age of five live with both parents. Although many single parents raised successful, well adjusted children, poverty and the lack of formal education made it exceedingly difficult for many others to secure decent jobs, adequate housing, affordable child care, and provide proper guidance and mentoring for their children. Despite a robust economy during the 1980s and 1990s, it appeared that the momentous civil rights gains of the 1960s had done little to improve the lives of most poor blacks or to prepare them for the future.

The violent response of African Americans and Latinos in 1992, following the exoneration of white police officers who had been charged in the violent beating of Rodney King, an African American who had been stopped for speeding and driving recklessly in Los Angeles, revealed that the West's racial problems remained every bit as serious and unresolved as those of any other region of the nation. Rodney King's arrest and beating by multiple police officers was captured on videotape and shown repeatedly on local and national news stations, and this violent response by the LAPD clearly represented an offense that should have been prosecuted in the minds of the majority of African American westerners as well as many whites. Nevertheless, an all-white jury in Simi Valley, a suburb of Los Angeles, exonerated the white officers on all charges. The Los Angeles riots of 1992 began almost as soon as the verdict was reached. The rebellion, known commonly as the Rodney King riots, began on April 29 and continued until May 4, exceeding the 1965 Watts riot in both its destruction of property and loss of life. The death toll in 1992 reached fifty-four people, and the fighting and skirmishes left hundreds of others injured or wounded. Officials estimated property damage at nearly $1 trillion, a staggering sum. When one measures the 1992 Los Angeles rioting against these two indicators, it emerges as the most destructive urban riot of the twentieth century and one of the most destructive riots in American history.

The Los Angeles riot also differed from earlier race riots in the West and the nation in several important respects. Many of the Los Angeles rioters and looters were Latinos. Some members of the Latino community had also been disappointed with the opportunity that the West had promised when measured against the stark reality of their lives. Occupying low-wage jobs that offered little upward mobility and attending low-performing schools, Latinos, a classification that in L.A. included Mexican Americans, Salvadorians, Nicaraguans, and people from an array of other Latin American and Caribbean countries, had shared little in the boom times of the 1980s and early 1990s. Latinos also began increasingly to occupy housing in neighborhoods that African Americans had formerly dominated such as South Central Los Angeles. By 1992, Latinos, in fact, comprised a majority of residents in this community. Unlike many African Americans, who had been long-standing victims of police brutality in Los Angeles and felt personally aggrieved by the Rodney King beating, Latinos, writes historian Douglas Flamming, "appeared to be motivated by the desire to get a little something for themselves and their families in the midst of this chaos." Finally, the 1992 Los Angeles riots transpired in a city with a black mayor, Tom Bradley, and one in which African Americans had made important political progress since World War II. The large-scale violence and the scale of destruction and loss of life revealed that even the presence of black elected officials did little to address some of the most serious problems that plagued Los Angeles and other western cities as the twentieth century was coming to a close.

The 1992 L.A. riots also revealed serious strains between the African American and Korean communities, tensions that had predated the violence by more than a decade. During the melee, black and Latino rioters targeted Korean-owned shops and businesses in the South Central area and in nearby Korea Town. More than 2,000 Korean-owned businesses were burned or looted by rioters, roughly one-half of the total number of businesses that were destroyed. That Korean-owned businesses, which included small grocery stores, bazaars, and liquor stores were destroyed while black and Latino businesses in proximity were not damaged, was hardly coincidental. Some Latino and Korean business owners reported, in fact, that groups of roving black men "tagged" with spray paint Korean shops before they were torched by looters. H. Eric Schockman, a political scientist and an expert on black-Korean relations, confirmed this opinion when he stated, "I think it was very methodical." Schockman and others noted that Korean shopkeepers and businesspersons became highly visible targets, much like Jews had been in the 1960s when black rioters destroyed their businesses in urban ghettos throughout the nation.

Although Koreans became scapegoats for many of the ills of urban life in western cities like L.A., African Americans also felt that Koreans and other Asian businesspersons gave little back to their communities and often felt contempt for the local residents who supported their establishments. Black residents of South Central complained, for example, that few Korean businesses employed African Americans, relying instead on family members or Latinos as employees. Similarly, many African Americans felt that Korean shop owners disrespected them and viewed them with deep suspicion. Leonard Brown, a lifelong resident of South Central, stated, "They just see you as black. We're supposed to be stupid, so they treat us that way." Some contend that these tensions had come to a head a year before the verdict in the trial of the white officers who beat Rodney King, when a Korean shop owner named Soon Ja Du pointed a gun at the back of Latasha Harlins, a fifteen-year-old African American girl, and pulled the trigger, killing her instantly. Although the shooting was caught on videotape and Harlins had only been accused of shoplifting by the store owner, a judge placed Soon Ja Du on five years' probation after she was convicted of voluntary manslaughter. The verdict outraged African Americans in South Central and in many other western communities and explains, at least in part, the outrage and fury unleashed by some rioters after Rodney King's assailants were acquitted by a suburban jury. It had become apparent that African Americans and Korean Americans would need to mend their fractured relationship in the future if they hoped ever to live as peaceful neighbors in the West.

Conclusion

At the turn of the twenty-first century, African American westerners could take solace in the fact that virtually every overt sign of legal racial discrimination had been eradicated. Through their collective struggle, as well as the commitment of progressive whites, Hispanics, and the courts, black westerners had overcome decades of segregation and de facto discrimination. It would have been unimaginable in the 1960s, in the wake of the cataclysmic urban riots in cities like Los Angeles and Oakland, that African American politicians would serve as mayors, police chiefs, councilmen, and city managers of numerous western cities.

But had these changes brought about full equality, and had black political empowerment resulted in greater access and equity for African American westerners in general? Here, unfortunately, the record was far more mixed, and blacks in the American West entered the new century cautiously optimistic. Two qualities that African Americans had proven consistently during their nearly five centuries in the American West were their resilience and ability to adapt to new and difficult circumstances. As African American westerners looked toward the future, they took considerable pride in the progress that they had achieved collectively. For many of them, however, much work remained unfinished.

Suggested Readings

Dreyfuss, Joel and Charles Lawrence III. *The Bakke Case: The Politics of Inequality.* New York: Harcourt Brace and Jovanovich, 1979.

Frear, Yvonne Davis. "Juanita Craft and the Struggle to End Segregation in Dallas, 1945–1955." Sam W. Haynes and Cary D. Wintz, eds. *Major Problems in Texas History: Documents and Essays.* Boston: Houghton Mifflin Company, 2002.

Gutierrez, Henry J. "Racial Politics in Los Angeles: Black and Mexican American Challenges to Unequal Education in the 1960s." *Southern California Quarterly* 78 (1996): 51–86.

Hartman, Chester. *City for Sale: The Transformation of San Francisco.* Berkeley: University of California, 2002.

Kelly, Samuel E. and Quintard Taylor. *Dr. Sam, Soldier, Educator, Advocate, Friend: An Autobiography.* Seattle: University of Washington Press, 2010.

Lawson, Steven F. *Running for Freedom: Civil Rights and Black Politics in America Since 1941,* 2nd ed. New York: Wiley, 1997.

Foley, Neil. *Quest for Equality: The Failed Promise of Black-Brown Solidarity.* Cambridge: Harvard University Press, 2010.

Richardson, James. *Willie Brown: A Biography.* Berkeley: University of California Press, 1996.

Shakur, Sanyika. *Monster: The Autobiography of an L.A. Gang Member.* New York: Grove Press, 2004.

Self, Robert. *American Babylon: Race and the Struggle for Postwar Oakland.* Princeton: Princeton University Press, 2003.

Rogers, Mary Beth. *Barbara Jordan: American Hero.* New York: Random House, 1998.

White, Michael. *White Metropolis: Race, Ethnicity, and Religion in Dallas, 1841–2001.* Austin: University of Texas Press, 2006.

Epilogue

African Americans did find opportunity in the American West, but they also experienced considerable hardship, discrimination, intermittent racial violence, and failed expectations there. Ironically, the earliest African American settlers who came West with the Spanish explorers and settled in New Spain in the sixteenth and seventeenth centuries possessed a broader range of freedom than those blacks who migrated west and settled in U.S. territory following the 1848 Treaty of Guadalupe-Hidalgo at the conclusion of the War with Mexico. Thus a black scout such as Esteban de Dorantes, despite his status as an enslaved person, played an important role in the exploration of New Spain. Similarly, black women such as Isabel de Olvera, one of many Spanish-speaking black settlers who resided in New Spain in the early 1600s, possessed multiple identities, intermarried with Indians and other Spanish castas, settled communities, and were widely respected.

Rather than feeling like outcasts, nineteenth-century black westerners brought considerable optimism and enthusiasm with them to the West. Whether they arrived as mountain men, gold miners, or in search of cheap land like many white immigrants, black westerners had high expectations that they would succeed. They also believed that their experience in the region would prove more advantageous economically and politically, and that it was a place where they could carve out a better life for their children and future generations. As African Americans settled in such diverse western communities as

Helena, Montana, Topeka, Kansas, Denver, Colorado, Tulsa, Oklahoma, Seattle, Washington, and San Antonio, Texas, they brought an array of expectations and desires. They also established numerous institutions that had served as pillars of Africans American communities for many generations in other regions of the country. Black community institutions such as schools, churches, newspapers, lodges, fraternities, and women's clubs united disparate black residents across class and generational lines. They also reminded black westerners that they were not alone in their day-to-day struggles and provided hope, fellowship, and solace in any unfamiliar environment.

While black westerners had much in common with white immigrants who moved West during the nineteenth and twentieth century, the African American experience was unique in many respects. No white immigrant, despite his or her social class or previous status, grappled with the heritage of slavery and the stigma that bondage represented. Similarly, white immigrants never faced the pernicious and systematic discrimination laws that relegated many black westerners to a second-class, inferior status. African Americans, irrespective of their education or social position, unlike white immigrants, had to fight to obtain basic citizenship rights in the western states and territories. Joining forces with national protest organizations such as the NAACP, black westerners challenged Jim Crow laws, demanding the right to vote, educate their children in integrated schools, and live in integrated neighborhoods. Like African American activists in other regions of the nation, black westerners placed an enormous faith in the U.S. Constitution. By the early decades of the twentieth century, federal courts up to the U.S. Supreme Court proved more willing to overturn long-established racial practices when they outlawed the "Grandfather Clauses." By mid-century, the Supreme Court outlawed segregation in public education in *Brown* v. *Board of Education of Topeka* (1954), arguably one of the most significant Supreme Court cases of the twentieth century.

African Americans also faced considerably more violence than white immigrants who went west. Although the number of lynchings in the West never rivaled that of the Deep South, Texas, in particular, recorded nearly three hundred African American victims of this heinous crime. Black westerners also faced race riots and retribution from angry white mobs in western communities such as Tulsa, Oklahoma, where the entire Greenwood District was burned and looted by angry white mobs in 1921, and at least twenty-one African Americans lost their lives. These black men and women learned that white westerners could be every bit as brutal and vicious as white southerners, and that their lives could be just as expendable as their black southern counterparts on the whim of hostile whites.

World War II changed the West more profoundly than any single event in the twentieth century. Black migrants, particularly those from the southern states, renewed their faith in the West by moving to the region in massive numbers. Emboldened by a national commitment to defeat nazism and fascism abroad, African Americans were also committed to ending discrimination at home. So as black migrants came west during the war by the hundreds of thousands to work in West Coast shipyards and defense industries, they also challenged discriminatory policies within many of those workplaces as well as in the U.S. armed forces. This wartime activism set the stage for the modern civil rights movement in the West and the nation during the 1950s and 1960s.

The West also differs from the rest of the nation because of its unique mixture of racial minorities. Hispanics and Asians, particularly Chinese immigrants, outnumbered African Americans in many communities until World War II. Because of the region's rich racial and ethnic diversity, African Americans often shared schools, neighborhoods, and public space with members of these groups in such cities as Seattle, Denver, Portland, Los Angeles, and San Francisco. Like African Americans, these racial and ethnic minorities faced discrimination and their own degree of second-class citizenship in the West. Organized labor in California viewed the Chinese as serious competitors, and federal law restricted further Chinese immigration to the United States in 1882 through the

Chinese Exclusion Act. Japanese immigrants who came west also faced discrimination. Following Japan's bombing of Pearl Harbor on December 7, 1941, Japanese Americans in the United States faced increased discrimination, culminating in their forcible removal at the hands of the federal government from their homes, farms, and businesses along the West Coast and incarceration in camps overseen by armed guards throughout the duration of the war.

The common hardships African Americans and other racial minorities faced in the West brought surprisingly little collaboration between these groups. By World War II, African American, Asian, and Hispanic leaders were becoming somewhat more likely to serve on interracial committees and the boards of prestigious civic and statewide organizations than in the past. Only on rare occasions did members from these groups coalesce to fight a common grievance. As Scott Kurashige showed in his important book, *The Shifting Ground of Race: Black and Japanese Americans in the Making of Multiethnic Los Angeles*, African Americans and Japanese Americans came together in 2000 to save the Holiday Bowl, a multicultural bowling alley that served as a symbol of community pride and a shared public space, from demolition. Many ethnic and racial groups also participated in the demonstrations led by CORE in the San Francisco Bay Area between 1963 and 1964. Similarly, hundreds of black, white, Hispanic, Native American, and Asian students participated in the year-long strike at San Francisco State University in 1968, which culminated in the creation of a Black Studies Program.

But coalitions between African Americans and other racial minorities in the West proved the exception rather than the rule. Hispanics, the largest ethnic minority in most western communities, seldom embraced the overtures of African American leaders to join their own struggle for civil rights with the one that blacks waged for full citizenship. Cultural and language barriers probably kept blacks and Hispanics apart in some instances, but many Hispanic leaders also insisted that the two struggles were quite different. As Neil Foley and others have argued, many important Hispanic leaders insisted that Hispanics be racially defined as white, rather than as Mexican or Latin American, and that it would be disadvantageous, therefore, to join a struggle for civil rights where skin color was central to determine a group's legal status. In some instances, Hispanics joined white segregationists in Arizona and Texas to deny African Americans access to public accommodations and service at their businesses. "If Mexican restaurants would refuse to serve Negroes, Anglo restaurants might begin serving Mexicans," explained Manuel Avila, a member of the American G.I. Forum, a Mexican American civil rights organization. For this reason, "Mexicans must say to Negroes, I'm White and you can't come into my restaurant." Avila's position may well have represented the views of numerous Hispanic leaders in the West. For example, Felix Tijerina, the president of League of United Latin American Citizens, refused to serve African American patrons at a chain of restaurants he owned in Houston, a policy that remained in force until the passage of the 1964 Civil Rights Act. Under these circumstances, it is surprising that any significant alliances developed between African Americans and Mexican Americans in the West.

With or without the support of other racial minorities, African Americans continued to challenge inequality in many ways. These challenges took on a new urgency during the 1960s, as black westerners combined their long struggle for full equality and greater access to jobs, housing, and education with the national civil rights movement. In the wake of the 1965 Watts riot in Los Angeles, black westerners clearly voiced their discontent at the slow, piecemeal reforms that earlier African American leaders had accepted as stepping stones to full equality. The time for full access to racial equality, in their minds, had arrived. Gradualism was a thing of the past.

Since the 1970s, black westerners have adopted new strategies in their quest to overcome decades of ingrained prejudice, indifference, and racial inertia. Black western politicians have achieved surprising success in their bids to become mayors of major western cities such as Seattle, Denver, Los Angeles, and San Francisco, to name just a few. Moreover, African Americans succeeded in gaining entry to state legislatures, as well as being elected to Congress. The charismatic African American congresswoman Barbara Jordan serves as one of the best examples, as in 1966 she became the first black person elected to the Texas State Senate since Reconstruction. She also became the first African American woman to serve in that body. Still other western cities elected African Americans to an array of local offices such as city manager, police chief, and school boards. The desire to enter politics was part of a broader strategy as well as an assumption that change in race relations would come about if more African Americans held significant political positions.

African American businesspersons and entrepreneurs also made significant progress since the 1970s, and some individuals have climbed the corporate ladder with an ease and rapidity that their parents would never have thought possible. Black students also increasingly began to break the unspoken racial barriers in some of the most prestigious western colleges and universities such as Stanford University, the University of California, Berkeley, the University of California, Los Angeles, the University of Washington, and the University of Texas at Austin. These were remarkable gains when measured against the decades-long struggle for access and inclusion that African Americans had waged during the era of the Gold Rush, in the wake of World War I, or during the massive migration of black southerners to western cities and territories during World War II.

And, yet, despite gains like these, the West by the turn of the twenty-first century continued to represent a paradox to many African Americans. They could not disregard the region's racist past, but they remained cautiously optimistic about their place in the region's future. Will opportunity be available for those who are willing to work hard and educate themselves, irrespective of their skin color? Some black westerners answered this question by returning to the South or to other Sunbelt states, a pattern replicated in other regions of the nation. The majority of black westerners, anchored by jobs, mortgage payments, family obligations, and kinship networks remained in the region, hopeful that the West would at long last fulfill its promise to serve as a bellwether region for the rest of the nation and truly become a welcoming home for all of its people.

Bibliographical Essay

Overview

Unlike many established fields in African American history, the general literature on the African American experience in the American West is relatively small. The best general introduction is Quintard Taylor, *In Search of the Promised Land* (New York, 1998). Douglas Flamming's, *African Americans in the West* (Santa Barbara, CA, 2009) updates many of Taylor's arguments and contains an excellent discussion on the current and future state of scholarship on blacks in the West. Less expansive in its coverage, but nonetheless the product of many decades of exhaustive scholarship, is W. Sherman Savage, *Blacks in the West* (Westport, CT, 1976). Two excellent essays that explore the historiography of African Americans in the western states and territories are Lawrence B. De Graaf, "Recognition, Racism, and Reflections on Western Black History," *Pacific Historical Review* (February 1975) and Quintard Taylor, "From Esteban to Rodney King: Five Centuries of African American History in the West," *Montana: The Magazine of Western History* (Winter 1996), 2–23. African Americans are seldom mentioned in western history textbooks published prior to the 1960s, so broad histories of the West are of little value. More useful in reconstructing the role of African Americans in the broader story of the settlement of the West are Richard White, *"It's Your Misfortune and None of My Own": A*

New History of the American West (Norman, OK, 1991) and Walter Nugent, *Into the West: The Story of Its People* (New York, 1999). Less expansive in its coverage is Gerald D. Nash, *A Brief History of the American West since 1945* (New York, 2001). Several edited collections contain important material on African Americans in the West. Among these are Suchen Chan, Douglas Henry Daniels, Mario T. Garcia, and Terry P. Wilson, eds., *People of Color in the American West* (Lexington, MA, 1994) and Quintard Taylor and Shirley Ann Wilson Moore, eds., *African American Women Confront the West, 1600–2000* (Norman, OK, 2003). Far broader in its scope, however, is Quintard Taylor, Lawrence B. De Graaf, and Kevin Mulroy, eds., *Seeking El Dorado: African Americans in California, 1769–1997* (Seattle, 2001).

Chapter One

Numerous scholars have cited the Spanish origins of the black presence in the West. Esteban's journey throughout the Americas has particularly intrigued historians. Consult Cleve Hallenbeck, ed., *The Journey of Fray Marcos de Niza* (Dallas, 1987); A. D. F. Bandelier, ed., *The Journey of Alvar Nunez Cabeza de Vaca* (New York, 1905); David J. Weber, *The Mexican Frontier, 1821–1846: The American Southwest under Mexico* (Albuquerque, 1982); Jack D. Forbes, "Black Pioneers: The Spanish-Speaking Afroamericans of the Southwest," *Phylon* (Fall 1966). Considerably less material has been published on Spanish-speaking black women. On the role of Isabel de Olvera, see George P. Hammond and Agapito Rey, eds., *Don Juan de Onate: Colonizer of New Mexico, 1595–1628* (Albuquerque, 1953). Numerous scholars have studied the role of color and caste in Mexico and Latin America. The best accounts are Magnus Morner, *Race Mixture and the History of Latin America* (Boston, 1967) and Morner, ed., *Race and Class in Latin America* (New York, 1970). For a broad survey of Spanish-speaking persons of African descent in Texas, see Alwyn Barr, *Black Texans: A History of Negroes in Texas, 1528–1971*, 2d.

ed. (Norman, OK, 1996). The early black presence in San Diego has been documented by David J. Weber in "A Black American in Mexican San Diego: Two Recently Discovered Documents," *Journal of San Diego History* 20 (1974): 29–32.

The role of African Americans in the founding and settlement of Los Angeles has been documented in David J. Weber, *Foreigners in Their Native Land: Historical Roots of the Mexican Americans* (Albuquerque, 1973); Lonnie Bunch III, *Black Angelos: The Afro-American in Los Angeles, 1850–1950* (Los Angeles, 1988); and Quintard Taylor, *In Search of the Racial Frontier* (New York, 1998). California's early black settlers, especially those who came with the Spanish explorers and during the Gold Rush, are covered superbly in Rudolph Lapp, *Blacks in Gold Rush California* (New Haven, CT, 1977). Shorter accounts of African Americans in California during the Gold Rush can be found in Albert S. Broussard, "Slavery in California Revisited: The Fate of a Kentucky Slave in Gold Rush California," *Pacific Historian* (Spring 1985): 17–21. J. S. Holliday, *The World Rushed In: The California Gold Rush Experience* ((New York, 1981) is a much broader study of the gold rush. Also W. H. Brands, *The Age of Gold* (New York, 2003), a lively account of the California Gold Rush, is useful in reconstructing the mood and feeling of this era. On the struggle of the slave Archy Lee to gain his freedom, see Rudolph Lapp, *Archy Lee, A Fugitive Slave Case* (San Francisco, 1969) and Lapp, *Blacks in Gold Rush California* (New Haven, CT, 1977); William F. Franklin, "The Archy Lee Case: The California Supreme Court Refuses to Free a Slave," *Pacific Historical Review* 33 (May 1963): 137–154; and Lapp, "Negro Rights Activities in Gold Rush California," *California Historical Society Quarterly* 45 (March 1966): 3–20.

The most complete discussion on African Americans in nineteenth-century Hawaii, although scant, appears in Miles M. Jackson, ed., *They Followed the Trade Winds: African Americans in Hawaii, Social Process in Hawaii* 43 (2004). More specialized studies of the early black experience in Hawaii include Marc Scruggs, "Anthony

Allen: A Prosperous American of African Descent in Early Nineteenth Century Hawaii," *Hawaiian Journal of History* 26 (1992): 55–92. Betsey Stockton, the first black female missionary in Hawaii, continues to attract the attention of scholars in many fields. See John A. Andrew III, "Betsey Stockton: Stranger in a Strange Land," *Journal of Presbyterian History* 52 (1974): 157–66 and Constance K. Escher, "She Calls Herself Betsey Stockton," *Princeton History* 10 (1991): 71–101.

Unlike Hawaii, there is considerable material on the African American presence in Texas. William Goyens' life and experiences have been covered by Victor H. Treat, "William Goyens: Free Negro Entrepreneur," in *Black Leaders: Texans for Their Times,* eds., Alwyn Barr and Robert A. Calvert (Austin, 1981), and Alwyn Barr, *Black Texans: A History of Negroes in Texas, 1528–1995,* 2d ed. (Norman, OK, 1996). The best study of Stephen F. Austin and the Austin colony is Gregg Cantrell, *Stephen F. Austin, Empresario of Texas* (New Haven, CT, 1999). The literature on slavery in Texas is voluminous. The single best volume is Randolph B. Campbell, *An Empire for Slavery: The Peculiar Institution in Texas* (Baton Rouge, LA, 1989). Also useful are T. Lindsey Baker and Julie P. Baker, eds., *Till Freedom Cried Out: Memories of Texas Slave Life* (College Station, TX, 1997) and Ron Tyler and Lawrence Murphy, eds., *The Slave Narratives of Texas* (Austin, 1974). The most complete collection of slave narratives, however, which contains numerous narratives from Texas slaves, is George P. Rawick, ed., *The American Slave: A Composite Autobiography* (Westport, CT, 1972–79). On slave resistance in Texas, consult Paul D. Lack, "Dave: A Rebellious Slave," in *Black Leaders: Texans for Their Times,* eds., Alwyn Barr and Robert A. Calvert (Austin, 1981).

Although many western scholars have cited the presence of African Americans in the West as fur trappers and traders, few have written full-scale biographies of these individuals. On James Beckwourth's life and career, see Thomas D. Bonner, ed., *Life and Adventures of James Beckwourth* (Lincoln, NE, 1972); Delmont R.

Oswald, "James P. Beckwourth," in LeRoy Hafen, ed., *The Mountain Men and the Fur Trade of the Far West* (Glendale, CA, 1968), and Hafen, "The Last Years of James P. Beckwourth," *Colorado Magazine* 5 (August 1928): 134–39. A much broader study of African Americans on the frontier is Kenneth W. Porter, *The Negro on the American Frontier* (New York, 1971).

California, which attracted a sizable black migration and contained the largest free black community outside of Texas, is the focus of Lapp, *Blacks in Gold Rush California* (New Haven, CT, 1977) and Douglas Henry Daniels, *Pioneer Urbanites: A Social and Cultural History of Black San Francisco* (Philadelphia, 1980). An excellent comparative study of racial minorities in nineteenth-century California is Arnoldo De León, *Racial Frontiers: Africans, Chinese, and Mexicans in Western America, 1848–1890* (Albuquerque, 2002). The struggle to obtain political and civil rights is California has been covered admirably by Albert S. Broussard, *Black San Francisco: The Struggle for Racial Equality in the West, 1900–54* (Lawrence, 1993) and Philip M. Montesano, "San Francisco Black Churches in the Early 1860s: Political Pressure Groups," *California Historical Society Quarterly* 52 (Summer 1973): 145–52. The role of Philip Alexander Bell, a pioneering black journalist, is examined in John H. Telfer, "Philip Alexander Bell and the *San Francisco Elevator,*" *San Francisco Historical and Cultural Society Monograph* (August 1966).

The struggle to break down discriminatory barriers in California schools is the subject of Charles M. Wollenberg, *All Deliberate Speed: Segregation and Exclusion in California Schools, 1855–1975* (Berkeley, 1976), and Susan Bragg, "Knowledge is Power: Sacramento Blacks and the Public Schools, 1854–1860," *California History* 75 (1996): 214–21. The political activities of California's black community has been documented carefully by Howard H. Bell, "Negroes in California, 1849–1859," *Phylon* 28 (1967): 151–60, and Lynn M. Hudson, "A New Look, or I'm Not Mammy to Everybody in California': Mary Ellen Pleasant, a Black Entrepreneur," *Journal of the West* 32 (1993): 35–40. For a more complete view of Mary

Ellen Pleasant as both a businesswoman and civil rights leader in San Francisco, see Hudson, *The Making of "Mammy Pleasant": A Black Entrepreneur in Nineteenth-Century San Francisco* (Urbana, IL, 2003). An excellent first-person account of a black businessman, activist, and community leader is Mifflin Gibbs, *Shadow and Light: An Autobiography* (New York, 1968). James Fisher, "The Struggle for Negro Testimony in California, 1851–1863," *Southern California Quarterly* 51 (December 1969): 313–34, evaluates the protracted struggle of black Californians to obtain the right to testify in court against whites. See also Brainerd Dyer, "One Hundred Years of Negro Suffrage," *Pacific Historical Review* 41 (February 1968): 1–20. For additional examples of black activism and political leadership in California, see Odell A. Thurman, "The Negro in California before 1890," *Pacific Historian* 19 (1975): 321–46.

Anti-black legislation and Negro Exclusion laws in the western states are covered in Eugene Berwanger, *The Frontier Against Slavery: Western Anti-Negro Prejudice and the Slavery Extension Controversy* (Urbana, IL, 1967) and Robert K. Dykstra, *Bright Radical Star: Black Freedom and White Supremacy on the Hawkeye Frontier* (Cambridge, MA, 1993). James W. Pilton examines the migration of African Americans to British Columbia during the 1850s in Pilton, "Negro Settlement in British Columbia, 1858–1871," M.A. thesis, University of British Columbia, 1951. Two recent accounts, though less thorough than Pilton's scholarship, are Malcolm Edwards, "The War of Complexional Distinction: Blacks in Gold Rush California and British Columbia," *California Historical Quarterly* 66 (1977): 34–45, and Crawford Kilian, *"Go Do Some Great Things": The Black Pioneers of British Columbia* (Vancouver, 1978).

The role of black westerners in the Civil War has generally escaped the attention of scholars, including the majority of western historians. On the role of African Americans in Texas, see Randolph B. Campbell, *An Empire for Slavery* (Baton Rouge, LA, 1989) and Ira Berlin, ed., *Freedom: A Documentary History of Emancipation, 1861–1867, series II: The Black Military Experience* (Cambridge, MA,

1982). The role and participation of black Kansans, however, has been documented more thoroughly. See Quintard Taylor, *In Search of the Racial Frontier* (New York, 1998), Henry Clay Bruce, *The New Man: Twenty-nine Years a Slave, Twenty-Nine years a Free Man* (New York, 1969), Richard B. Sheridan, "From Slavery in Missouri to Freedom in Kansas: The Influx of Black Fugitives and Contrabands into Kansas, 1854–1864," *Kansas History* 12 (Spring 1989). Sheridan's article also discusses the role of the Underground Railroad in Kansas. Several scholars take issue with the interpretation that white Kansans possessed benevolent attitudes toward African Americans, stressing instead that the majority of Kansans did not favor racial equality. See, for example, James Rawley, *Race and Politics:"Bleeding Kansas" and the Coming of the Civil War* (Philadelphia, 1969) and Albert Castel, "Civil War Kansas and the Negro," *Journal of Negro History* 52 (April 1966), 125–38. The best account of black Civil War soldiers, including those who served in Kansas regiments, remains Dudley Cornish, *The Sable Arm: Black Troops in the Union Army, 1861–1865* (New York, 1966). Robert J. Chandler examines the role of the Republican Party to assist African Americans during the Civil War. See Chandler, "Friends in Time of Need, Republicans and Black Civil Rights in California during the Civil War Era," *Arizona and the West* 24 (Winter 1982): 319–40. The role of a pivotal Kansas politician and officer who supported African American participation in the Civil War is discussed in Wendell Holmes Stephenson, *The Political Career of General James H. Lane* (Topeka, 1930). The role of black soldiers in the battle of Honey Springs is covered in detail in Lary C. Rampp and Donald L. Rampp, *The Civil War in the Indian Territory* (Austin, 1975).

Chapter 2

Juneteenth has become one of the most celebrated African American holidays in the nation. For its origins, see Alwyn Barr, *Black Texans: A History of African Americans in Texas, 1528–1995,* 2d ed. (Norman,

OK, 1996). Elizabeth Hayes Turner has evaluated how Juneteenth and its meaning has changed over time in "Juneteenth: Emancipation and Memory," eds. Gregg Cantrell and Elizabeth Hayes Turner, *Lone Star Past: Memory and History in Texas* (College Station, TX, 2007).The fate of African Americans in post–Civil War Texas is the subject of Lawrence D. Rice, *The Negro in Texas, 1874–1900* (Baton Rouge, LA, 1971). A far more compelling account of how blacks in Texas and throughout the former Confederate states fared immediately after the Civil War is Leon Litwack, *Been in the Storm So Long: The Aftermath of Slavery* (New York, 1979). Dan T. Carter also captures the indiscriminate violence that black Texans faced in the wake of the Civil War in *When the War Was Over: The Failure of Self-Reconstruction in the South, 1865–1867* (Baton Rouge, LA, 1985). The individual struggle of Azeline Hearne, an African American woman in Texas who fought to protect her land from predatory whites during the era of Reconstruction, is the subject of Dale Baum, *Counterfeit Justice: The Judicial Odyssey of Texas Freedwoman Azeline Hearne* (Baton Rouge, LA, 2009). The creation of public and private black colleges in Texas following the Civil War has been well documented. The best studies include Alton Hornsby, "The Freedman's Bureau Schools in Texas, 1865–1870," *Southwestern Historical Quarterly* 76 (April 1973): 397–417; Alwyn Barr, *Black Texans* (Norman, OK, 1996); James M. McPherson, "White Liberals and Black Power in Negro Education, 1865–1915," *American Historical Review* 75 (June 1970): 1357–86; and George R. Woolfolk, *Prairie View: A Study in Public Conscience, 1878–1946* (New York, 1962). The best overview of private black colleges is Michael R. Heintze, *Private Black Colleges in Texas, 1865–1954* (College Station, TX, 1985). There are several excellent general histories of black education in the South that contain useful material on Texas. They include James D. Anderson, *The Education of Blacks in the South, 1860–1935* (Chapel Hill, NC, 1988); and Henry Allen Bullock, *A History of Negro Education in the South from 1619 to the Present* (Cambridge, MA,1967).

Several important studies have appeared on nineteenth-century western black politicians. Among the best is Douglas Hales, *A Southern Family in White and Black: The Cuneys of Texas* (College Station, TX, 2003). Hales' work is the first book-length study of Norris Wright Cuney and his descendants. Several books and articles have examined George Ruby's career. Among them are Carl H. Moneyhon, "George T. Ruby and the Politics of Expediency in Texas," in Howard N. Rabinowitz, ed., *Southern Black Leaders of the Reconstruction Era* (Urbana, IL, 1982) and Randall Woods, "George T. Ruby: A Black Militant in the White Business Community," *Red River Valley Historical Review* 1 (1974): 269–80. Other useful studies that examine the role of black political leaders in Texas include Merlene Pitre, *Through Many Dangers, Toils, and Snares: The Black Leadership of Texas, 1868–1900* (Austin, 1985); Alwyn Barr, *Reconstruction to Reform: Texas Politics, 1876–1906* (Austin, 1971); Brewer, *Negro Legislators of Texas*; Barr, "Black Legislators of Reconstruction Texas," *Civil War History* 32 (December 1986): 340–52; Greg Cantrell, *Feeding the Wolf: John B. Rayner and the Politics of Race, 1850–1918* (Wheeling, IL, 2001) and Cantrell, *Kenneth and John B. Rayner and the Limits of Southern Dissent* (Urbana, IL, 1993). A short though useful article that explores the life and political career of Matthew Gaines has been written by Ann Patton Malone, "Matt Gaines: Reconstruction Politician," in eds., Alwyn Barr and Robert A. Calvert, *Black Leaders: Texans for Their Times* (Austin, 1981). Carl Moneyhon also notes the importance of Gaines' political career in *Republicanism in Reconstruction Texas* (Austin, 1980).

Considerably less material is available on the early African American communities along the Pacific Coast. On Oregon's black community, including its leadership and struggles to gain equal rights, see Elizabeth McLagan, *A Peculiar Paradise: A History of Blacks in Oregon, 1788–1940* (Portland, 1980). For a survey of Colorado's black politicians, consult Eugene Berwanger, "Hardin and Langston: Western Black Spokesman of the Reconstruction Era," *Journal of Negro History* 64 (Spring 1979). Berwanger's *The West and Reconstruction* (Urbana, IL, 1981), is also important in understanding the role of African Americans in the broader picture of Reconstruction politics in the western states and territories. Historian Nell Painter cites the activities of Edward McCabe briefly in *Exodusters: Black Migration to Kansas after Reconstruction* (New York, 1976). To reconstruct the early civil rights activities of black San Franciscans, see Albert S. Broussard, *Black San Francisco* (Lawrence, 1993) and Douglas Henry Daniels, *Pioneer Urbanites* (Philadelphia, 1980).

The literature on the Buffalo Soldiers is extensive, as these men have often been relegated to iconic status rather than treated as authentic historical figures. The best short history, however, remains William H. Leckie, *Buffalo Soldiers: A Narrative of the Negro Calvary in the West* (Norman, OK, 1967). In addition, numerous fine studies examine the role of African American soldiers in the western states and territories. See James N. Leiker, *Racial Borders: Black Soldiers Along the Rio Grande* (College Station, TX, 2002) and Leiker, "Black Soldiers at Fort Hays, Kansas, 1867–1869: A Study in Civilian and Military Violence," *Great Plains Quarterly* 17 (Winter 1997): 3–17; William A. Dobak and Thomas D. Phillips, *The Black Regulars, 1866–1898* (Norman, OK, 2001); and Arlen Fowler, *The Black Infantry in the West, 1869–1891* (Westport, CT, 1971). The first study that examines the lives and voices of the Buffalo Soldiers through documents and primary sources is Frank N. Schubert, *Voices of the Buffalo Soldiers: Records, Reports, and Recollections of Military Life and Service in the West* (Albuquerque, 2009). An excellent anthology that has appeared recently is Bruce A. Glasrud and Michael N. Searles, eds., *Buffalo Soldiers in the West: A Black Soldiers Anthology* (College Station, TX, 2007). This volume also contains an extensive bibliography on the Buffalo Soldiers.

The careers of individual soldiers, although scare, are confined almost exclusively to the officers corps. On the life and military career of Henry O. Flipper, see Flipper, *The Colored Cadet at West Point: Autobiography of Lieutenant Henry Ossian Flipper* (Lincoln, NE, 1998). A different perspective regarding Flipper's innocence is portrayed by Charles M. Robinson III, *The Fall of a Black Officer:*

Racism and the Myth of Henry O. Flipper (Norman, OK, 2008). Bernard Nalty has written a solid general history of African Americans in the military, including some important work on Henry Flipper and the Buffalo Soldiers. See Nalty, *Strength for the Fight: A History of African Americans in the Military* (New York, 1986). Colonel Charles Young's life is explored in Brian G. Shellum, *Black Cadet in a White Bastion: Charles Young at West Point* (Lincoln, NE, 2006). Although no one to date has written a book or article on the Buffalo Soldiers' role in protecting the national parks in the West, the website of the National Park Service contains some useful information.

African American cowboys continue to fascinate both scholars and the general public, and considerable scholarship has been devoted to their multifaceted roles. The best starting point is Philip Durham and Everett L. Jones, *The Negro Cowboys* (New York, 1965). The many jobs and responsibilities that African American cowboys performed in the West are explored carefully and meticulously in Sara R. Massey, ed., *Black Cowboys of Texas* (College Station, TX, 2005). For biographies of individual black cowboys, consult Bailey C. Hanes, *Bill Pickett, Bulldogger: The Biography of a Black Cowboy* (Norman, OK, 1989); and Michael Searles, "Taking Out the Buck and Putting in a Trick: The Black Working Cowboy's Art of Breaking and Keeping a Good Cow Horse," *Journal of the West* 44 (Spring 2005): 53–60. An account of Bose Ikard can be found in James Evetts Haley, *Charles Goodnight, Cowman and Plainsman* (Norman, OK, 1949). Equally important is Richard Slatta, *Cowboys of the Americas* (New Haven, CT, 1990). Kenneth W. Porter has also written widely on black cowboys and African Americans who worked on the western frontier. See Porter, *The Negro on the American Frontier* (New York, 1971).

Numerous books cite the presence of blacks on the cattle drives. See, for example, Terry C. Jordan, *Trails to Texas: Southern Routes of Western Cattle Ranching* (Lincoln, NE, 1981); Kenneth Porter, "Negro Labor in the Western Cattle Industry," *Labor History* 10 ((Summer 1969): 346–74. An informative essay on black cowboys in Kansas is C. Robert Haywood, "'No Less a Man': Blacks in Cow Town Dodge City, 1876–1886," *Western Historical Quarterly* 19 (May 1988). Art T. Burton has broken new ground and written a recent account of Bass Reeves, an African American deputy marshal. See Burton, *Black Gun, Silver Star: The Life and Legend of Frontier Marshal Bass Reeves* (Lincoln, NE, 2006). Useful material on African American cowboys can also be located in Ronnie C. Tyler, Douglas E. Barnett, and Roy R. Barkley, eds., *The New Handbook of Texas, 6 vols.* (Austin, 1996) and Howard Lamar, ed., *The New Encyclopedia of the American West* (New Haven, CT, 1998). Brief accounts of Henrietta Williams Foster and Johanna Jolly can be found in Sara Massey, ed., *Black Cowboys of Texas* (College Station, TX, 2005). Unfortunately, African American women remain under-represented in the broader literature on black cowboys.

The best discussions of black rural life in Texas are provided by Barr, *Black Texans* (Norman, OK, 1996). Debra Reid has also written an engaging study of black Texans who worked with the Texas Extension Service. See Reid, *Reaping a Greater Harvest: African Americans, the Extension Service, and Rural Reform in Jim Crow Texas* (College Station, TX, 2007). The Populist appealed to African Americans in Texas, and Gregg Cantrell's study of John B. Rayner is excellent. See Cantrell, *Kenneth and John B. Rayner and the Limits of Southern Dissent* (Urbana, IL, 1993). Other important works on blacks and the Populist Party include Jack Abramowitz, "John B. Rayner: A Grass-Roots Leader," *Journal of Negro History* 36 (April 1951) and Roscoe Martin, *The People's Party in Texas* (Austin, 1970). The best case study of blacks and the Populist Party is Lawrence Goodwyn, "Populist Dreams and Negro Rights: East Texas as a Case Study," *American Historical Review* 78 (1971): 1435–56. Any discussion of African American westerners and the Populist should be supplemented with Robert C. McMath, Jr., *American Populism: A Social History, 1877–1898* (New York, 1993).

African American migration to rural areas of the West proved the exception, but a number of small farming and ranching com-

munities thrived. On black settlement in the rural West, see Norman
L. Crockett, *The Black Towns* (Lawrence, 1979); Louis R. Harlan,
Booker T. Washington: The Wizard of Tuskegee, 1901–15 (New York,
1983); Delores Nason McBroome, "Harvests of Gold: African Amer-
ican Boosterism, Agriculture, and Investment in Allensworth and
Little Liberia," in Lawrence B. de Graaf, Kevin Mulroy, and Quintard Taylor, eds., *Seeking El Dorado: African Americans in California*
(Seattle, 2001); and Kenneth Hamilton, *Black Towns and Profit: Pro-
motion and Development in the Trans-Appalachian West, 1877–1915*
(Urbana, IL, 1991). A small black population also settled in Deerfield, Colorado, a rural community. On Deerfield see George H.
Wayne, "Negro Migration and Colonization in Colorado," *Journal
of the West* 15 (January 1976): 112–17. On black towns in Kan-
sas, consult Nell Painter, *Exodusters: Black Migration to Kansas after
Reconstruction* (New York, 1976) and Robert Athearn, *In Search of
Canaan: Black Migration to Kansas, 1879–1880* (Lawrence, 1978).
Oklahoma's race relations and the changing status of African Ameri-
cans can be found in Jimmie Lewis Franklin, *Journey Toward Hope:
A History of Blacks in Oklahoma* (Norman, OK, 1982).

Two excellent books examine the role of African American
women in the West. They are Gretchen Lemke-Santangelo, *Abiding
Courage: African American Migrant Women and the East Bay Community* (Chapel Hill, NC, 1996) and Quintard Taylor and Shirley
Ann Wilson Moore, eds., *African American Women Confront the
West, 1600–2000* (Norman, OK, 2003). Students should supple-
ments these books with a solid, though dated, historiographical
essay, Lawrence B. de Graaf, "Race, Sex, and Region: Black Women
in the American West, 1850–1920," *Pacific Historical Review* (February 1980): 285–314. Also important is Willi Coleman, "African
American Women and Community development in California,
1848–1900," in Lawrence B. de Graaf, Kevin Milroy, and Quintard Taylor, eds., *Seeking El Dorado: African Americans in California*
(Seattle, 2001). The long struggle for equality that African American
women in Texas waged for respect and equality is told by Ruthe Win-

egarten, *Black Texas Women: 150 Years of Trial and Triumph* (Austin, 1995). For general studies of African American women in the nursing and teaching professions, see Darlene Clark Hine, *Black Women in White: Racial Conflict and Cooperation in the Nursing Profession, 1890–1950* (Bloomington, IN, 1989) and Stephanie J. Shaw, *What a Woman Ought to Be and to Do: Black Professional Women Workers During the Jim Crow Era* (Chicago, 1996). Charlotta Bass tells her own story in a privately published account, Charlotta A. Bass, *Forty Years: Memoirs from the Pages of a Newspaper* (Los Angeles, 1960). George Albert Flippin's life has been reconstructed by Albert S. Broussard, "George Albert Flippin and Race Relations in a Rural Western Community," *Midwest Review* (1990): 1–15.

The Tulsa race riot has been examined by many scholars, including Scott Ellsworth, *Death in a Promised Land: The Tulsa Race Riot of 1921* (Baton Rouge, LA, 1982). Two recent studies of this horrific event include James S. Hirsch, *Riot and Remembrance: The Tulsa War and Its Legacy* (Boston, 2002) and Alfred L. Brophy, *Reconstructing the Dreamland: The Tulsa Riot of 1921: Race, Reparations and Reconciliation* (New York, 2003). Although scholarship on African American professional women continues to lag behind work on black men, J. Clay Smith, Jr., has written a broad history of black female attorneys, although his brief biographical sketches lack detailed analysis. See Smith, Jr., *Rebels in Law: Voices in History of Black Women Lawyers* (Ann Arbor, MI, 2000). Pauli Murray, who later became the first African American woman to be ordained an Episcopal priest, has written widely about her life. On her upbringing and career as a lawyer, see Pauli Murray, *Proud Shoes* (Boston, 1999). A more recent book examines her four-decade relationship with Caroline Ware, a prominent white southern reformer. See Anne Firor Scott, ed., *Pauli Murray and Caroline Ware: Forty Years of Letters in Black and White* (Chapel Hill, NC, 2008). The trials and tribulations of western women of all races who were incarcerated are examined by Anne Butler, *Gendered Justice in the American West: Women Prisoners in Men's Penitentiaries* (Urbana, IL, 1997). Butler also addresses the widespread disparity of western black women who were incarcerated in "Still in Chains: Black Women in Western Prisons, 1865–1915," *Western Historical Quarterly* 20 (February 1989): 18–35.

Chapter 3

While urban history in the American West has lagged behind scholarship in other regions of the nation, many solid monographs have been published in the past twenty years. Among the best are Albert S. Broussard, *Black San Francisco: The Struggle for Racial Equality in the West, 1900–54* (Lawrence, 1993); Quintard Taylor, *The Forging of a Black Community: Seattle's Central District from 1870 through the Civil Rights Era* (Seattle, 1994); Shirley Ann Moore, *To Place Our Deeds: The African American Community in Richmond, California, 1910–1963* (Berkeley, 2000); Dolores McBroome, *Parallel Communities: African Americans in California's East Bay, 1850–1963* (New York, 1993); and Douglas Henry Daniels, *Pioneer Urbanites: A Social and Cultural History of Black San Francisco* (Philadelphia, 1980). Matthew Whitaker examines Phoenix's black community and the role of black activism in the Mountain West in *Race Work: The Rise of Civil Rights in the Urban West* (Lincoln, NE, 2005). A useful study of minority groups, including African Americans in Phoenix, is Bradford Luckingham, *Minorities in Phoenix: A Profile of Mexican American, Chinese American, and African American Communities, 1860–1992* (Tucson, 1994). Thomas Cox has written a solid history of Topeka's black community, although no scholar has studied the black community of Wichita, the state's largest city, in a similar manner. See Thomas C. Cox, *Blacks in Topeka, Kansas: 1865–1915* (Baton Rouge, LA, 1982). No comparable studies of the African American community in such western cities as Denver, Salt Lake City, San Diego, Albuquerque, Omaha, and many of the inter-mountain states in the West have been published.

Likewise, no comprehensive studies of the black communities of either Dallas or Houston have been published to date, but students can consult many important articles on black leadership, race relations, and community building in those cities. For example, Merline Pitre has written *In Struggle Against Jim Crow: Lulu B. White and the NAACP, 1900–1957* (College Station, TX, 1999), an excellent study of Lulu B. White, an NAACP official in Houston. Two recent books, Douglas Flamming, *Bound for Freedom: Black Los Angeles in Jim Crow America* (Berkeley and Los Angeles, 2005) and Josh Sides, *L.A. City Limits: African Americans from the Great Depression to the Present* (Berkeley, 2003), present a detailed picture of Los Angeles' black community and will serve as models for other urban historians.

The plight of black workers in the West has been documented widely by urban historians, and students should first consult the wide range of local histories on specific cities. The best comprehensive source remains Quintard Taylor, *In Search of the Racial Frontier* (New York, 1998). The quest of black westerners to make progress in trade unions has been documented sporadically, and the majority of studies focus on Texas. Ernest Obadele-Starks examines the plight of black workers in the Upper Texas Gulf Coast in *Black Unionism in the Industrial South* (College Station, TX, 2000). Michael R. Botson, Jr., reveals the long, difficult, though ultimately successful struggle that black Houstonians waged to gain equality in the Hughes Tool Company in *Labor, Civil Rights, and the Hughes Tool Company* (College Station, TX, 2005). The plight of African American workers in the San Francisco East Bay is the subject of Lawrence P. Crouchett, Lonnie Bunch, and Martha Kendall Winnacker, *Visions Toward Tomorrow: The History of the East Bay Afro-American Community, 1852–1977* (Oakland, 1989). Delilah L. Beasley, a black columnist for the *Oakland Tribune*, published a useful study in 1918, but it should be used with considerable caution because it contains numerous factual errors. See Beasley, *The Negro Trail Blazers of California* (1919). A more recent and favorable view of Beasley is provided by Lynn M. Hudson, "This is Our Fair and Our State": African Americans and the Panama-Pacific International Exposition," *California History* 87 (2010): 26–45. Several urban histories have noted the importance of black seaman and longshoreman in the West. Each of these studies also notes that these workers achieved more success in gaining access to white unions that their counterparts in other industries. See, for example, Broussard, *Black San Francisco* (Lawrence, 1993), Taylor, *The Forging of a Black Community* (Seattle, 1994), and Barr, *Black Texans* (Norman, OK, 1996). On the struggle of African American workers in Los Angeles to gain access to unions, consult Josh Sides, *L.A. City Limits* (2003).

Few histories of African American western families have been published. Albert S. Broussard has written a three-generation history of the Stewart and Flippin families, and his study illuminates many important aspects of gender, employment, race relations, and leadership. See Broussard, *African American Odyssey: The Stewarts, 1854–1963* (Lawrence, 1998). The plight of black attorneys in the West and the nation is the subject of J. Clay Smith, Jr., *Emancipation: The Making of the Black Lawyer, 1844–1944* (Philadelphia, 1999). On the tragic struggle of one western black attorney to gain acceptance in the legal profession and find steady employment, see Albert S. Broussard, "McCants Stewart: The Struggles of a Black Attorney in the Urban West," *Oregon Historical Quarterly* 89 (1988): 157–79. Buck Colbert Franklin's memoir is one of the most unique in western history, in part because he lived and worked among Indians in the Oklahoma Territory. On Franklin's remarkable life, see John Hope Franklin and John Whittington Franklin, eds., *My Life and an Era: The Autobiography of Buck Colbert Franklin* (Baton Rouge, LA, 1997). A small number of black male professionals in California have written memoirs. On the life and public career of J. Alexander Somerville, consult his autobiography, *Man of Color* (1949). The racial activism of the African American dentist and civil rights leader Jack J. Kimbrough has been documented by Albert S. Broussard in "Percy Steele, Jr., and the Urban League," *California History* 83 (2006): 7–23. The life and political activism of the Reverend Clayton Russell is covered briefly in Mark Wild, *Street Meeting: Multiethnic Neighborhoods in Early Twentieth-Century Los Angeles*

(Berkeley, 2008). S. R. Martin, Jr., has written a remarkable account of his own life as well as that of his father, Reverend S. R. Martin, in *On the Move: A Black Family's Western Saga* (College Station, TX, 2009).

The western jazz scene has been documented carefully in Los Angeles and Kansas City, but in few other cities. The best studies are Clora Bryant, Buddy Collette, et al., *Central Avenue Sounds: Jazz in Los Angeles* (Berkeley, 1998) and Jacqueline C. Djedje and Eddie S. Meadows, eds., *California Souls: Music of African Americans in the West* (Berkeley, 1998). Douglas Henry Daniels has reconstructed the remarkable activities of the Oklahoma City Blue Devils in *One O'Clock Jump: The Unforgettable History of the Oklahoma City Blue Devils* (Boston, 2007). Similarly, the motion picture industry, which thrived in Los Angeles and discriminated widely against African American actors, has been studied by Thomas Cripps, *Slow Fade to Black* (New York, 1977); and Don Bogle, *Toms, Coons, Mulattoes, Mammies, and Bucks: An Interpretive History of Blacks in American Film,* 3d ed. (New York, 1994). A more recent study by Bogle is also useful, *Bright Boulevards, Bold Dreams: The Story of Black Hollywood* (New York, 2006). The important career of the black film maker Oscar Micheaux is covered in his autobiography, Micheaux, *The Conquest: The Story of a Negro Pioneer* (Lincoln, NE, 1994).

There is no single study of black businesses in the West comparable to the excellent studies of black banks and insurance companies in the southern states. Alwyn Barr offers the most thorough discussion of African American businesses in Dallas and Houston in *Black Texans* (Austin, 1996). James M. SoRelle also discusses the importance of black businesses in the Bayou City in "The Emergence of Black Business in Houston, Texas: A Study of Race and Ideology," in Howard Beeth and Cary D. Wintz, eds., *Black Dixie: Afro-Texans History and Culture in Houston* (College Station, TX, 1992). Alan Govenar has compiled a wonderfully rich collection of photographs of African Americans and black businesses in Texas. See Govenar, *Portraits of Community: African American Photography in Texas* (Austin, 1996). The broad array of black businesses in Los Angeles, including the Somerville Hotel and the Golden State Mutual Life Insurance Company, is examined in Flamming, *Bound for Freedom* (Berkeley, 2005).

Few studies exist of either housing patterns or housing discrimination in the West but most that do so examine the broader context of community studies and racial discrimination in western cities. One of the few exceptions is Lawrence B. de Graaf, "The City of Black Angels: The Emergence of the Los Angeles Ghetto, 1890–1930," *Pacific Historical Review* 39 (August 1970): 323–52. A broad study that also examines housing discrimination and restrictive covenants is Loren Miller, *The Petitioners: The Story of the Supreme Court of the United States and the Negro* (New York, 1966). Matthew C. Whitaker's study of Phoenix, Arizona, contains substantial material on the struggle of African Americans to obtain housing on a nondiscriminatory basis. See Whitaker, *Race Work: The Rise of Civil Rights in the West* (Lincoln, NE, 2005). Most black westerners lived among people of various ethnic and racial groups, even when pockets of housing segregation existed. Mark Wild's book *Street Meeting* (Berkeley, 2008), came to a similar conclusion in Los Angeles. On residential integration in San Francisco, consult Broussard, *Black San Francisco* (Lawrence, 1993).

Numerous historians have documented the campaigns of African Americans and their allies to stamp out racial discrimination in the West. For a representative group of books and articles, see Albert S. Broussard, "Organizing the Black Community in the San Francisco Bay Area," *Arizona and the West* (1981): 335–54; Merlene Pitre, *In Struggle Against Jim Crow* (College Station, TX, 1999); and Quintard Taylor, "The Civil Rights Movement in the Urban West: Black Protest in Seattle, 1890–1940," *Journal of Negro History* 80 (Winter 1995): 1–14. On the national campaign to ban the film *The Birth of a Nation,* consult Thomas Cripps, "The Reaction of the Negro to the Motion Picture Birth of a Nation," in August Meier and Elliott Rudwick, eds., *The Making of Black America: Essays in*

Negro Life and History (New York, 1969) and Cripps, *Slow Fade to Black: The Negro in American Film, 1900–1942* (New York, 1977). The standard work on the NAACP's successful role in overturning the White Primary in Texas is Darlene Clark Hine, *Black Victory: The Rise and Fall of the White Primary in Texas* (Columbia, MO, 2003).

The NAACP's role in fighting segregation has been documented thoroughly by historians. Its role in working with organized labor is less well known. To assess the NAACP's contribution to the Brotherhood of Sleeping Car Porters, consult William H. Harris, *Keeping the Faith: A. Philip Randolph, Milton Webster, and the Brotherhood of Sleeping Car Porters, 1925–37* (Urbana, IL, 1977). A more recent work is Eric Arnesen, *Brotherhoods of Color: Black Railroad Workers and the Struggle for Equality* (Cambridge, MA, 2002). On the role of the NAACP and its reluctance in supporting the Scottsboro Boys, see Dan T. Carter, *Scottsboro, A Tragedy of the American South,* rev. ed. (Baton Rouge, LA, 1979). A recent book that evaluates the role of the NAACP in the long struggle for racial equality is Patricia Sullivan, *Lift Every Voice: The NAACP and the Making of the Civil Rights Movement* (New York, 2009).

Several good studies examine the role of the National Urban League in fighting for racial justice in the West. On the role of the Urban League in Omaha and Lincoln, Nebraska, see Dennis Mihelich, "The Formation of the Lincoln Urban League," *Nebraska History* 68 (Summer 1987): 63–73; and Mihelich, "World War II and the Transformation of the Omaha Urban League," *Nebraska History* 60 (Fall 1979): 401–23. Quintard Taylor and Douglas Flamming note the important role that the Urban League played in Los Angeles and Seattle in securing jobs for African Americans. See Flamming, *Bound for Freedom* (Berkeley, 2005) and Taylor, *The Forging of a Black Community* (Seattle, 1994). Less attention has been devoted to Marcus Garvey's influence in the West. Emory J. Tolbert's *The U.N.I.A. and Black Los Angeles: Ideology and Community in the American Garvey Movement* (Los Angeles, 1980) is the only book-length account of Garvey's role in a western city. Considerable material on Garvey's role in the West, can, however, also be obtained in the Marcus Garvey Papers published by the University of California Press. Albert S. Broussard evaluates the role of the Garvey movement in San Francisco in *Black San Francisco* (Lawrence, 1993).

Few western urban historians have examined the Great Depression and the New Deal's affect on African Americans in western cities. A good starting point is Dennis Mihelich, "The Lincoln Urban League: The Travail of Depression and War," *Nebraska History* 70 (Winter 1989): 303–16. Josh Sides examines the pernicious impact that the Great Depression had on Los Angeles in *L.A. City Limits* (Berkeley, 2003). Douglas Flamming's, *Bound for Freedom* (Berkeley, 2005) devotes several chapters to this era. Similarly, Albert S. Broussard devotes an entire chapter to the Great Depression and the New Deal in *Black San Francisco* (Lawrence, 1993). Alwyn Barr's discussion of the New Deal's impact on black Texans is excellent and includes material on blacks who lived in rural areas as well as cities. See Barr, *Black Texans* (Austin, 1996). There has been considerable interest in the role of Lyndon Baines Johnson and the National Youth Administration. Christi L. Bourgeois has written an important essay on Johnson's support of black Texans. See Bourgeois, "Stepping over the Lines: Lyndon Johnson, Black Texans, and the National Youth Administration, 1935–1937," *Southwestern Historical Quarterly* 91 (October 1987): 149–72. Two scholars, John A. Salmond and Calvin W. Gower, analyze the Civilian Conservation Corps' policy toward race. See John A. Salmond, "The Civilian Conservation Corps and the Negro," *Journal of American History* 52 (June 1965): 75–88; Calvin W. Gower, "The Struggle of Blacks for Leadership in the Civilian Conservation Corps," *Journal of Negro History* 61 (April 1976): 123–35. The difficulty that black farmers experienced in Texas during the Great Depression, including the deleterious policy of the Agricultural Adjustment Administration that drove many black tenants and sharecroppers off the land, is cited in Robert A. Calvert, Arnoldo De León, and Gregg Cantrell, *The History of Texas,* 4th ed. (Wheeling, IL, 2008). Maury Maverick's alliance with San Antonio's black community is explored in Judith Kaaz Doyle, "Maury Maverick and Racial Politics in San Antonio, Texas, 1938–1941," *Journal of Southern History* 53 (May 1987): 194–224. For general biographical information of Maverick's political career, consult Richard B. Henderson, *Maury Maverick: A Political Biography* (Austin, 1970).

The role of the Communist Party and radical organizations in the West can be gleaned from Josh Sides, "'You Understand My Condition'" The Civil Rights Congress in the Los Angeles African-American Community, 1946–1952," *Pacific Historical Review* 67 (May 1998): 233–57. On Langston Hughes' evolving radicalism, see Arnold Rampersad, *The Life of Langston Hughes, vol. 1:1902–1941: I, Too, Sing, America* (New York, 1986). For a recent overview of the role of African Americans during the Great Depression and the New Deal, see Albert S. Broussard, "The Worst of Times: African Americans in the Great Depression," in *Great Depression: People and Perspectives,* ed., Hamilton Cravens (Santa Barbara, CA, 2009).

Chapter 4

Many historians have examined World War II and stress the impact of this global conflict on transforming race relations in the American West. The best coverage of the war years can be found in Albert S. Broussard, *Black San Francisco* (Lawrence, 1993). Broussard devotes four chapters to World War II and its impact on San Francisco's black community. Other important studies of the war's significance in the West include Josh Sides, "Battle on the Home Front: African American Shipyard Workers in World War II Los Angeles," *California History* 75 (Fall 1996): 250–63, and Alonzo Smith and Quintard Taylor, "Racial Discrimination in the Workplace: A Study of Two West Coast Cities during the 1940's," *The Journal of Ethnic Studies* 8 (Spring 1980): 35–54. Historian Gerald Nash argued that the war had a profound effect on the entire West. See Nash, *The American West Transformed: The Impact of the Second World War* (Bloomington,

IN, 1985). Lawrence B. De Graaf argues that World War II was the beginning of a long process of change that would take place in the West in eradicating racial discrimination in "Significant Steps on an Arduous Path: The Impact of World War II on Discrimination against African Americans in the West," *Journal of the West* 35 (January 1996): 24–33.

We have a far better understanding of the role of gender during World War II, as well as the insidious discrimination that African American women faced. The best general introduction to this subject is Karen Tucker Anderson, "Last Hired, First Fired: Black Women Workers during World War II," *Journal of American History* 69 (June 1982): 82–97. Shirley Ann Moore and Gretchen Lemke-Santangelo each argue that African American women played an important role in community building in the San Francisco Bay Area. See Moore, *To Place Our Deeds* (Berkeley, 2000) and Lemke-Santangelo, *Abiding Courage* (Chapel Hill, NC, 1996). Equally informative is Lemke-Santangelo, "Women Made the Community": African American Migrant Women and the Cultural Transformation of the San Francisco East Bay Area," in Quintard Taylor and Shirley Ann Wilson Moore, eds., *African American Women Confront the West* (Norman, OK, 2003). Charles Wollenberg has an excellent discussion of the struggle of black workers to gain admission into the predominately white Boilermakers unions in "James v. Marinship: Trouble on the New Black Frontier," *California History* 60 (Fall 1981). Charles S. Johnson, the distinguished black sociologist, conducted an extension study of black workers and race relations in San Francisco, *The Negro War Worker in San Francisco* (San Francisco, 1944). Marilynn Johnson examines how the war affected Oakland and the East Bay in *The Second Gold Rush: Oakland and the East Bay in World War II* (Berkeley, 1993). A valuable first-person account of working conditions in Bay Area shipyards is provided by Katherine Archibald, *Wartime Shipyards: A Study in Social Disunity* (Urbana, IL, 2006).

A small number of first-person accounts have also been written by black migrants who came West during World War II. On the life of S. R. Martin and his settlement in San Francisco's Fillmore District, see *On the Move* (College Station, TX, 2009). Cy Wilson Record examines the joy and the frustration of black migrants in Richmond in "Willie Stokes at the Golden Gate," *The Crisis* 56 (June 1949):175–76. Quintard Taylor's study of black war workers in Seattle, *The Forging of a Black Community* (Seattle, 1994), remains the standard work for that city. Little comparative work exists on racial minorities in the West during World War II. A recent work that examines the role and contributions of Mexican Americans in the war effort is Maggie Rivas-Rodriguez, *Mexican Americans and World War II* (Austin, 2005). A similar work by Scott Kurashige, *The Shifting Ground of Race: Black and Japanese Americans in the Making of Multiethnic Los Angeles* (Princeton, 2008), examines the interrelationship of African Americans and Japanese Americans in twentieth-century Los Angeles and how each group has shaped the city's race relations. The most comprehensive study that examines the role of racial minorities during World War II is Mark Brilliant, *The Color of America Has Changed: How Racial Diversity Shaped Civil Rights Reform in California, 1941–1978* (New York, 2010).

Several important studies have broadened our understanding of African Americans in Nevada and the inter-Mountain West. Claytee White's engaging article, "Eight Dollars a Day and Working in the Shade": An Oral History of African American Migrant Women in the Las Vegas Gaming Industry," breaks new ground in several important areas. The impact of World War II on Texas was also profound. Bernadette Pruitt examines black migration during the war years in "For the Advancement of the Race: African-American Migration to Houston, 1914–1940," *Journal of Urban History* 31 (May 2005). Michael R. Botson, Jr., illustrates how African American workers struggled to gain acceptance and full equality within the Hughes Tool Company in *Labor, Civil Rights, and the Hughes Tool Company* (College Station, TX, 2005).

The majority of western historians ignore Alaska and Hawaii when they evaluate the impact of World War II on the West. However, several important studies note the importance of these U.S. territories. On Hawaii, see Beth Bailey and David Farber, *The First Strange Place: The Alchemy of Race and Sex in World War II Hawaii* (New York, 1992). Albert S. Broussard also examines race relations in Hawaii as well as factors that led to the creation of Hawaii's first NAACP chapter in "The Honolulu NAACP and Race Relations in Hawaii," *Hawaiian Journal of History* 39 (2005): 115–33. A special issue on African Americans in Hawaii, "They Followed the Trade Winds: African Americans in Hawaii," appeared in *Social Processes in Hawaii* 43 (2004). Brief accounts of the role that African Americans played in Alaska during World War II can be found in Lael Morgan, "Writing Minorities Out of History: Black Builders of the Alcan Highway," *Alaska History* 7 (Fall 1992): 1–13 and Heath Twichell, *Northwest Epic: The Building of the Alaska Highway* (New York, 1992).

Robert L. Allen has written the definitive work on the Port Chicago Mutiny, *The Port Chicago Mutiny* (New York, 1993). Allen's fine book can be supplemented with a briefer description of this rebellion by Charles Wollenberg, "Blacks vs. Navy Blue: The Mare Island Mutiny Court Martial," *California History* 58 (Spring 1979): 62–75, and Peter Vogel, "The Last Wave from Port Chicago," *Black Scholar* 13 (1982): 30–47.

The struggle of African American workers to gain membership in the Boilermakers Union along the entire Pacific Coast has been examined by numerous scholars, including Albert S. Broussard, Quintard Taylor, William H. Harris, and Charles Wollenberg. Unfortunately, there is no significant biographical sketch of Joseph James or any other African American leader who pressed for full equality within these unions. Harris' fine article, "Federal Intervention in Union Discrimination: FEPC and West Coast Shipyards during World War II," *Labor History* 11 (1981): 325–47, is the best introduction to the subject. Three broader studies of the Bay Area shipyards also provide important information on African American workers. For example, Charles Wollenberg's, *Marinship at War: Ship-*

building and Social Change in Wartime Sausalito (Berkeley, 1990), analyzes the wartime production of ships at Marinship, one of the major Bay Area shipbuilders. Similarly, Mark Foster's, *Henry J. Kaiser, Builder in the Modern American West* (Austin, 1989) is useful in reconstructing this era. The best study, however, remains Marilynn S. Johnson, *The Second Gold Rush: Oakland and the East Bay in World War II* (Berkeley, 1993).

The struggle of African American war workers to find housing in western cities has been cited by numerous scholars. Josh Sides, *L.A. City Limits* (Berkeley, 2003), provides the best description of housing shortages in wartime Los Angeles. Yet Keith Collins, *Black Los Angeles: The Maturing of a Ghetto, 1940–1950* (Saratoga, CA, 1980), and Russell A. Buchanan, *Black Americans and World War II* (Santa Barbara, 1977), are both useful. So is Arthur C. Verge, *Paradise Transformed: Los Angeles during the Second World War* (Dubuque, IA, 1993). Quintard Taylor examines the long history of African Americans in Seattle's Central District in *The Forging of a Black Community* (Seattle, 1994). Clement Vose evaluates the efforts of the NAACP and the U.S. Supreme Court to eliminate restrictive covenants in *Caucasians Only: The Supreme Court, the NAACP and the Restrictive Covenant Cases* (Berkeley, 1967). To compare the plight of African Americans with Asians in finding housing in the West, see Charlotte Brooks, "Sing Sheng vs. Southwood: Housing, Race, and the Cold War in 1950s California," *Pacific Historical Review* 73 (August 2004). Stuart McElderry traces the decline of Portland's African American community in "Building a West Coast Ghetto: African-American Housing in Portland, 1910–1960," *Pacific Northwest Quarterly* 92 (2001): 137–48. A recent study that examines a community in Portland, Oregon, that was transformed racially during World War II is provided by Karen J. Gibson, "Bleeding Albina: A History of Community Disinvestment, 1940–2000," *Transforming Anthropology* 15 (2007): 3–25.

There is considerably less material on race relations in the West than one might expect, particularly in light of the importance of

World War II to western history. Kevin Allen Leonard has provided
one of the few accounts of multiracial activity in "Brothers Under
the Skin?: African Americans, Mexican Americans, and World War
II in California," in Roger W. Lotchin, ed., *The Way We Really Were*
(Urbana, IL, 2000). Shana Bernstein's *Bridges of Reform: Interracial
Civil Rights Activism in Twentieth-Century Los Angeles* (New York,
2011) is important because it reveals a long history of interracial
activism in one western city. Quintard Taylor provides an insightful
discussion of black migration and race relations in wartime Portland
and Seattle in "The Great Migration: The Afro-American Communities of Seattle and Portland during the 1940s," *Arizona and the West*
23 (Summer 1981): 109–26. Similarly, the literature on racial conflict during World War II is limited. One exception is Kevin Allen
Leonard, *The Battle for Los Angeles: Racial Ideology and World War
II* (Albuquerque, 2006). Matthew Whitaker also examines racial
conflict and the role of the Phoenix branch of the NAACP in *Race
Work* (Lincoln, NE, 2005). The best account of Howard Thurman's
life remains his autobiographical writings. The letters between Thur-
man and Dr. Howard Fiske appear in Thurman, *First Footprints: The
Dawn of the Idea of the Church of the Fellowship of All Peoples* (San
Francisco, 1975). For the founding and early work of Fellowship
Church, consult Thurman, *Footprints of a Dream: The Story of the
Church for the Fellowship of All Peoples* (New York, 1959). A brief
collection of Thurman's principal writing appears in Walter Fluger
and Catherine Tumber, eds., *A Strange Freedom: The Best of Howard
Thurman on Religious Experience and Public Life* (Boston, 1998). The
Beaumont, Texas, race riot has been covered thoroughly by James
A. Burran, "Violence in an 'Arsenal of Democracy': The Beaumont
Race Riot, 1943," *East Texas Historical Review* 14 (Spring 1976). On
race conflict in World War II Hawaii, see Beth Bailey and David
Farber, *The First Strange Place* (New York, 1992).

On the awakening of black politics in the West, see Broussard,
Black San Francisco (Lawrence, 1993) and Lawrence P. Crouchett,
William Byron Rumford: The Life and Public Services of a California

Legislator (El Cerrito, CA, 1984). Quintard Taylor, Matthew Whitaker, and Josh Sides also examine African American interest in politics in Seattle, Phoenix, and Los Angeles. The life and public career of Willie L. Brown, Jr., is examined by James Richardson, *Willie Brown: A Biography* (Berkeley, 1996). Richardson covered Brown's political career as a reporter for the *Sacramento Bee*. Richardson's book, however, was published prior to Brown's election as mayor of San Francisco. An important discussion of biracial coalitions and politics in Los Angeles' black community is provided by Raphael J. Sonenshein in *Politics in Black and White: Race and Politics in Los Angeles* (Princeton, 1993).

Chapter 5

The status of African Americans in the postwar West remains perhaps the most understudied area of western black history. Nonetheless, a surprising number of books and articles have been written on athletes, musicians, and creative artists. African Americans played an important role in both collegiate and professional sports in the western states, and Albert S. Broussard's article, "George Albert Flippin and Race Relations in a Western Rural Community," *Midwest Review* (1990) illuminates the significance of a superb black athlete at the University of Nebraska. Two recent studies of African Americans in collegiate football in the West are provided by Lane Demas in "Sport History, Race, and the College Gridiron: A Southern California Turning Point," *Southern California Quarterly* 89 (Summer 2007): 169–193, and *Integrating the Gridiron: Black Civil Rights and American College Football* (Newark, NJ, 2010). Demas' book, which examines a number of case studies, is one of the best single accounts of race, civil rights and politics in collegiate sports. Numerous studies of Jackie Robinson have been published, yet Robinson framed his own life carefully in *I Never Had it Made: An Autobiography* (New York, 1995). Arnold Rampersad's *Jackie Robinson, A Biography* (New York, 1997) is an excellent account of Robinson's public and private career written by a distinguished literary scholar. Hispanics also broke the color line in major league baseball and played with African Americans in the United States, Mexico, and Latin America. The best discussion of their contribution and collective struggle is Adrian Burgos, Jr., *Playing America's Game: Baseball, Latinos, and the Color Line* (Berkeley, 2007).

Wilt Chamberlain's collegiate career at the University of Kansas is told by Gary M. Pomerantz, *Wilt, 1962* (New York, 2005). Similarly, Bill Russell's brilliant collegiate career and his difficult adjustment to the University of San Francisco campus and coach Phil Woolpert's system appears in Aram Goudsouzian, "The House That Russell Built: Bill Russell, the University of San Francisco, and the Winning Streak That Changed College Basketball," *California History* 84 (2007). Goudsouzian's recent book on Russell's professional career, *King of the Court: Bill Russell and the Basketball Revolution* (Berkeley, 2010), should also be consulted. Ray Sanchez, *Basketball's Biggest Upset* (El Paso, TX, 1992) traces the incredible run of the Texas Western Miners in 1966 when they defeated the heavily favored University of Kentucky Wildcats in the NCAA championship basketball game. The legacy of this victory is examined by Frank Fitzpatrick, *And the Walls Came Tumbling Down: Kentucky, Texas Western, and the Game that Changed American Sports* (New York, 1999). The fictionalized film "Glory Road," also tells this story, but, like any Hollywood drama produced for a mass audience, while good entertainment, the film must be viewed with caution. A far more compelling study of the slow decline of segregation in college sports is provided by Charles H. Martin in *Benching Jim Crow: The Rise and Fall of the Color Line in Southern College Sports, 1890–1980* (Urbana, IL, 2010). Mickey Herskowitz's *The Legend of Bear Bryant* (New York, 1987) tells how coach Bear Bryant was finally convinced to integrate the University of Alabama football team in the early 1970s after his all-white team received a sound thrashing by USC.

Black westerners dominated professional sports as much as they dominated collegiate athletics. On Willie Mays' phenomenal baseball career, consult Willie Mays with Lou Sahadi, *Say Hey: The Autobiography of Willie Mays* (New York, 1988). An entertaining study of Mays' career, though largely hagiography, is provided by Charles Einstein, *Willie's Time, A Memoir* (New York, 1979). A recent biography of Mays' career, though also largely uncritical, is provided by James S. Hirsch in *Willie Mays: The Life, The Legend* (New York, 2010). Roy Campanella's career with the Brooklyn Dodgers is examined in his autobiography, *It's Good to Be Alive* (Lincoln, NE, 1995). The integration of baseball, including teams in the western states, is covered carefully by Jules Tygiel in *Baseball's Great Experiment: Jackie Robinson and His Legacy, 25th Anniversary ed.* (New York, 2008).

Numerous historians in western black history have noted the role that black professionals have played in providing leadership to civil rights organizations. One such study is provided by Albert S. Broussard in "Percy Steele, Jr. and the Urban League," *California History* 83 (2006). Linda Williams traces the role of Clara Luper in breaking down racial barriers in Oklahoma City in "Clara Luper and the Civil Rights Movement in Oklahoma City, 1958–1964," in Quintard Taylor and Shirley Ann Wilson Moore, eds., *African American Women Confront the West, 1600–2000* (Norman, OK, 2003). These studies can be supplemented by two excellent books on black professional women and racial activism. Consult Stephanie J. Shaw, *What a Woman Ought to Be and Do: Black Professional Women Workers During the Jim Crow Era* (Chicago, 1996), and Deborah Gray White, *Too Heavy a Load: Black Women in Defense of Themselves, 1894–1994* (New York, 1999). A recent study that explores the activism of African American women and their quest for racial justice is Bettye Collier-Thomas, *Jesus, Jobs, and Justice: African American Women and Religion* (New York, 2010). Howard Thurman's remarkable career is chronicled in Thurman, *With Head and Heart: The Autobiography of Howard Thurman* (New York, 1979).

The role of black professional women in strengthening their communities and fighting for civil rights and racial justice in the West is examined in Matthew Whitaker, *Race Work* (Lincoln, NE,

2005). An early study that examines the role of Vivian Osborne Marsh in California is B. Joyce Ross, "Mary McLeod Bethune and the National Youth Administration: A Case Study of Power Relationships in the Black Cabinet of Franklin D. Roosevelt," in John Hope Franklin and August Meier, eds., *Black Leaders of the Twentieth Century* (Urbana, IL, 1982). The history and role of Delta Sigma Theta is provided by Paula Giddings, I*n Search of Sisterhood: Delta Sigma Theta and the Challenge of the Black Sorority Movement* (New York, 1988).

Many modern scholars have mistakenly cited Greensboro, North Carolina, as the site of the first sit-ins in the civil rights movement. Yet Gretchen Eick demonstrates in *Dissent in Wichita* (Urbana, IL, 2007) that events both in Oklahoma City and Wichita, Kansas, predated those in Greensboro. Two articles by Ronald Walters are also valuable. See Walters, "The Great Plains Sit-in Movement, 1958–60," *Great Plains Quarterly* 16 (Spring 1996): 85–94 and "Standing Up in America's Heartland: Sitting-in before Greensboro," *American Vision* 8 (February 1993): 20–23. The starting point for any serious reading of the *Brown* decision is Richard Kluger, *Simple Justice: The History of Brown v. Board of Education and Black America's Struggle for Equality* (New York, 1975). Other important works on this monumental Supreme Court decision include James T. Patterson, *Brown v. Board of Education: A Civil Rights Milestone and Its Troubled Legacy* (New York, 2001) and Charles J. Ogletree, Jr., *All Deliberate Speed: Reflections on the First Half Century of Brown v. Board of Education* (New York, 2004). An excellent study that examines the significance of the *Brown* decision within the broader context of the black freedom struggle is Harvard Sitkoff, *The Struggle for Black Equality: 1954–1992, rev. ed.* (New York, 1993). Cheryl Brown, the plaintiff, also wrote a brief remembrance of this case. See Cheryl Brown Henderson, "Landmark Decision: Remembering the Struggle for Equal Education," *Land and People* (Spring 1994): 2–5.

Quintard Taylor and Albert S. Broussard provide the most detailed discussions of the modern civil rights movement in the

West in their important studies, *In Search of the Racial Frontier* (New York, 1998) and *Black San Francisco* (Lawrence, 1993). Mary Melcher evaluates the interracial leadership of the Phoenix civil rights movement in "Blacks and Whites Together: Interracial Leadership in the Phoenix Civil Rights Movement," *Journal of Arizona History* 32 (Summer 1991):195–216. The role of CORE in the West and the nation is examined thoroughly in August Meier and Elliott Rudwick, *CORE: A Study in the Civil Rights Movement, 1942–1968* (New York, 1973). The campaign to integrate public schools in Berkeley and the ensuing protest is the subject of W. J. Rorabaugh, *Berkeley at War: The 1960s* (New York, 1989). Regrettably, there is no biography of either Tracy Simms or any other grassroots leader in the San Francisco Bay Area. Valuable material on Simms can, however, be located at the California Labor Archive, San Francisco State University. The 1965 Watts riot is covered in detail in Gerald Horne, *Fire This Time: The Watts Uprising and the 1960s* (Charlottesville, VA, 1995). San Antonio, Texas, the third largest city in the Lone Star State, integrated its lunch counters and public accommodations without a single incident of racial violence. The San Antonio story is told by Robert A. Goldberg, "Racial Change on the Southern Periphery: The Case of San Antonio, Texas, 1960–1965," *Journal of Southern History* 49 (1983).

The Black Panther Party continues to fascinate historians and journalists, and numerous studies have appeared in recent years that document the activities of this black militant organization and its role in organizing local communities. Several first-person accounts by former party members are especially valuable. For example, consult Bobby Seale, *Seize the Time: The Story of the Black Panther Party and Huey P. Newton* (New York, 1968) and Eldridge Cleaver, *Soul on Ice* (New York, 1968). Also important are Cleaver, *Post-Prison Writings and Speeches* (New York, 1969), David Hilliard and Lewis Cole, *This Side of Glory: The Autobiography of David Hilliard and the Story of the Black Panther Party* (Boston, 1993), and Hilliard, ed., *The Black Panther Party Service to the People Programs* (Albuquerque,

2008). Gilbert Moore, a black journalist who covered the Black Panthers extensively during the 1960s, wrote *Rage* (New York, 1993). Elaine Brown, a former chairwoman of the Black Panther Party, has written one of the most compelling narratives, one that also illuminates the role of gender and discrimination against women within the organization. See Brown, *A Taste of Power: A Black Woman's Story* (New York, 1992). Two broad studies of the Black Power movement also illuminate many aspects of the Black Panthers. They are William L. Van Deburg, *New Day in Babylon: The Black Power Movement and American Culture, 1965–1975* (Chicago, 1992) and Peniel E. Joseph, *Waiting 'Til the Midnight Hour: A Narrative History of Black Power* (New York, 2007). The best discussion of the FBI's COINTELPRO program is provided by David J. Garrow's, *The F.B.I. and Martin Luther King, Jr.* (New York, 1983).

Chapter 6

Steven F. Lawson's *Running for Freedom: Civil Rights and Black Politics in America Since 1941,* 2d ed. (New York, 1997) provides an excellent overview of the ceaseless quest for equality in the postwar era as well as the conservative backlash that sweep through the nation. Tom Bradley's rise and important political career are examined by Raphael J. Sonenshein, *Politics in Black and White: Race and Politics in Los Angeles* (Princeton, 1993). Sonenshein's perceptive article, "Coalition Building in Los Angeles: The Bradley Years and Beyond," in De Graaf, Mulroy, and Taylor, eds, *Seeking El Dorado: African Americans in California* (Seattle, 2001), addresses the successful coalitions that African Americans forged with other racial and ethnic groups in Los Angeles to elect the city's first African American mayor. Henry J. Gutierrez's "Racial Politics in Los Angeles: Black and Mexican American Challenges to Unequal Education in the 1960s," *Southern California Quarterly* 78 (1996): 51–86, is also important in illuminating the strategies that two non-white groups used in Los Angeles to improve their status. Neil Foley's *Quest for Equality: The*

Failed Promise of Black-Brown Solidarity (Cambridge, MA, 2010) takes a dimmer view of attempts to form coalitions by Hispanics and African Americans. Robert Self's *American Babylon: Race and the Struggle for Postwar Oakland* (Princeton, 2003) evaluates the early political leadership in Oakland's African American community, including the activities of the East Bay Democratic Club. Congresswoman Barbara Jordan's life and public career is examined skillfully by Mary Beth Rogers, a former colleague at the Lyndon B. Johnson School of Public Affairs, in *Barbara Jordan: American Hero* (New York, 1998). Willie L. Brown's mercurial life and career is captured by James Richardson's *Willie Brown: A Biography* (Berkeley, 1996). Alwyn Barr's *Black Texans* (Norman, OK, 1996) captures the modern struggle for civil rights in Texas, including the dramatic increase there in African American voting. Michael Phillips has written an engaging study, that examines race relations in Dallas among African Americans, Mexican Americans, Jews, and the city's white elite in *White Metropolis: Race, Ethnicity, and Religion in Dallas, 1841–2001* (Austin, 2006). Yvonne Davis Frear provides a short though incisive critique of a major civil rights leader in Dallas, Texas, in "Juanita Craft and the Struggle to End Segregation in Dallas, 1945–1955," in Sam W. Haynes and Cary D. Wintz, eds., *Major Problems in Texas History: Documents and Essays* (Boston, 2002).

Only a handful of scholars have examined urban poverty and the impact of deindustrialization in the West. Robert Self's pathbreaking book *American Babylon* provides the most detailed example. Also useful is Gretchen Lemke-Santangelo's "Deindustrialization, Urban Poverty and African American Community Mobilization in Oakland, 1945 through the 1990s," in de Graaf, Mulroy, and Taylor, eds., *Seeking El Dorado: African Americans in California* (Seattle, 2001). Students who wish to compare western cities with other regions of the nation should consult Thomas J. Sugrue, *The Origins of the Urban Crisis: Race and Inequality in Postwar Detroit* (Princeton, 1996). Gang violence has been a conspicuous feature of many western cities, but none more so than Los Angeles. Leon Bing, a former journalist, reveals in graphic detail the inner world of these gangs in *Do or Die* (New York, 1992). Numerous African American and Hispanic gang members have written accounts of their lives as gang bangers. Among the most gripping is Sanyika Shakur, *Monster: The Autobiography of an L.A. Gang Member* (New York, 2004).

To ascertain how urban redevelopment affected African Americans and others in one western city, consult Chester Hartman, *City for Sale: The Transformation of San Francisco* (Berkeley, 2002). Lawrence B. de Graaf has written widely about the process of black suburbanization in southern California. I would especially consult his essay "African American Suburbanization in California, 1960 through 1990," in de Graaf, Mulroy, and Taylor, eds., *Seeking El Dorado: African Americans in California* (Seattle, 2001). Karen J. Gibson examines the process of gentrification and racial change in one of Portland's longstanding black neighborhoods in Bleeding Albina: A History of Community Disinvestment, 1940–2000," *Transforming Anthropology* 15 (2007): 3–25.

African Americans and Mexican Americans who sought greater access to colleges and universities prior to the 1960s generally faced a rude awakening. Many western colleges, however, established affirmative action programs after 1965, which gradually increased the number of these under-represented groups but caused considerable angst and occasionally protests by whites. One black administrator's personal account is provided by Samuel E. Kelly and Quintard Taylor, *Dr. Sam, Soldier, Educator, Advocate, Friend: An Autobiography* (Seattle, 2010). On the significance and legacy of the U.S. Supreme Court's *Bakke* decision, see Joel Dreyfuss and Charles Lawrence III, *The Bakke Case: The Politics of Inequality* (New York, 1979). A broad study of affirmative action that places *Bakke* and other cases in historical perspective is Terry H. Anderson, *The Pursuit of Fairness: A History of Affirmative Action* (New York, 2004). For information on more recent Supreme Court cases, one should consult the *Washington Post* or the *New York Times*. Thomas Sugrue's recent study of race relations and civil rights in the North, *Sweet Land of Liberty: The*

Forgotten Struggle for Civil Rights in the North (New York, 2008), which regrettably ignores the majority of western states, is important nonetheless in illuminating many issues that black westerners also confronted at the close of the twentieth century. Cecil Williams, who served as pastor of the Glide Memorial Church in San Francisco, and whose ministry focused on empowering the poor and the dispossessed of all races and genders, tells his story in *No Hiding Place: Empowerment and Recovery for Our Troubled Communities* (New York, 1992).

Index

Expectations of Equality: A History of Black Westerners
Developmental editor and copy editor: Andrew J. Davidson
Production editor: Linda Gaio
Proofreader: Claudia Siler
Typesetter: Bruce Leckie
Printer: McNaughton & Gunn